21世纪经济管理新形态教材·物流学系列

物流专业英语
Logistics English
（第2版）

于　丹 ◎ 主编

清华大学出版社
北京

内 容 简 介

　　物流产业在国际上被喻为经济发展的加速器,其将对中国经济的健康发展产生积极的影响。本书以深入浅出的英语语言系统地介绍现代物流基础概念和相关知识,选材内容涵盖供应链管理、物流系统、物流服务、库存、运输、仓储、包装、配送、物流信息、物流成本控制、物流策略管理、第三方物流、国际物流和顾客服务等,并配以丰富的练习和教学辅助资源。

　　本书可作为高等学校物流管理与物流工程专业本科生教材,也可作为工程硕士和其他相关专业学生的学习用书,亦可供物流专业人士或英语爱好者阅读参考。

图书在版编目(CIP)数据

物流专业英语 / 于丹主编. —2 版. —北京:清华大学出版社,2020.7(2025.1重印)
(21 世纪经济管理新形态教材·物流学系列)
ISBN 978-7-302-55113-3

Ⅰ.①物… Ⅱ.①于… Ⅲ.①物流–英语 Ⅳ.①F25

中国版本图书馆 CIP 数据核字(2020)第 049479 号

责任编辑:高晓蔚
封面设计:李伯骥
责任校对:王凤芝
责任印制:丛怀宇

出版发行:清华大学出版社
　　　　　网　　　址:https://www.tup.com.cn,https://www.wqxuetang.com
　　　　　地　　　址:北京清华大学学研大厦 A 座　　　　邮　　编:100084
　　　　　社 总 机:010-83470000　　　　　　　　　　　邮　　购:010-62786544
　　　　　投稿与读者服务:010-62776969,c-service@ tup.tsinghua.edu.cn
　　　　　质量反馈:010-62772015,zhiliang@ tup.tsinghua.edu.cn
　　　　　课件下载:https://www.tup.com.cn,010-83470332
印 装 者:天津鑫丰华印务有限公司
经　　销:全国新华书店
开　　本:185mm×260mm　　　印　张:17.75　　　　字　数:388 千字
版　　次:2014 年 1 月第 1 版　2020 年 8 月第 2 版　　印　次:2025 年 1 月第 6 次印刷
定　　价:49.00 元

产品编号:085329-02

前　言

随着时代的发展,现代经济越来越多样化,因此产生了各种各样的行业。物流作为一个新兴的行业,也在日益快速地发展,给人们的生活带来了极大的影响。《物流专业英语》是物流管理和物流工程专业本科生的专业英语教材。本书自2014年第1版出版以来,受到广大师生的欢迎。随着物流行业实践的发展,以及教学需求的提升,我们对教材进行了完善与更新。本书内容系统、题材广泛,涵盖物流领域的主要知识,专业性强,深度适当,注重实用。具体特色如下。

(1) 教材共12课,每课包括5篇文章。课文A为精读材料,课文B、C、D、E为泛读材料。5篇文章均围绕同一主题。课文A一般为该主题的概述,课文B、C、D、E多就该主题的某一具体方面或具体例子展开讨论。对于课文A,要求能正确理解和熟练掌握其内容。对于课文B、C、D、E,要求能掌握中心大意,抓住主要事实,其后的核心概念则便于学生更系统地掌握专业英语知识。

(2) 本书每篇课文后附有大量练习题,包括简答题、填空题、选择题、词组英文释义、英汉互译、短文选词填空等,旨在巩固和拓展学生所学的内容。完成练习后,可按书后说明扫码获取练习参考答案。

(3) 课文中生词均用粗体标出,并在课后进行注释,以便于阅读和记忆。物流术语相当于骨架材料,要想用英语来说物流、听物流,就需要关于物流行业的单词积累,所以学会物流英语的第一步就是背诵物流专业术语。本书对首次出现的专业术语进行注释,对重点句型、疑难句进行翻译。书后附录列示了汉英、英汉物流术语解释,英汉物流常用词汇,物流英语基本概念,便于学习者阅读和查询。

本书涵盖物流专业几乎所有基础知识。内容包括:供应链管理、物流系统、物流服务、库存、运输、仓储、包装、配送、物流信息、物流成本控制、物流策略管理、第三方物流、国际物流和顾客服务等。内容全面、条理清晰、通俗易懂、实用性强。不但可作为高等学校物流管理与物流工程专业本科生教材,也可以作为工程硕士和其他相关专业学生的学习用书,亦可供物流专业人士阅读参考。

本书旨在提高读者实际使用英语的能力,使学生掌握有关物流专业方面的英文基本词汇、基本表达方法和较完整的英美国家物流专业知识体系,较快地提高读者阅读物流方面的科技文章和技术手册等资料的能力。所以从这一角度出发,本书亦可作为高校专业英语教材或参考资料,还可供英语爱好者使用,使其在获得相当的物流知识的同时,学习英语达到事半功倍的效果。

本书由辽宁石油化工大学于丹负责全书的构思,其中第一章到第四章由辽宁石油化工大学于丹编写,第五章到第八章由辽宁石油化工大学李玥编写,第九章到第十二章由辽宁石油化工大学任彬编写,全书最后由于丹统稿。本书在编写过程中,借鉴了许多国内外教材、论文、网站资料,引用了部分资料,并在书中加以注明。在编写过程中得到澳大利亚的 Gary John Mahoney 的鼎力支持,感谢他对这本书所付出的时间与心血。王浦策也为本书的出版给予了大力的支持,在此一并表示感谢。

由于水平和时间的限制,本书难免有疏漏和错误之处,敬请同行及读者批评指正。

编者

2020 年 5 月

Contents

Chapter 1

Logistics from A Historical Perspective
物流历史回顾

📚 Section A   Overview Logistics   物流概述

A characteristic of today's society is its dependence on a wide variety of goods and services which are produced by a multitude of business organizations. These companies are highly competitive with each other in supplying goods and services. This competition occurs in three areas: in determining customers' wants, in arranging the production of goods to satisfy those wants, and in making those goods available to the customers. The last responsibility is the special objective of industry's newest management function—business logistics.

Logistics has always been a central and essential feature of all economic activities. There are few aspects of human activity that do not ultimately depend on the flow of goods from point of origin to point of consumption. [1] Without logistics, no materials can be moved, no operations can be done, no products are delivered, and no customers are served.

Logistics has been playing a fundamental role in global development for almost 5,000 years by now. Since the construction of the pyramids in ancient Egypt, logistics has made remarkable strides. [2] Time and again, brilliant logistics solutions have formed the basis for the transition to a new historical and economic era. [3] Quite frankly, from approximately 1950 to 1980, limited appreciation was shown for the importance of logistics **discipline**. [4]

The practice of logistics in the business sector, starting in the later half of the twentieth century, is considered as the development of enterprises " accelerator" and the 21st century "gold industry." Examples of this fundamental progress include the invention of the sea-cargo container and the creation of novel service systems during the 20th century.

In an effort to avoid potential misunderstanding about the meaning of logistics, this book adopts the current definition **promulgated** by the Council of Logistics Management (CLM) [5], one of the world's most prominent organizations for logistics professionals.

According to the CLM, " Logistic is the process of planning, **implementing**, and controlling the efficient cost-effective flow and storage of raw materials, in process inventory, finished goods, and related information from point of origin to point of consumption for the purpose of conforming to customer requirement."

According to Coyle, Bardi and Langley, there are four subdivisions of logistics:

- Business logistics—this is the same as the definition from the CSCMP and approach we are adopting in our discussion.
- Military logistics—all that is necessary to support the operational capability of military forces and their equipment in order to ensure readiness, reliability, and efficiency.
- Event logistics—management of all involved (activities, facilities, and personnel) in organizing, scheduling, and deploying the resources necessary to ensure the occurrence of an event and efficient withdrawal afterwards.
- Service logistics—acquisition, scheduling, and management of facilities, personnel, and materials needed to support and sustain a service operation.

Logistics is the management of the physical and information flows of products and of all activities related to these flows. [6] The physical flows of products include the movement of raw materials from suppliers (physical distribution).The information flows of products cover reports and documentation relating to goods movement. The activities related to these flows include: storage, inventory, packaging, materials handling, communication, site selection, and transportation. Thus, the logistics objective **encompasses** the delivery of products in correct quantities and qualities whenever they are required.

Logistics is changing at a rapid and accelerating rate. There are some reasons: pressure to change by the development of the system itself, more flexible and accurate logistic planning and controlling through computer data processing, being flexible in handling markets of different sizes for better competition, and competitive pressures leading to more efforts to improve customer service.

This definition has been further **augmented** to include: the potential contribution of logistics to achieving the goals of commercial enterprise is based upon (1) the integrated management of all activities related to inventory to achieve operating objectives at lowest possible costs, [7] and (2) the **proactive** use of logistics to help achieve customer satisfaction. [8] This definition needs to be analyzed in closer detail.

New Words

1. discipline *vt.*训练;使有纪律;处罚;使有条理 *n.*训练;纪律;学科;符合行为准则的行为(或举止)

2. promulgate *vt.*宣扬(某事物);传播;公布;颁布(法令、新法律等)

3. implement *vt.*实施,执行;使生效,实现;落实(政策);把……填满 *n.*工具,器械;家具;手段;[法]履行(契约等)

4. encompass *vt.*围绕,包围;包含或包括某事物;完成

5. augment *vt.*增强,加强;增加,增添;(使)扩张,扩大 *n.*增加,补充物

6. proactive *adj.*前摄的;积极主动的;主动出击的;先发制人的

Phrases

1. supplying goods   商品供应
2. management function   管理功能
3. economic activity   经济活动
4. fundamental role   基本角色
5. logistics discipline   物流学科
6. customer requirement   客户需求
7. military logistics   军事物流
8. integrated management   综合管理
9. play a (an) ...role in ...   扮演……角色,起……作用
10. in an effort to   企图,努力想,试图要

Notes

1. There are few aspects of human activity that do not ultimately depend on the flow of goods from point of origin to point of consumption.

几乎人类所有的活动都最终依赖于货物从产地到消费地点的流动。

2. Since the construction of the pyramids in ancient Egypt, logistics has made remarkable strides.

自古埃及建造金字塔以来,物流业已取得了很大的进步。

3. Time and again, brilliant logistics solutions have formed the basis for the transition to a new historical and economic era.

很多良好的方案不断地为物流业向新的历史与经济时期的转变奠定了基础。Time and again,一次又一次地,不断地。

4. Quite frankly, from approximately 1950 to 1980, limited appreciation was shown for the importance of logistics discipline.

其实,大约在 1950 年到 1980 年间人们才对物流学科的重要性有所了解。

5. Council of Logistics Management,简称 CLM,是全球最有影响的物流专业组织。于 2005 年 1 月 1 日正式更名为美国供应链管理专业协会(Council of Supply Chain Management Professionals,CSCMP)。物流管理协会(Council of Logistics Management,CLM) 成立于 1963 年,凭借会员的积极参与和杰出才能,协会一直致力于推动物流业的发展,为物流从业人员提供教育的机会和信息。为实现这一目标,物流协会向行业人士提供了种类繁多的项目、服务、相关活动,促进从业人员的参与,了解物流业,从而对物流事业作出贡献。

6. Logistics is the management of the physical and information flows of products and of all activities related to these flows.

物流是对产品的实际流动与信息流动,及对与这些流动相关活动的管理。

7. the integrated management of all activities related to inventory to achieve operating objectives at lowest possible costs

用最低成本对所有库存相关活动进行综合管理,以达成操作目标

8. the proactive use of logistics to help achieve customer satisfaction

充分运用物流业来帮助实现客户满意度

Section B What is the Scope of Logistics Activities?
物流活动的范围

The word "logistics" comes from the Greek logistikë, which translates as "the art of calculating" using concrete items, in contrast with arithmetike, which was the art of calculating using abstract concepts. The latter eventually evolved into the modern concepts of **arithmetic** and **algebra.**

Figure 1-1 Military logistics at the wartime

Historically, the concept of logistics stems from specific facets of industrial and military management.[1] However, the modern **interpretation** of the term "logistics" has its origins in the military, where it was used to describe the activities related to the **procurement** of ammunition and essential supplies to troops located at the front (see Figure 1-1).

Military logistics is the discipline of planning and carrying out the movement and maintenance of military forces. [2] In its most comprehensive sense, [3] it is those aspects or military operations. The field of logistics has become much broader than initially defined.

In the industrial and commercial sector, logistics is often called "business logistics" or "industrial logistics". Modern industrial logistics is related to the effective and efficient flow of materials and information that are of vital importance to customers and clients in various sections of the economic society.[4] It covers a variety of activities which include, but are not limited to, the following:

- Souring
- Purchasing
- Warehousing
- Inventory management
- Product distribution
- Transportation
- Customer service

Logistics is usually thought of in connection with military or manufacturing operations.

However, there can be projects involved in logistics (e.g. building a bridge to move troops) and logistics involved in projects (e.g. supplying materials to a construction site). It is not surprising, then, that these two disciplines interact and learn from each other.

Social and political **implications** also result from logistics. Social and cultural unity is achieved. The exchange of goods leads to an exchange of ideas and culture. The accompanying personal contacts encourage a national and international outlook, replacing narrow local or provincial views. From a political perspective, logistics contributes to a strong national defense.[5] The nation's investment in transportation facilities (roads, highways, ports, etc.) is in response to logistics needs. The political influence extends also to the economic and safety regulations of transport carriers. In fact, the nation's transportation network reflects a political as well as an economic base.

More recently, logistics has been viewed on a much broader scale and the field of logistics has been growing at a rapid pace, stimulated primarily by the technological, sociological, and economic trends in our world today. Some well-known logistics companies include UPS, FedEx etc (see Table 1-1).

In summary, logistics occupies a major role in an economy. Economic, social, and political benefits are realized, affecting both the interests of the nation and its individual citizens.

Table 1-1　Global industrial logistic companies

	Company	Business	Sales (million dollar)	Net Profit (million dollar)	Increase in Profit(%)
1	Deutshe Post/Danzas Group	Express, forwarder, logistics	30,858	2,245	7.3
2	UPS	Logistics, forwarder, express	29,771	2,934	15.2
3	FedEx	Air cargo, logistics	19,629	584	5.5
4	Nippon Express	Truck, forwarder, logistics	14,211	215	2
5	Union Pacific	Railway	11,878	842	16
6	Stinnes/Schenker	Forwarder, logistics	11,345	142	2.2
7	TPC/TNT/CTI Group	Express, logistics	9,374	496	9.3
8	A.P.Moller	Shipping, logistics	9,338	119	3.5
9	BNSF	Railway, logistics	9,025	1,019	23.4
10	NYK	Shipping, logistics	9,152	287	7.7

New Words

1. arithmetic　　*n.*算术,计算;算法

2. algebra　　*n.*代数学,代数

3. interpretation　　*n.*解释,说明;翻译;表演,演绎;理解

4. procurement　　*n.*获得,取得;采购

5. implication　　*n.*含义;含蓄,含意,言外之意;卷入,牵连,牵涉,纠缠;[逻辑学]蕴涵,蕴含

Phrases

1. transportation facility　　运输工具

2. concrete item　　具体实物

3. abstract concept　　抽象概念

4. essential supply　　重要的、必要的供应

5. stem from　　来源于

6. result from　　由于

7. in response to　　回答;响应

8. safety regulations　　安全规程,安全守则

Notes

1. Historically, the concept of logistics stems from specific facets of industrial and military management.

从历史角度看,物流这一概念来源于工业及军事管理的一些特定方面。

2. Military logistics is the discipline of planning and carrying out the movement and maintenance of military forces.

军事物流是关于军事行动的计划与实施,及军事力量的维持。

3. in its most comprehensive sense

从更广泛的角度来看

4. Modern industrial logistics is related to the effective and efficient flow of materials and information that are of vital importance to customers and clients in various sections of the economic society.

现代工业物流是关于材料与信息的高效率流动,而这些材料和信息对经济社会的多个领域的顾客来说都是至关重要的。

5. From a political perspective, logistics contributes to a strong national defense.

从政治角度来看,物流有利于增强国防力量。

Section C　Logistics Strategies　物流策略

Efficient management of the flow of goods from point-of-origin to point-of-consumption at the macro society or micro firm levels requires successfully planning, implementing, and controlling a multitude of logistics activities. [1]

Effective logistics resolves around five key issues—movement of product, movement of information, time/service, cost and integration. [2]

The increasing rate of change in technologies and markets and the search for competitive advantage has led to a new focus on logistics strategy and management. The modern organization in a free market needs to be agile, able to make rapid decisions, in order to respond to the changing **circumstances** and thereby gain an advantage over its competitors. [3] Logistics strategy appears as a subset of the overall strategy. It is about **formulating** a long-term plan for the supply chain, as distinct from solving the day-to-day issues and problems that inevitably occur. [4] Logistics must be consistent with corporate goals and strategies of organization. Logistics provides the interface between the external and internal environments, and consists of five interrelated components:

- Configuration/facilities network strategy
- Coordination or organization strategy
- Customer service strategy
- Integrated inventory strategy
- Information technology strategy

As businesses continue to globalize, attention has increasingly turned to international logistics strategies. The international strategy is an element of the internationalization strategy of **manufacturing** companies. The decision about which international logistics strategy to choose can be made only within the context of the overarching internationalization strategy. When a company creates international logistics strategies, it is defining the service levels at which its logistics organization is at its most cost effective. Wal-Mart's business has been able to grow rapidly and now become well-known company, because the cost savings as well as international logistics strategies and distribution systems and supply chain management have made **tremendous** achievements.

New Words

1. circumstance　　n.境况;境遇;(尤指)经济状况;命运;环境;事件;境遇;机遇
2. formulate　　v.构想出;规划;确切地阐述;用公式表示
3. manufacturing　　n.制造业,工业　　adj.制造业的,制造的　　v.(大规模)制造(manufacture 的现在分词);捏造;加工;粗制滥造(文学作品)
4. tremendous　　adj.极大的,巨大的;可怕的,惊人的;极好的

Phrases

1. competitive advantage　　竞争优势
2. overall strategy　　总体战略
3. external and internal environment　　内外环境
4. distribution system　　分销系统

5. supply chain management　供应链管理

6. search for　寻找,搜索

7. lead to　导致,通向

8. respond to　对……做出回应,响应

9. supply chain　供应链,供给链,供需链

10. consistent with　符合,与……一致

11. consist of　由……组成,构成 consist(of)：由……组成;包含

12. turn to　转变;变成

13. as well as　也;和……一样;不但……而且……

14. logistics strategies　物流策略

Notes

1. Efficient management of the flow goods from point-of-origin to point-of-consumption at the macro society or micro firm levels requires successfully planning, implementing, and controlling a multitude of logistics activities.

无论是宏观社会还是微观企业,要使货物从产地高效流通到消费地,必须成功地计划、执行和控制各种物流活动。

2. Effective logistics resolves around five key issues—movement of product, movement of information, time/service, cost and integration.

有效的物流是围绕着五个要素展开的——产品的流动、信息的流动、时间/服务、成本和一体化。

3. The modern organization in a free market needs to be a agile one, able to make rapid decisions, in order to respond to the changing circumstances and thereby gain an advantage over its competitors.

自由市场中的现代组织必须反应敏捷,并能够对环境的变化做出快速的决定,从而获得超过其竞争对手的优势。

4. It is about formulating a long-term plan for the supply chain, as distinct from solving the day-to-day issues and problems that inevitably occur.

与那些不可避免的几乎每天发生的情况和问题不同的是,这是关于制订长期供应链计划。

📚 Section D　Using Logistics as A Competitive Weapon
物流作为一种竞争武器

Logistics is a hot topic in China and the whole world. Although it is anything but a newborn baby, lots of people still have limited awareness of, and knowledge about logistics. [1]

The purpose of logistics is to gain a competitive advantage in the marketplace. By improving customer service performance, expanding **geographical** markets, and increasing market **penetration** of present markets, logistics contributes to additional sales. It increases **revenue**.[2]

Logistics has the "7R" characteristics, namely: the right product with the right quality in the right quantity has to be delivered at the right time and right place to the right customer at the right cost.

Logistics supports competitiveness and availability as a whole by meeting the ends-customer demands in supplying what is needed in the form it is needed, when it is needed at a competitive cost.

Service advantage

Increase and maintain customer service levels across all dimensions and channels, from delivery performance to **ad-hoc** customer response and last minute order changes. Logistics is an **integral** part of the customer service or marketing mix. Service now plays a major role in customers' buying decisions and logistics is targeted at customer service. Excellence in logistics can result in strong customer relationships, and improve the firm's value to the customer.

Time advantage

Reduce overall cycle time—from order placement or demand **projection** to customer delivery and availability to a matter of hours and days. [3] Time measures how long a customer has to wait in order to receive a given product or service. Speeding up the supply chain processes may help to maintain the customers, because they don't want to wait, especially for those prepared to pay more to get what they want.

Cost advantage

Logistics accounts for a major **portion** of a company's value chain costs, and savings through improved logistics strategies and improved processes go straight to the bottom line. Many products are supported from a supply chain point of view by low-cost manufacture, distribution, servicing and the like, such as "own brand". Examples of products that compete on low price are "own brand" supermarket goods that reduce operation cost and advertising cost of major brands. Because of the low cost, Tesco[4] can develop and offer responsible products at affordable prices to as many consumers as possible through its own brand ranges (See Figure 1-2).

New Words

1. geographical   *adj.*地理学的,地理的
2. penetration   *n.*渗透,穿透;[军]突破;洞察力
3. revenue   *n.*(土地、财产等的)收入,收益,所得,[复数]总收入
4. ad-hoc   *n.*点对点;对等式
5. integral   *adj.*完整的;积分的;必需的   *n.*整体;积分

Figure1-2　Tesco's Own Brand Products

6. projection　　*n.*预测;规划,设计;[心]投射;突起物

7. portion　　*n.*一部分

Phrases

1. appropriate to　将(某物)分配给

2. as a whole　作为一个整体;总的来说

3. integral part　主要的部分,组成部分

4. customer service　客户服务,售后服务

5. be targeted at　以……为目标

6. result in　导致,结果是

7. speed up　加速,使加速

8. supply chain　供应链

9. bottom line　底线,最低限度

10. additional sales　额外销售额

11. marketing mix　市场营销组合

12. own brand　自有品牌,又称为商店品牌,是指零售企业从设计、原料、生产到经销全程控制的产品,由零售企业指定的供应商生产,贴有零售企业品牌,在自己的卖场进行销售,实质上是零售业的OEM产品。其特点是自产自销商品,省去许多中间环节,使用自有品牌的商品可以少支付广告费,进行大批量生产、销售,可以取得规模效益,降低商品的销售成本。

Notes

1. Logistics is a hot topic in China and the whole world. Although it is anything but a newborn baby, lots of people still have limited awareness of, and knowledge about logistics.

　物流在中国乃至全世界都是一个热门话题。虽然它已经不是一个新生事物了,但是不少人对物流的认识仍然有限。

be aware of something 意识到

2. By improving customer service performance, expanding geographical markets, and

increasing market penetration of present markets, logistics contributes to additional sales. It increases revenue.

通过改善客户服务,拓展地域市场,以及提高目前市场渗透率,物流有助于增加销售和总体收入。

3. Reduce overall cycle time—from order placement or demand projection to customer delivery and availability to a matter of hours and days.

降低总周期时间,即包括从下订单到客户交付和使用,甚至降低到小时和天。

4. Tesco:乐购是以生产"康师傅"方便面闻名的台湾顶新国际集团于 1997 年创立的连锁超市品牌,2006 年由英国最大的零售商——Tesco 控股经营,全名为"Tesco 乐购"。截至 2008 年 10 月,Tesco 乐购在华东、华北和华南三个区域拥有 58 家大卖场。

Section E　Logistics Industry in China　中国的物流行业

During the past few years, China's logistics industry witnessed rapid growth. "According to the statistics of **National Development and Reform Commission**, National Bureau of statistics of China and **China Logistics and Purchasing Association**, during the 10th Five-Year Plan period, the total amount of social logistics reached RMB 158.7 trillion." [1] The figure has increased by 1.4 times compared with that of the 9th Five-Year Plan period. According to the industry report in 2006, the total amount of social logistics accounted for 18.6% of GDP in 2005, which has dropped from 19.4% in 2000. That means the total amount of social logistics exceeded RMB 1.2 trillion in 2005.

Logistics is a **perspective** industry in China.

Firstly, governments pay more attention to logistics and investment in logistics infrastructure is increasing year by year in China. The roads, railways and ports are getting much better. The logistics technique and equipment are being enhanced, too. The logistics industry is booming in Pearl River Delta, Yangtze River Delta and Bohai Sea Rim Economic Zone. At the same time, Northeast China are strengthening the **consolidation** and **coordination**, constructing the vast environment for the development of logistics industry. [2] China's economic developing strategies are becoming **explicit**, and related policies are being carried out gradually. These will have profound influence on the logistics Industry.

Secondly, the rapid development of related industries, such as chain sales, auto, steel, medicine, and coal industry, arouses the development of the industry of logistics.

Thirdly, managers have realized the importance of operating efficient and **integrated** logistics. China's modern logistics is enhancing its operating efficiency, performing more obvious functions in supporting and promoting economic development. Integrated **transportation**, storage and delivery will lower the cost and achieve more benefit in enterprises and society. Nowadays, more and more enterprises have paid attention to **value-adding** activities, which would greatly promote the industry. [3]

After entering WTO, China's logistics market is opening up to the outside world logistics enterprises. The entering of foreign enterprises will reorganize and integrate in the competitive environment in China. The year of 2006 is the first year of China's 11th Five-Year Plan, and is also the first year when logistics is opened up completely.

It is obvious that state owned, private owned and foreign funded enterprises will survive and thrive in the competitive markets. [4] However, the related risks must be **put into account**, and it should be cautious when choosing investment projects.

New Words

1. perspective　*n.* 观点;远景;透视图　*adj.* 透视的
2. consolidation　*n.* 巩固;合并;团结
3. coordination　*n.* 协调,调和;对等,同等
4. explicit　*adj.* 明确的;清楚的;直率的;详述的
5. integrated　*adj.* 综合的;完整的;互相协调的　*v.* 整合;使……成整体(integrate 的过去分词)
6. transportation　*n.* 运输;运输系统;运输工具;流放

Phrases

1. National Development and Reform Commission　国家发展与改革委员会
2. China Logistics and Purchasing Association　中国物流与采购协会
3. value-adding　价值增值的
4. put into account　将考虑在内

Notes

1. "According to the statistics of National Development and Reform Commission, National Bureau of statistics of China and China Logistics and Purchasing Association, during the 10th Five-Year Plan period, the total amount of social logistics reached RMB 158.7 trillion."

据国家发改委、国家统计局、中国物流与采购协会统计,"十五"期间,社会物流总量达到 158.7 万亿元人民币。

2. At the same time, Northeast China are strengthening the consolidation and coordination, constructing the vast environment for the development of logistics industry.

与此同时,中国东北地区正在加强整合与协调,为物流业的发展营造广阔的环境。

3. Nowadays, more and more enterprises have paid attention to value-adding activities, which would greatly promote the industry.

如今,越来越多的企业重视增值活动,这将极大地促进行业的发展。

4. It is obvious that state owned, private owned and foreign funded enterprises will survive and thrive in the competitive markets.

很明显,国有、私营和外资企业将在竞争激烈的市场中生存和发展。

🎯 Core Concepts　核心概念

1. Logistics is referred to the article flow, but not including the flow of the people.

物流是指商品货物的流动,但不包括人的流动。

2. The concept of article in logistics includes tangible goods and intangible service, such as customer service, freight agents and logistics network design.

物流中物品的概念包括有形的实体货物和无形的服务,例如:客户服务、货运代理及物流网络设计。

3. Logistics documents generally refer to documentations required to complete all processes of logistic, such as contracts, bills, and notes.

物流单证泛指实现一切物流过程的各种文件,例如合同、账单、票据。

4. The external logistics is about the macro-economic activities, like international trade and global investment.

社会物流是指宏观经济活动,如:国际贸易和全球投资。

5. The four key procedures in the internal logistics are supply, production, distribution and reverse.

企业物流中四个关键程序是:供给、生产、配送和逆向物流。

6. A standardized logistic system ensures better time management, location choices and distribution capacities.

标准化的物流系统确保高效的时间管理、适当的位置选择和更好的配送能力。

7. Logistics system includes customer service, packaging, transportation, storage, distribution processing and information control.

物流系统包括客户服务、包装、运输、仓储、配送及信息管控。

8. Market share is the proportion of sales of goods or service provided by one company to the industry sales of such goods or service.

市场份额是指某家产品销售公司提供的货物或服务在整个市场所占的比例。

9. Customer Relationship Management (CRM) is software to manage the relationship and communication between customers and suppliers.

客户关系管理(CRM)是用来管理客户和供应商之间的关系和交流的软件系统。

10. A logistics model is a standardized module that is used to regulate the cargo transportation, manage logistics facilities and equipments.

物流模型是用来调节货物运输、管理物流设施与设备的标准模块。

11. A logistic center consists of a series of integrated logistic activities, processes, equipments, and information network.

物流中心是由一系列的综合的物流活动、过程、设备及信息网络组成。

12. Customized logistics refers to a logistic system or process specifically designed to cater to an individual customer's requirements and needs.

定制物流是专门设计用来满足个别用户需求的物流系统和过程。

13. Logistics alliance refers to the long-term cooperation and business relationship between logistics supplier and customers.

物流联盟是指在物流服务商和客户间形成的长期合作的业务联系。

14. Time value in logistics refers to the differences in value of the same goods in different time.

物流的时间价值是指同样的货物在不同的时间具有不同的价值。

15. Location value in logistics refers to the differences in value of the same goods in different locations.

物流的空间价值指的是同样的货物在不同地点具有不同价值。

16. Logistics vehicles include ships, trucks, trains and aircrafts used in the logistics process。

在物流过程中使用的运输工具包括轮船、卡车、火车和飞机。

Exercises 练习

Ⅰ. Answer the follow questions in English.

1. What is the characteristic of today's society mentioned in the article? Where might the competitions between business organizations come from?

2. According to this article, why is logistics so important?

3. What kind of role could be played by logistics in constructing pyramids in ancient Egypt?

4. What is CLM?

5. What is logistics? Please conclude a definition by yourself.

6. Where does the word "logistics" come from?

7. What is the difference between logistike and arithmetike?

8. How was logistics initially used in the military?

9. What is modern industrial logistics?

10. What activities may the modern industrial logistics cover ?

11. What are the five components that the logistics include?

12. What are the "7R" characteristics that logistics has?

13. What advantages does the logistics have?

Ⅱ. Choose the best word or phrase that fits the sentence.

1. These companies are highly competitive _____ each other in supplying goods and services.

    A. on   B. with   C. for   D. in

2. Time and again, brilliant logistics solutions have formed the basis for the transition to a new _____ and economic era.

　　A. history　　　　　　B. historical　　　C. historic　　　　D. political

3. The physical flows of products include the movement of raw materials from _____.

　　A. wholesalers　　　　B. suppliers　　　C. consumers　　　D. retailers

4. Logistics is the _____ of the physical and information flows of products and of all activities related to these flows.

　　A. management　　　　B. manager　　　C. charge　　　　D. control

5. The potential contribution of logistics to _____ the goals of commercial enterprise is based upon.

　　A. achieve　　　　　　B. achieving　　　C. achievement　　D. achieved

6. The field of logistics has become much broader than initially _____.

　　A. define　　　　　　B. defining　　　C. definition　　　D. defined

7. Logistics is usually thought of in connection with military or _____ operations.

　　A. manufacturing　　　B. manufacture　　C. manufacturer　　D. manufactured

8. The exchange of goods leads to an _____ of ideas and culture.

　　A. change　　　　　　B. interchange　　　C. exchange　　　D. changing

9. The nation's investment in transportation facilities (roads, highways, ports, etc.) is in _____ to logistics needs.

　　A. respond　　　　　　B. responsible　　　D. responsibility　　D. response

10. In fact, the nation's transportation network reflects a political _____ an economic base.

　　A. but　　　　　　　B. other than　　　C. as well as　　　D. rather than

11. Logistics must be _____ with corporate goals and strategies of organization.

　　A. persistent　　　　　B. associated　　　C. constant　　　D. consistent

12. As businesses continue to _____, attention has increasingly turned to international logistics strategies.

　　A. urbanize　　　　　B. modernize　　　C. globalize　　　D. localize

13. By improving customer service performance, expanding geographical markets, and increasing market penetration of present markets, logistics _____ additional sales.

　　A. contributes to　　　B. attributes to　　　C. due to　　　　D. owes to

14. Logistics accounts for a major _____ of a company's value chain costs, and savings through improved logistics strategies and improved processes go straight to the bottom line.

　　A. proportion　　　　　B. portion　　　C. section　　　　D. piece

15. Because of the low cost, Tesco can develop and offer responsible products at _____ prices to as many consumers as possible through its own brand ranges.

　　A. afford　　　　　　B. unacceptable　　　C. affordable　　　D. favorite

Ⅲ. Match each word on the left with its corresponding meaning on the right.

A.	B.
1. essential	(a) unusual or striking
2. ultimately	(b) having a quality that thrusts itself into attention
3. origin	(c) a detailed list of all the items in stock
4. remarkable	(d) just in time
5. prominent	(e) the act of getting possession of something
6. inventory	(f) absolutely necessary; vitally necessary
7. distribution	(g) the smallest possible quantity
8. acceleration	(h) as the end result of a succession or process
9. implementing	(i) the act of distributing or spreading
10. procurement	(j) the place where something begins

Ⅳ. Fill in the blanks with words or phrases from the list below.

playing …role in	conforming to	on low price	depend on
in connection with	in an effort to	speeding up	internal
investment in	related to		

1. There are few aspects of human activity that do not ultimately _____ the flow of goods from point of origin to point of consumption.

2. Logistics has been _____ a fundamental _____ global development for almost 5,000 years now.

3. _____ to prevent the crisis getting worse, the government is making its best to work out a positive policy.

4. All the processes are actually working for only one purpose of _____ customer requirement.

5. Logistics is the management of the physical and information flows of products and of all activities _____ these flows.

6. Logistics is usually thought of _____ military or manufacturing operations.

7. The nation's _____ transportation facilities (roads, highways, ports, etc.) is in response to logistics needs.

8. Logistics provides the interface between the external and _____ environments.

9. _____ the supply chain processes may help to maintain the customers, because they don't want to wait, especially for those prepared to pay more to get what they want.

10. Examples of products that compete _____ are "own brand" supermarket goods that reduce operation cost and advertising cost of major brands.

Ⅴ. Translate the following sentences into Chinese.

1. U.S. shippers say there are innumerable issues to keep in mind when setting up supply chain and logistics operations in China. However, most agree that becoming successful in the region requires customization with several logistics partners.

2. Smith is adamant about integrating department, for example, purchasing department must have open communication with its import and export departments.

3. Companies are in a race to leverage emerging markets—both as lower-cost supply sources and as new sources of revenue.

4. Eight of history's ten largest mergers occurred in 2006; so the fact that mergers and acquisition (M&A) will be biggest and more frequent than ever should not come as a surprise.

5. Guangdong's key ports realized cargo throughput of 886 million tones in 2008, up 6.19 percent year on year.

Ⅵ. Translate the following sentences into English.

1. 美国经济高度发达,也是世界上最早发展物流业的国家之一。

2. 20 世纪 60 年代,随着世界经济环境的变化,美国现代化市场营销的观念逐步形成,客户服务成为企业经营管理的核心要素。

3. 据了解,世界 500 强中的 400 多家企业在中国都有投资,其中 90%左右的外资企业选择了物流外包。

4. 一个成功的物流企业,必须具备较大的运营规模,建立有效的地区覆盖,具有强大的指挥和控制中心。

5. UPS 是全球最大的投递机构,全球最大的包裹递送公司,同时也是全球最大的专业运输和物流服务提供商。

Ⅶ. Fill in the blanks with words from the list below and each word can be used once.

Since the 40-year reform and opening up, the development and evolution of Chinese logistics industry has experienced three stages: Agglomeration (凝聚) on the eastern coastal region in the early (before 1999); Gradient propulsion from eastern to the middle and west region (1999—2008); Overall layout __1__ balanced in the national area (after 2008). From the __2__ of Chinese logistics industry development in space and time shows that: Chinese logistics industry pattern of __3__ development and regional economic development __4__ that from gradients to equilibrium is coincide; Logistics industry gathering in areas with better location and __5__ ; and __6__ international industrial transfer accelerated the space evolution of the logistics industry layout; Urban agglomeration becomes an __7__ base for the development of __8__ logistics industry; It is __9__ the __10__ area of the development of Chinese logistics industry in the future.

A) important	B) regional	C) seriously
D) relatively	E) Domestic	F) modern
G) core	H) evolution	I) revolution
J) too	K) also	L) strategy
M) method	N) transportation	O) communication

Chapter 2

Inventory Management
库 存 管 理

Section A What is Inventory? 库存的定义

Inventory represents one of the most important assets that most businesses possess, because the **turnover** of inventory represents one of the primary sources of revenue generation and **subsequent** earnings for the company's **shareholders** or owners. [1] Decisions on inventory are both high risk and high impact throughout the supply chain. Inventory committed to supporting future sales drives a number of **anticipatory** supply chain activities. [2] Without the proper inventory management, lost sales and customer **dissatisfaction** may occur. Inventory must be maintained at a proper level and provided in a timely fashion, otherwise production efficiencies will erode, as in the case of a service or manufacturing business, or sales will **plummet**, as in the case of a wholesaling or retailing business.

Formulation of an inventory policy requires an understanding of the role of inventory in manufacturing and marketing. [3] Inventory serves five purposes within the firm: (1) it enables the firm to achieve economies of scale; (2) it balances supply and demand; (3) it enables specialization in manufacturing; (4) it provides protection in demand and order cycle; and (5) it acts as a buffer between critical interfaces within the channel of distribution. [4]

There are several different categories or types of inventory. The first is called materials and **components**. This usually consists of the essential items needed to create or make a finished product, such as gears for a bicycle, microchips for a computer, or screens and tubes for a television set.

The second type of inventory is called work in progress inventory (WIP). This refers to items that are partially completed, but are not the entirely finished product.

The third and most common form of inventory is called completely finished goods. These are the final products that are ready to be purchased by customers and consumers. Finished goods can range from cakes to furniture to vehicles. Most people think of the finished goods as being part of an inventory stock, but the parts that create them are held accountable in inventory as well.

The raw materials, work-in-process goods and completely finished goods are considered to be the portion of a business' assets that can be calculated with money and they are ready or will be ready for sale.

There are many different ways that companies handle their inventory. Overall it depends on what kind of business it is. For example, a food manufacturer who makes canned meat may take into account every single piece of that can in its inventory. The materials used to make the can, the labels, the meat, and the spice filling could all be part of the overall analysis of inventory.[5] Keeping track of inventory can be a complex process. Several different people are involved in logistics. This can include everything from the owner of the company to the transportation company that delivers the goods to the manufacturing plant. By using complex systems such as **barcode** integration, every piece of inventory from the smallest parts to the largest finished product can be tracked and observed. You may wonder why companies keep such a close eye on their inventory. Without inventory control, millions of dollars could be lost each year just because there was no accountability for everything involved in making a product.

New Words

1. turnover　*n.*翻滚,翻倒,弄翻,逆转,转向;半圆形的小馅饼;营业额,成交量,证券交易额;[体育运动]易手,失球　*adj.*可翻下的,或折转的

2. subsequent　*adj.*后来的;随后的;作为结果而发生的;附随的

3. shareholder　股东,投资者;股民

4. anticipatory　*adj.*预期的;提早发生的

5. dissatisfaction　*n.*不满,不平;令人不满的事物

6. plummet　*vi.*垂直落下;骤然跌落　*n.*铅锤;坠子;重压物

7. component　*n.*(机器、设备等的)构成要素,零件,成分;成分;[物理化学]组分;[数学]分量;(混合物的)组成部分

8. barcode　*n.*条形码

Phrases

1. be committed to　致力于

2. consist of　由……构成;包含

3. range from ... to ...　在从……到……的范围或幅度内变动或变化

4. be considered to be　被认为是

5. depend on　依靠;依赖;取决于

6. keep an eye on　照看;留意;密切注视

7. retailing business　零售业

8. involve in　参与;包含;涉及

Notes

1. Inventory represents one of the most important assets that most businesses possess,

because the turnover of inventory represents one of the primary sources of revenue generation and subsequent earnings for the company's shareholders or owners.

库存是大多数企业拥有的最重要的资产标志之一,因为存货周转代表着公司的股东或业主创收和后续盈利的主要来源之一。

2. Inventory committed to supporting future sales drives a number of anticipatory supply chain activities.

以支持未来销售为目的的库存能够驱动一系列预期供应链活动。

3. Formulation of an inventory policy requires an understanding of the role of inventory in manufacturing and marketing.

库存策略的制定要求了解库存在制造及营销中的作用。

4. (4) it provides protection in demand and order cycle; and (5) it acts as a buffer between critical interfaces within the channel of distribution.

(4)保护需求周期和订货周期;(5)在分销渠道的主要环节起缓冲作用。

5. The materials used to make the can, the labels, the meat, and the spice filling could all be part of the overall analysis of inventory.

用来制作罐头、标签、肉、香料填充的材料都可能是总体库存分析的一部分。

Section B   Inventory Carrying Cost   库存执行成本

Inventory costs are important for three reasons. First, inventory costs represent a significant component of total logistics costs in many companies. [1] Second, the inventory levels that a firm maintains at points in its logistics system will affect the level of service the firm can provide to its customers. Third, cost trade-off decisions in logistics frequency depend on and ultimately affect inventory carrying cost. [2]

The cost to carry inventory measures the **overhead** that an organization carries to support its inventory. In addition to the money originally spent to purchase it, more money will be spent on upkeep while inventory sits in your possession. The longer the inventory is there, the more it will cost in upkeep. Carrying cost is usually expressed as a percentage that represents the cents per dollar that will be spent on inventory overhead per year.

Assuming an annual inventory carrying cost percentage of 20 percent, the annual inventory expense for an enterprise with $100 million in average inventory would be $20 million.

Inventory Carrying Cost = Inventory Carrying Rate (See above) × Annual Inventory Expense (20% × $100). While the **calculation** of inventory carrying expense is basic, determining the appropriate carrying cost percent is less obvious.

Inventory carrying costs consist of a number of different factors or elements, and the importance of these factors can vary from product to product.

There are four major components of inventory carrying cost: **obsolescence**, storage space cost, insurance cost, and taxes.

Obsolescence

Inventory obsolescence means inventory is no longer salable because of **pilferage**, fire or technical, fashion obsolescence and price decline.[3] Obsolescence cost results from **deterioration** of product during storage. For example, **perishable** items such as meat, bread, fruit and **pharmaceuticals** whose guarantee period is short, which make them with little or no value after the **expiration** date, which affects the consumption. By contrast, a book loses its value more slowly through time. Obsolescence also includes financial loss when a product no longer has fashion appeal or no longer has any demand.

Storage Cost

Storage cost includes handling costs associated with moving products into and out of inventory, as well as storage costs such as rent, heating, cooling and lighting. Some products have very specialized storage requirements, for example, ice cream must be stored at a temperature below −18℃ (see Table 2-1).

Table 2-1　Storage Temperature for Food

Products	Storage temperature(℃)	Products	Storage temperature(℃)
Meat	−2~4	Ice cream	−18
Fish	−1~1	Milk	2~5

Insurance Cost

Insurance of inventory against fire, flood, theft and other **perils**. Insurance cost is an expense based upon estimated risk or loss over time, which is not uniform across products. For example, high-value products are easily stolen, which causes higher insurance costs. In addition, hazardous products also cause high insurance costs. Be especially aware of chemical products that require high cost storage precautions and fire control methods as these may increase fire insurance costs.

Taxes

Taxes represent yet another component of inventory carrying costs. Inventory tax is what we call the property tax on business inventories. High inventory levels resulting in high tax costs can be significant in determining specific locations. The tax rate and means of assessment vary by location. Many governments have high inventory taxes that they're levying against businesses to enhance their own cash flow in this economy. [4] The more inventories you have in stock, the more you're going to pay in taxes. For companies, managing his inventory more effectively may save an enormous amount of cash. Firms must consider tax when calculating inventory carrying cost.

Not surprisingly, an increase or decrease in the carrying cost percentage will affect the relevant inventory expenses.

New Words

1. overhead   *adj.*上面的,高架的;头顶上的;(费用等)经常的,管理的   *n.*天花板;管理费用,经常费用;船舱的顶板;[体](网球等的)扣杀   *adv.*在头顶上;在空中;在楼上;向上

2. calculation   *n.*计算,估算,计算的结果

3. obsolescence   *n.*废弃;陈旧过时;<生>(器官的)废退

4. deterioration   *n.*恶化;变坏;退化;堕落

5. pilferage   *n.*行窃,偷盗;小偷小摸

6. perishable   *adj.*易腐烂的;易腐败的;易毁灭的;易消亡的   *n.*容易腐坏的东西(尤指食品)

7. pharmaceutical   *adj.*制药的,配药的   *n.*药物

8. expiration   *n.*满期;截止;呼气;(气的)呼出

9. peril   *n.*极大危险;危险的事(或环境)

Phrases

1. in addition to   除了;除……之外;加之

2. result from   起因于;由……造成

3. expiration date   截止日期

4. by contrast   相比之下;与之相比;与之相反

5. no longer   不再

6. storage cost   仓储成本,保管费用

7. be aware of   知道;意识到

8. cash flow   资金流动

9. inventory carrying cost   保管费用,库存费用

10. insurance cost   保险费

Notes

1. First, inventory costs represent a significant component of total logistics costs in many companies.

首先,库存成本在许多公司的总物流成本中占据很大比重。

2. Third, cost trade-off decisions in logistics frequency depend on and ultimately affect inventory carrying cost.

第三,物流系统中的成本权衡决策时常取决于库存保管成本,并最终对其产生影响。

3. Inventory obsolescence means inventory is no longer salable because of pilferage, fire or technical, fashion obsolescence and price decline.

库存废旧是指库存不再适销,其原因可能是偷盗、火灾或者技术过时、样式陈旧和价格下降。

4. Many governments have high inventory taxes that they're levying against businesses to enhance their own cash flow in this economy.

许多国家的政府对企业收取较高的库存税以增加现有经济下的现金流。

Section C   JIT   准时制物流

To progress further, one needs to **address** not only the specific demand factors for spares, but to **evaluate** these factors in terms of the overall inventory requirements. [1] Too much inventory may **ideally** respond to the demand for spares. However, this may be costly, with a great deal of capital tied up in the inventory.

Perhaps the most widely discussed **approach** to inventory management is the Just-in-Time, or JIT approach. In today's business environment people often refer to a JIT manufacturing process, JIT inventories, or a JIT delivery system.

The **commonsense** phrase "just in time" is an inventory strategy that strives to improve a business return on investment by reducing in-process inventory and **associated** carrying costs. JIT can improve a manufacturing organization's return on investment, quality, and efficiency; it suggests that inventories should be available when a firm needs them—not any earlier, nor any later. From an historical view, Ford Motor Company [2] was a **marvelous** example of Just-in-Time manufacturing, but his ideas on inventory were not widely held. At that time, some retailers attempted to run their production or ordering off of a sales mix report or their experience. In many cases producing or ordering too much product opens the window for waste. The goal with JIT is to limit the window and keep the waste to a minimum.

After World War Ⅱ, operations research developed theories on inventory management which determined optimized lot sizes, reorder points, and distribution stocking levels. In the 1970's, an absolutely different theory was developed in Japan, used by Toyota Motor Corporation[3]. Just-In-Time production method is also called the Toyota Production System. The concept that inventory should be kept at a minimum, lots should be very small, and products should be built "on demand" rather than stocked ran contrary to the current manufacturing "wisdom" in the US.[4] However, **Just-in-Time** models proved to have significant advantages in capital reduction, plant **throughput**, quality assurance and market responsiveness. The benefits of Japanese manufacturing techniques began to dawn on the US manufacturing community in the 1980's. This theory suggested that finding and "feeding" the bottleneck workstation in a manufacturing plant would allow all other processes to hold to a steady and predictable pace. JIT can improve a manufacturing organization's return on **investment**, quality, and efficiency.

" Waste is considered anything other than the absolute minimum resources of material, machines, and manpower required to add value to the product." This is in direct contrast to the traditional philosophy of "just in case", in which large inventories of safety stocks are held in event they are needed. [5]

New Words

1. address　*n.*(收件人的)称呼和地址;演讲,演说;谈吐;殷勤,求爱　*vt.*忙于,专注于;讲演;处理;在……写姓名地址

2. evaluate　*vt.*评价;求……的值(或数);对……评价;[数学、逻辑学]求……的数值　*vi.*评价,估价

3. ideally　*adv.*完美地;理想地;观念上地;理论上地

4. approach　*n.*方法;途径;接近

5. commonsense　*adj.*常识的,具有常识的

6. associated　*adj.*有关联的;联合的

7. marvelous　*adj.*引起惊异的;不可思议的;非凡的;神乎其神

8. Just-in-Time　*n.& adj.*及时的;及时盘存调节法的;适时制的,零库存的

9. throughput　*n.*生产量,生产能力,吞吐量;流率

10. investment　*n.*投资,投资额;[军]封锁;(时间、精力的)投入;值得买的东西

Phrases

1. in terms of　依据;按照

2. be respond to　对……做出反应

3. attempt to　尝试;企图;试图

4. in many cases　在许多情况下

5. absolutely different　完全不同

6. rather than　而不是

7. inventory management　存货[库存]管理

8. manufacturing community　制造业社区

Notes

1. To progress further, one needs to address not only the specific demand factors for spares, but to evaluate these factors in terms of the overall inventory requirements.

为了进一步发展,我们需要解决的不仅是具体的备件需求因素,而且要对这些整体库存需求方面的内容进行评估。

2. Ford Motor Company:创办者是美国汽车工程师与企业家亨利·福特(Henry Ford,1863年7月30日—1947年4月8日)。福特汽车公司是世界上第一家使用流水线大批量生产汽车的公司。

3. Toyota Motor Corporation:丰田汽车公司是一家总部设在日本爱知县丰田市和东京都文京区的汽车工业制造公司,隶属于日本三井财阀。丰田汽车公司自2008年始逐渐取

代通用汽车公司而成为全世界排行第一位的汽车生产厂商。其旗下品牌主要包括凌志、丰田等系列高、中、低端车型等。

4. The concept that inventory should be kept at a minimum, lots should be very small, and products should be built "on demand" rather than stocked, ran contrary to the current manufacturing "wisdom" in the US.

库存应保持在最低限度,批量产量应该非常小,产品应该按需求生产,而不是库存,这恰恰与当前美国的制造业"智慧"背道而驰。

5. "Waste is considered anything other than the absolute minimum resources of material, machines, and manpower required to add value to the product." This is in direct contrast to the traditional philosophy of "just in case", in which large inventories of safety stocks are held in event they are needed.

"用于增加产品价值的原料、机器和人力超过了起码数量即被认为浪费。"该思想与传统的"以防万一"形成了直接的对照,后者常常保管大量安全库存以备需要。

📚 Section D　ABC Analysis　ABC 分析法

ABC analysis is based on the Pareto principle. Vilfredo Pareto was an Italian economist who made an **observation** that a **preponderance** of the wealth was concentrated in the hands of a relatively small percentage of the population.[1] In the context of inventory control, Pareto's Principle is important because it recognizes that all the individual items which comprise the total inventory are not of equal relative importance. After the nineteenth-century the Italian philosopher **illustrated** graphically the fact that a small **proportion** of the population owned most of the wealth in Italy. It is sometimes called 80/20 rule, as 20% of the population owned 80% of the wealth.

ABC analysis is a business term used to define an inventory categorization technique often used in materials management. ABC analysis provides a mechanism for identifying items that will have a significant impact on overall inventory cost, while also providing a mechanism for identifying different **categories** of stock that will require different management and controls.

When carrying out an ABC analysis, inventory items are valued (item cost multiplied by quantity issued/consumed in period) with the results then ranked. The results are then grouped typically into three bands. These bands are called ABC codes. One issue with ABC analysis involves a determination of what percentage of items should be **classified** as A, B and C, respectively. It's important to recognize that either too high or too low a percentage of A items may reduce the potential efficiencies to be gained from the classification technique.[2]

A class inventory will typically contain items that account for 80% of total value, or 20% of total items. A items could be the ones with the highest criticality.

B class inventory will account for around 15% of total value, or 30% of total items. B items could be those with moderate **criticality**.

C class inventory will account for the remaining 5%, or 50% of total items. C items could have low criticality (see Figure 2-1).

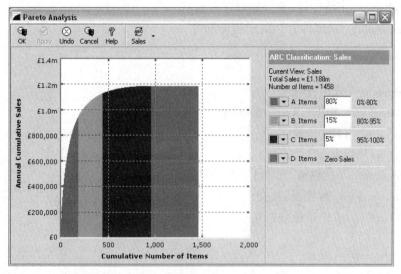

Figure 2-1   ABC Analysis

Each organization should tailor its inventory system to its own **peculiarities**. Organizations may choose to group their inventory into more than three classifications, but the principle is the same.

The ABC approach can also be used in other analyses such as:

- Spend per supplier in a portfolio: few suppliers will represent most of the spend.
- Number of orders per supplier: few suppliers will have most of the orders in a portfolio.
- Number of items bought per supplier: few suppliers will deliver most of the articles in a portfolio.

Before proceeding further, it should be noted that some companies are adding a fourth classification, D, to ABC analysis. D stands for "dogs," also referred to as dead inventory or excess inventory. The ABC method can be used for material, purchased parts, **subassemblies**, component parts, or products, depending on what form of inventory the company usually carries.

New Words

1. observation   *n.*观察;观察力;注意;观察报告
2. preponderance   *n.*优势
3. proportion   *n.*比,比率;[数学]比例(法);面积;相称,平衡
4. illustrated   *n.*有插画的报章杂志   *adj.*有插图的   *v.*给……加插图(illustrate 的过去式和过去分词);说明;表明;(用示例、图画等)说明
5. category   *n.*种类,类别;派别

拓展资源

6. classified　　*v.*分类(classify 的过去式和过去分词)

7. criticality　　*n.*危险程度;临界

8. peculiarity　　*n.*特性;特质;怪癖;奇形怪状

9. subassembly　　*n.*部件,组件;子组件部件

Phrases

1. in terms of　依据;按照

2. be based on　根据,以……为基础

3. group into　(使)分成

4. stand for　代表

5. account for　(在数量、比例上)占

6. be referred to　被提及;被交付

7. ABC analysis　帕累托分析法

Notes

1. Vilfredo Pareto was an Italian economist who made an observation that a preponderance of the wealth was concentrated in the hands of a relatively small percentage of the population.

维弗雷多·帕累托是意大利经济学家,他观察到,大量财富集中在少数人手中。

2. It's important to recognize that either too high or too low a percentage of A items may reduce the potential efficiencies to be gained from the classification technique.

重要的是,要认识到 A 中过高或过低的百分比项可能减少从分类技术中获得的潜在效率。

Section E　Economic Order Quantity　经济订货量

A long-standing issue in **inventory** management concerns how much inventory should be ordered at a particular time. The typical inventory order size problem, referred to as the economic order quantity (EOQ), deals with calculating the proper order size **with respect to** two costs: the costs of carrying the inventory and the costs of ordering the inventory. [1]

If there were no inventory carrying costs, customers would hold an **immense** inventory and avoid the vagaries of reordering. **Alternatively**, if there were no costs to ordering, one would continually place orders and maintain **virtually** no inventory at all, aside from safety stocks. [2] There are, however, costs of carrying inventory and costs of ordering inventory, Inventory **carrying costs** are in direct proportion to order size; that is, the larger the order, the greater the inventory carrying costs. **Ordering costs**, by contrast, tend to decline with the size of the order, but not in a **linear** relationship.

Although some view the EOQ as an outdated technique, others suggest that the EOQ allows "senior management to determine the money required to finance inventories, the length of time those funds are required, the source of that finance and the impact of its cost on the firm's profitability." [3].

The EOQ determines the point at which the sum of carrying costs and ordering costs are minimized, or the point at which carrying costs equal ordering costs. **Assuming** that carrying costs and ordering costs are accurate, the EOQ "is absolutely the most cost-effective quantity to order based on current operational costs." [4]

Mathematically, the EOQ can be calculated in two ways; one presents the answer in dollars, the other in units. In terms of dollars, suppose that $1 000 of a particular item is used each year, the order costs are $25 per order **submitted**, and inventory carrying costs are 20 percent. The EOQ can be calculated using this **formula**:

$$EOQ = \sqrt{2AB/C}$$

Where

EOQ = the most economic order size, in dollars

A = annual usage, in dollars

B = **administrative** costs per order of placing the order

C = carrying costs of the inventory (expressed as an annual percentage of the inventory dollar value)

Thus:

$$EOQ = \sqrt{2\times1000\times25/0.2} = \sqrt{250\ 000} = 500 \text{ order size}$$

Alternatively, the EOQ can be calculated in terms of the number of units that should be ordered. Using the same information as in the previous example, and assuming that the product has a cost of $5 per unit, the relevant formula is:

$$EOQ = \sqrt{2DB/(IC)}$$

Where

EOQ = the most economic order size, in units

D = annual demand, in units (200 units; $1 000 value of inventory/ $5 value per unit)

B = administrative costs per order of placing the order

I = dollar value of the inventory, per unit

C = carrying costs of the inventory (expressed as an annual percentage of the inventory's dollar value)

Thus:

$$EOQ = \sqrt{2\times200\times25/(0.2\times5)} = \sqrt{10\ 000/1} = 100 \text{ units}$$

Although we've calculated EOQs, how do we know that the answers are correct? Because the EOQ is the point where carrying costs equal ordering costs, we need to calculate both of these costs (see Table 2-2). Ordering cost can be calculated by multiplying the number of orders per year times the ordering cost per order. For example, because an order size of

$ 1 000 means that we're ordering once a year, the ordering cost would be 1× $ 25, or $ 25.

Table 2-2　EOQ Cost Calculations

Number of Orders Per Year	Order Size ($)	Ordering Cost ($)	Carrying Cost ($)	Total Cost (Sum of Ordering and Carrying Cost) ($)
1	1 000	25	100	125
2	500	50	50	100
3	333	75	33	108
4	250	100	25	125
5	200	125	20	145

Because of the **assumption** of even outward flow of goods, inventory carrying costs are applied to one-half of the order size, a figure that represents the average inventory.[5] Average inventory is multiplied by the carrying costs of the inventory (expressed as a percentage of the dollar value). Thus, when ordering once per year, the order size of $ 1 000 is divided by 2, **yielding** $ 500. This, in turn, is multiplied by 0.20, resulting in a carrying cost of $ 100. The $ 25 ordering cost and $ 100 carrying cost are not equal, thus indicating that we haven't found the EOQ.

Recall that we calculated $ 500 (100 units) to be the EOQ. As shown in Table 2-2, a $ 500 order size means that we'll be ordering twice per year; the corresponding ordering costs are $ 50. Average inventory for a $ 500 order size is $ 250, meaning that our carrying costs are $ 50. Thus, we've proven that at an order size of $ 500, our ordering costs and carrying costs are equal. Table 2-2 presents the total cost calculations for several other order sizes. Note that ordering costs equal carrying costs at the EOQ and that the total cost is minimized as well.

Several caveats bear mention. First, EOQs, once calculated, may not be the same as the lot sizes in which a product is commonly bought and sold. Second, the simple EOQ formulation does not take into account the special discounts given to encourage larger orders or increased volumes of business.[6] Third, there is an implicit assumption of demand certainty; that is, demand is continuous and constant over time. The inclusion of one, or more, of these caveats will alter EOQ calculations.

New Words

1. inventory　*n.* 存货,存货清单;详细目录;财产清册

2. immense　*adj.* 巨大的,广大的;无边无际的;非常好的

3. alternatively　*adv.* 要不,或者;非此即彼;二者择一地;作为一种选择

4. virtually　*adv.* 事实上,几乎;实质上

5. linear　*adj.* 线的,线型的;直线的,线状的;长度的

6. assuming　*v.* 假设(assume 的现在分词)　*adj.* 傲慢的;不逊的;僭越的

7. submit　*v.* 递交；主张；屈服

8. formula　*n.* 公式，准则；配方；婴儿食品

9. administrative　*adj.* 管理的，行政的

10. assumption　*n.* 假定；设想；担任；采取

11. yielding　*v.* 出产（作物），产生（收益）；屈从；放弃；给（大路上的车辆）让路
（yield 的现在分词）

Phrases

1. with respect to　关于；至于
2. carrying cost　持有成本
3. ordering cost　订货成本

Notes

1. The typical inventory order size problem, referred to as the economic order quantity (EOQ), deals with calculating the proper order size with respect to two costs: the costs of carrying the inventory and the costs of ordering the inventory.

典型的库存订货批量问题，即经济订货量（Economic Order Quantity, EOQ），涉及按照库存持有成本和订货成本这两项成本，计算合理的订货批量问题。

2. Alternatively, if there were no costs to ordering, one would continually place orders and maintain virtually no inventory at all, aside from safety stocks.

另外，如果没有订货成本，顾客将不停地订货，除了安全存量以外，不存在其他库存。

3. Although some view the EOQ as an outdated technique, others suggest that the EOQ allows "senior management to determine the money required to finance inventories, the length of time those funds are required, the source of that finance and the impact of its cost on the firm's profitability."

虽然有些人认为经济订货量是一种过时的方法，但更多的人认为经济订货量有助于"高级管理者确定库存所需经费、经费占用时间、来源及其对企业盈利能力的影响"。

4. Assuming that carrying costs and ordering costs are accurate, the EOQ "is absolutely the most cost-effective quantity to order based on current operational costs."

如果持有成本与订货成本是准确的，经济订货量"就是使目前运营成本最低的订货量"。

5. Because of the assumption of even outward flow of goods, inventory carrying costs are applied to one-half of the order size, a figure that represents the average inventory.

由于假设物品的流动是均匀的，因此库存持有成本可以采用库存量的一半（即平均库存）来计算。

6. Second, the simple EOQ formulation does not take into account the special discounts given to encourage larger orders or increased volumes of business.

第二，简单的经济订货量公式并没有考虑为鼓励大宗订货或增大业务量所提供的特

别折扣优惠。

🎯 Core Concepts 核心概念

1. Storage is a process in which goods are stored, protected and managed.

存储是货物被存放、保护和管理的过程。

2. Every manufacturer and wholesaler need inventory.

每个制造商和批发商都需要存货。

3. Fixed Quantity System (FQS) is more accurate and convenient than Fixed Interval System (FIS).

定量定货方式比定期定货方式更加准确和便利。

4. "Twenty-Eighty" analysis method is the same as ABC classification.

"20-80"分析法和 ABC 分类方法类似。

5. Zero Inventory is guaranteed by the full market supply and Just in Time (JIT).

零库存的前提是充足的市场供应和准时制。

6. Cycle stock is the maximum inventory based on the maximum needs.

周转库存量是根据最大需要而定的最大库存量。

7. Safe stock refers to minimum inventory level given the forecasted market demand.

安全库存量是根据市场预期需求而定的最小库存量。

8. The average time when the goods is moved in and out of warehouse is inventory cycle time.

货物进出仓库的平均时间就是存货周转时间。

9. Inventory control is the method to keep the best inventory level and position with the minimum cost to satisfy the demand.

存货控制是以最佳存货水平和最低成本费用来满足需要的过程。

10. When the inventory is reduced to a specific level, purchase for new parts and material will start. It is called the Order Point System.

当存货减少到一定水平,新的零部件和原料的购买将开始,这被称为"订购点系统"。

11. Zero stock means zero inventory.

零库存意味着零存货。

12. Inspection is the operation to check the quantity, quality and package of the goods according to the contract and specific standards.

盘查是根据合同和相关标准检查货物数量、质量和包装的操作。

13. Commodity inspection is the process in which exported and imported goods are examined for their quantity, quality, package, place of production, safety and hygiene condition.

进出口商品检验是检查进出口货物的数量、质量、包装、产地和卫生安全状况的过程。

14. The purpose of Just in Time (JIT) is to meet demand instantly, with perfect quality

and punctuality.

"准时制"的目的是以高质量和高准时性来满足即时需要。

15. Zero stock is the best way for inventory control.

"零库存"管理是存货控制的最好方法。

Exercises　练习

Ⅰ. Answer the follow questions in English.

1. What is the definition of inventory?

2. What are the categories or types of inventory?

3. What are the ways that companies handle their inventory?

4. How to calculate inventory carrying cost?

5. What are the four major components of inventory carrying cost?

6. What does storage cost include?

7. What does insurance cost refer to?

8. What does high inventory levels result in?

9. What does JIT refer to?

10. What is ABC analysis?

Ⅱ. Choose the best word or phrase that fits the sentence.

1. _____ refers to a statement of taxable goods or of properties subject to customs duty.

　A. Declaration　　B. Submission　　C. Legislation　　D. Examination

2. _____ the warehouses in the factory is 6.

　A. A number of　B. A lot of　　C. Lots of　　D. The number of

3. Twenty dollars _____ all I need right now.

　A. being　　B. have been　　C. are　　D. is

4. The documentary bill is operated through _____ , therefore, it has certain advantages to both the sellers and buyers.

　A. agents　　B. buyers　　C. sellers　　D. banks

5. Everything _____ consideration, the price is reasonable.

　A. take into　　　　B. taking into

　C. being taken into　　D. taken into

6. Overhead and inventory carrying costs are always present but may _____ in a variety of ways.

　A. be allocating　B. be allocated　C. allocate　　D. allocated

7. Successful inventory management involves _____ the costs of inventory with the benefits of inventory.

A. balance　　　　B. balancing　　　　C. between　　　　D. among

8. It is necessary to establish adequate controls _____ inventory on order and inventory in stock.

A. under　　　　B. about　　　　C. on　　　　D. over

9. Today, the use of computer systems to control inventory is far more _____ for small business than ever before.

A. feasible　　　　B. practical　　　　C. acceptable　　　　D. easy

10. The degree of success in addressing these concerns is easier to gauge for some than for _____.

A. another　　　　B. those　　　　C. others　　　　D. other

11. Keeping _____ of inventory can be a complex process.

A. trace　　　　B. tackle　　　　C. track　　　　D. touch

12. Inventory carrying costs _____ a number of different factors or elements, and the importance of these factors can vary from product to product.

A. consist in　　　　B. consist of　　　　C. including　　　　D. compose

13. Not surprisingly, an increase or decrease in the carrying cost _____ will affect the relevant inventory expenses.

A. percent　　　　B. percentage　　　　C. proportion　　　　D. ratio

14. However, Just-in-Time models proved to have significant advantages in _____ reduction, plant throughput, quality assurance and market responsiveness.

A. money　　　　B. investment　　　　C. capital　　　　D. captain

15. JIT can improve a manufacturing organization's _____ on investment, quality, and efficiency.

A. return　　　　B. reward　　　　C. award　　　　D. turn

Ⅲ. Match each word on the left with its corresponding meaning on the right.

A.	B.
1. inventory	(a) a collection of things sharing a common attribute
2. component	(b) arrange or order by classes or categories
3. category	(c) a detailed list of all the items in stock
4. deterioration	(d) just in time
5. precaution	(e) an abstract part of something
6. classify	(f) laying out money or capital in an enterprise
7. JIT	(g) the smallest possible quantity
8. minimum	(h) balance among the parts of something
9. proportion	(i) a precautionary measure warding off danger
10. investment	(j) a symptom of reduced quality or strength

Ⅳ. Fill in the blanks with words or phrases from the list below.

are ready to	take into account	appeal	associated with
based upon	attempted	represents	handle
purchase	in stock		

1. Inventory _____ one of the most important assets that most businesses possess, because the turnover of the inventory represents one of the primary sources of revenue generation and subsequent earnings for the company's shareholders or owners.

2. These are the final products that _____ be purchased by customers and consumers.

3. There are many different ways that companies _____ their inventory.

4. A food manufacturer who makes canned meat may _____ every single piece of that can in its inventory.

5. In addition to the money originally spent to _____ it, more money will be spent on upkeep while inventory sits in your possession.

6. Obsolescence also includes financial loss when a product no longer has fashion _____ or no longer has any demand.

7. Storage cost includes handling costs _____ moving products into and out of inventory, as well as storage costs such as rent, heating, cooling and lighting.

8. Insurance cost is an expense _____ estimated risk or loss over time, which are not uniform across products.

9. The more inventories you have _____, the more you're going to pay in taxes.

10. At that time, some retailers _____ to run their production or ordering off of a sales mix report or their experience.

Ⅴ. Translate the following sentences into Chinese.

1. Just-in-time inventory management is an approach which works to eliminate inventories rather than optimize them.

2. Unless inventories are controlled, they are unreliable, inefficient and costly.

3. Inventory management includes the integrated management and control of assigned items of material.

4. One of the hottest supply chain technologies in 2007 was supply chain inventory optimization, an application that grew by 32% while the overall supply chain management space grew about 7%.

5. Experts agree one way to improve inventories is to shorten the supply chain by selectively moving some production closer to home.

Ⅵ. Translate the following sentences into English.

1. 在工业化国家里,物流是工业生产中增加利润的最后一关,这一点已经有共识。

2. 几个模式的成本特点各有千秋,决定了费率结构有所不同。

3. 从字面意思上看,库存指的是对做生意所需的任何必要的东西的存储。

4. 处于 JIT 管理中的货品、直接转运中的货品以及在长途运输中的货品都在存货控制管理的范围内。

5. 库存分析时应考虑有关的货物销售量和库存周转量,并在 ABC 的基础上完成。

Ⅶ. Fill in the blanks with words from the list below and each word can be used once.

The goal of the EOQ formula is to identify the optimal number of product units to order so that a company can minimize its costs related to buying, taking delivery of and storing the units. The economic order quantity (EOQ) __1__ can be modified to __2__ different production levels or order interval lengths, and __3__ with large supply __4__ and high variable costs use an algorithm in their computer software to determine EOQ.

EOQ is an important __5__ flow tool for management to minimize the cost of inventory and the amount of cash tied up in the __6__ balance. For many companies, inventory is the __7__ asset owned by the company, and these __8__ must carry sufficient inventory to meet the __9__ of customers. If EOQ can help minimize the level of inventory, the cash savings can be used for some other business __10__ or investment.

A) determine	B) businesses	C) cash
D) credit	E) formula	F) chains
G) material	H) needs	I) lowest
J) largest	K) corporations	L) transportation
M) purpose	N) invention	O) inventory

Chapter 3

Transportation and Transportation Management
运输与运输管理

Section A History of Transportation 运输的历史

Transportation system is a crucial factor in economic growth and in the transportation of regions and cities. When transport system is improved, transport services firms will gain lowered transport costs, time savings, more relaiblility, logistics services, etc.[1] All these attributes will help enhance economic performance and promote total factor productivity and endogenous growth.[2]

The history of transportation **spans** the entire history of man. Early **Paleolithic** and **Neolithic** man walked through his world on his own two legs, and couldn't transport more than he was able to carry on his back. In the late Neolithic, horse and camel began to be used after animal **domestication**,[3] but even then they could only carry what could be loaded onto or tied to their animals' backs. At some point early man became **ambitious** enough to want to move large stones or other heavy objects, and human **ingenuity devised** the log roller for this task.[4] There is evidence that many cultures in many geographic areas used simple log roller technology, but pyramid construction involved complex organization of labor and the physical movement of large stone blocks from their quarries to the pyramid sites. The means of transportation in logistics has changed dramatically in the long river of history (see Table 3-1).

Tab. 3-1 Partial List of Events on Transportation

3500 BC	Fixed wheels on carts were invented—the first wheeled vehicles in history Other early wheeled vehicles included the chariot River boats were invented—ships with oars
2000 BC	Horses were domesticated and used for transportation
181-234	The **wheelbarrow** was invented
770	Iron horseshoes improved transportation by horse
1492	Leonardo da Vinci first to seriously theorize about flying machines—with over 100 drawings that illustrated his theories on flight
1620	Cornelis Drebbel invented the first submarine—an human oared submersible

1662	Blaise Pascal invented the first public bus—a horse-drawn, regular route, schedule, and fare system
1740	Jacques de Vaucanson demonstrated his clockwork powered carriage
1783	First practical steamboat demonstrated by Marquis Claude François de Jouffroy d'Abbans—a paddle wheel steamboat
1783	The Montgolfier brothers invented the first hot air balloons
1787	Steamboat invented First self-propelled road vehicle invented by Nicolas Joseph Cugnot
1790	Modern bicycles invented
1801	Richard Trevithick invented the first steam powered locomotive (designed for roads)
1807	Isaac de Rivas makes a hydrogen gas powered vehicle—first with internal combustion power—however, very unsuccessful design
1807	First steamboat with regular passenger service invented by Robert Fulton—Clermont
1814	George Stephenson invented the first practical steam powered railroad locomotive
1862	Jean Lenoir made a gasoline engine automobile
1867	First motorcycle invented
1868	George Westinghouse invented the compressed air locomotive brake which enabled trains to be stopped with fail-safe **accuracy**
1871	First cable car invented
1885	Karl Benz built the world's first practical automobile powered by an internal combustion engine (See Figure 3-1)
1899	Ferdinand von Zeppelin invented the first successful dirigible—the Zeppelin
1903	The Wright Brothers invented and flew the first engine airplane
1907	Very first helicopter—unsuccessful design
1908	Henry Ford improved the assembly line for automobile manufacturing
1908	Hydrofoil boats co-invented by Alexander Graham Bell & Casey Baldwin—boats that skimmed water
1926	First liquid propelled rocket launched
1940	Modern helicopters invented
1947	First supersonic jet flight
1956	**Hovercraft** invented
1964	Bullet train transportation invented
1969	First manned mission (Apollo) to the Moon
1970	First jumbo jet
1981	Space shuttle launched

Source: http://inventors.about.com/, 2011

Thousands of years went by, and then, in our own times, **multifarious** advanced technologies are gaining ground. Transportation engineering increasingly involves the applications of advanced technologies known collectively as intelligent transportation systems (ITS), which have a broad spectrum of advanced technology. ITS encompass a broad range of wireless and wire line communications-based information and electronics technologies. When integrated into the transportation system's **infrastructure**, and in vehicles themselves, these technologies relieve congestion, improve safety and enhance the productivity (see Figure 3-1).

Figure 3-1　Karl Friedrich Benz in his first automobile.

(Reproduced courtesy of the Library of Congress.)

New Words

1. span　*n*.共轭(马、骡);跨度,墩距;一段时间;[航] 跨绳;*vt*.缚住或扎牢;跨越时间或空间;以掌测量;以手围绕测量类似测量

2. Paleolithic　*adj*.[考古]旧石器时代的

3. Neolithic　*adj*.新石器时代的;早先的,已经过时的

4. domestication　*n*.驯养,驯化

5. ambitious　*adj*.有雄心的;有野心的;有抱负的;炫耀的

6. ingenuity　*n*.足智多谋,心灵手巧;独创性;独出心裁,设计新颖;巧妙,精巧

7. devised　*v*.想出(devise 的过去式和过去分词);计划;设计;发明

8. wheelbarrow　*n*.独轮手推车

9. accuracy　*n*.精确(性),准确(性)

10. hovercraft　*n*.水翼船

11. multifarious　*adj*.许多的,多方面的;各式各样的;多样性的

12. infrastructure　*n*.基础设施;基础建设

Phrases

1. at some point　在某一时刻

2. intelligent transportation system　智能交通系统

3. a range of 一系列

4. integrate into   成为一体,融入;使并入

5. go by 时间逝去,从……旁经过,依照

Notes

1. When transport system is improved, transport services firms will gain lowered transport costs, time savings, more reliability, logistics services, etc.

当物流系统改善时,运输服务公司会获得更低的运输成本,节省更多的时间,从而提供更加可靠的物流服务等。

2. All these attributes will help enhance economic performance and promote total factor productivity and endogenous growth.

所有这些都会提高经济效益,提升全要素生产率和内生经济增长。

3. In the late Neolithic, horse and camel began to be used after animal domestication.

在新石器时代晚期,马和骆驼经过驯养后开始用于运输货物。

4. At some point, early man became ambitious enough to want to move large stones or other heavy objects, and human ingenuity devised the log roller for this task.

在人类社会的初期,人类就有足够的雄心去移动大石头或其他重物,从而利用其特有的聪明才智设计出圆木辊子来完成这项任务。

Section B   Basic Principles   基本原则

An industrialized society without efficient transportation system seems a contradiction in terms. [1] As a consumer, we often take for granted that products will move from where they are produced to where they are consumed with a minimum of difficulty— in terms of both time and cost. [2] The transportation sector of most industrialized economies is so pervasive that we often fail to comprehend the magnitude of its impact on our way of life. [3]

A formal definition of transportation is the element of economic activity which **accomplishes** the movement of persons and goods from one place to another. To an economist, the definition implies the supplying of place **utility**. To the marketing manger, it means the **completion** of another sale. To the production manager, transportation is the receipt of needed equipment or materials. To the logistician, transportation means a most useful tool for accomplishing an objective. [4] To the nation, transportation means thousands of jobs and the economies and output of mass production. And, finally, to the consumer, transportation is the satisfaction of needs and wants. This satisfaction is derived from the safe delivery of hundreds of thousands of goods into the hands of millions of people everywhere. One of transportation's most important roles is serving as a subsystem of logistics. Many people have the mistaken idea that transportation and logistics are **essentially** the same thing. But a logistics system, whether of an economy or a firm, is made up of many subsystems, inventory control, warehousing, material handling, packaging, site selection, communications, traffic management, and transportation. In most logistics systems, transportation is a logistics subsystem which achieves significance by its contribution to the overall **accomplishment** of logistics goals.

Whatever its relative importance is within the firm's logistics system, transportation performs the basic objective of place utility creation. Few firms are located geographically adjacent to both their sources of supply and markets. Materials and equipment must be placed at the manufacturing site to be useful in production. Products must be delivered to the market to effect sales. Transportation is the primary logistics subsystem which accomplishes the physical closure between supply, production, and consumption.

It is this closure between producer and consumer that allows the modern industrial economy to exist and function. Without transportation, the world's economy would be an **agrarian** one, operating at a subsistence level. Modern industry is dependent upon trade, and trade demands transportation.

Academic interest in transportation has also developed and **evolved**. Today, there are many institutions of higher learning with courses and programs and many excellent texts in transportation and transport management. [5] Transportation is the movement of people and goods from one location to another. Movement refers to the planning, monitoring and controlling of the movement through all the stages of the journey between origin and ultimate destination.

In order to be effective, movement organization must operate on a set of basic principles.

- Centralized control
- Regulation
- **Flexibility**
- Maximum utilization

Transportation influences, or is influenced by, many logistics activities to include:

1. Transportation costs that are directly affected by the location of the firm's plants, warehouses, **vendors**, retail locations, and customers.

2. Inventory requirements that are influenced by the mode of transport used. High-speed, high-priced transportation systems require smaller amounts of inventories in a logistics system, whereas slower, less-expensive transportation requires larger amounts of system wide inventory.

3. The transport mode that selects influences the packaging required, and carrier classification rules that dictate package choice.

4. The type of carrier that **dictates** a manufacturing plant's materials handling equipment, such as loading and unloading equipment and the design of the receiving and shipping docks.

5. An order-management methodology that encourages maximum consolidation of shipments between common points and enables a company to give larger shipments to its carriers and take advantage of volume discounts.

6. Customer service goals that influence the type and quality of carrier and carrier service selected by the seller.

These principles are important when evaluating transportation alternatives. Students should recognize that an individual country's topology, economy, infrastructure, and other macro environmental factors could result in a different transportation system. A lack of infrastructure makes it difficult to transport. According to the following example, Turkey has its strengths and weaknesses in transportation.

Strengths：

- Having two road bridge (see Figure 3-2) crossings between Asia and Europe and having a railway crossing being constructed.

Figure 3-2　Euro-Asia Continent Bridge

- Having a freight fleet with a high capacity capable of making international transport.
- Increasing freight demand between the EU countries and Asia and the Middle East.
- Having internationally institutionalized firms in road transport and a knowledge built up on the subject.

Weaknesses：

- Densities of the highway and railroad network are under EU averages.
- There is no balance between the shares of transport modes.
- There is no Transportation Master Plan that will enable the assessment of national transportation as a whole.
- The railroads in the main corridors are quite old and they have single track. moreover, the lines between the major cities aren't suited to high-speed train operations.

New Words

1. accomplish　*v.*完成；达到(目的)；实现(诺言、计划等)
2. utility　*n.*功用，效用；有用的物体或器械；公用事业公司；公用事业　*adj.*有多种用途的；各种工作都会做的；能在数个位置作替补的
3. completion　*n.*完成，结束；实现；[数]求全法；期满
4. essentially　*adv.*本质上，根本上；本来；"essential"的派生

5. accomplishment   *n.*成就;完成;技能;履行

6. agrarian   *adj.*土地的;农业的;农村的;促进农业利益的;*n.*平均地权论者

7. evolved   *v.*演变,进化(evolve 的过去式和过去分词);(动植物等)进化,进化形成

8. flexibility   *adj.*灵活性的

9. vendors   *n.*摊贩(vendor 的名词复数);小贩;(房屋等的)卖主;卖方

10. dictate   *n.*命令,规定,要求;*v.*大声讲或读;口授;支配;摆布

Phrases

1. mass production   大规模生产

2. derive from   来自

3. relative importance   相对重要性

4. adjacent to   与……毗连的

5. take advantage of   利用

6. traffic management   交通运输管理

7. order-management methodology   订单管理方法

Notes

1. An industrialized society without efficient transportation system seems a contradiction in terms.

缺乏高效的运输系统的工业化社会,就其措辞上是自相矛盾的。

2. As a consumer, we often take for granted that products will move from where they are produced to where they are consumed with a minimum of difficulty—in terms of both time and cost.

作为消费者,我们时常理所当然地认为产品从产地运到消费地不存在时间与费用问题。

3. The transportation sector of most industrialized economies is so pervasive that we often fail to comprehend the magnitude of its impact on our way of life.

工业化经济的运输部门遍地可及,致使我们无法了解它对我们生活方式的影响有多大。

4. To the logistician, transportation means a most useful tool for accomplishing an objective.

对于物流家来说,运输是指用来完成目标的最有用的工具。

5. Today, there are many institutions of higher learning with courses and programs and many excellent texts in transportation and transport management.

如今,很多高等院校开设有关运输和交通管理方面的课程、项目,拥有大量这方面的优秀文本资料。

Section C　Transportation Modes　运输模式

A wide range of transportation mode **alternatives** are available to support product or service. For example, if you want to travel abroad, the element of transportation will be involved throughout your journey, first to the domestic airport, then to the foreign one, and finally to your destination. All this transportation needs to connect up so that you neither miss your flight nor have to wait a long time for it.

Transportation mode (or form of transport) is a term used to **substantially** distinguish different ways to perform transport. The most **dominant** modes of transport are rail, road, water, pipeline, and air, but other modes also exist, including cable transport, and off-road transport. All modes are suitable for transporting goods, and most are suitable for transporting people.

Rail transportation

The railroads are distinguished by their ability to move mass quantities of goods over long distances in an economical manner. They interchange equipment and traffic with each other continuously, thereby providing service between all points served by the railroads. They also offer many services in addition to line-haul movement, including storage, in-transit activities, switching, and freight **consolidation**. Rail transportation has been the product of the industrial era, playing a critical role in the economic development of Western Europe, North America and Japan. It enhanced a major improvement of technology in land transport and has greatly made important changes in the movement of goods and people. The railroads own their facilities and right-of-way. A heavy fixed investment is required, therefore, to provide and maintain the physical plant. Tracks, terminals and rolling stock are **illustrative**; the costs associated with this investment are largely independent of the volume of traffic, e.g., depreciation, taxes, interest, and some maintenance. Rail transportation has its advantage in long-distance or medium distances movement of goods in large quantities at relatively low costs. Reliable transportation of goods is the primary and determining **precondition** for its quality. Comparing rail traffic with other traffic modes, we find out the rail traffic is undoubtedly the most reliable traffic mode. Rail transportation has so low an accident rate, not so for automobile, neither air transport.

These fixed costs, plus the **administrative** overhead costs of operating a railroad, create condition where more than one-half of total costs are of a fixed nature. Variable costs, such as fuel and direct labor, are relatively less important to a railroad than to all other modes except pipelines.

Air transportation

Air transportation was slow to take off after the Wright Brothers **breakthrough** at Kitty Hawk in 1903. More than ten years passed before first **faltering** efforts to launch scheduled passenger services. By the eve of World War II, air travel was quite **literally** taking off, borne aloft by important advances in technology. War again encouraged the rapid growth of air transportation. In the years since the beginning of the Jet Age, commercial aircraft have advanced markedly in **capacity** and range. Yet the limitations that structure air transportation are mainly human creations. Relatively inexpensive air transport has also been crucial to the growth of tourism.

The aircraft is the fastest method of transport of the five modes. While still dwarfed by other transportation modes, carrying less than three-tenths of 1 percent of all freight, domestic air freight has become increasingly important in recent years. Air freight is usually limited to valuable products such as furs and computers or **perishable** products such as flowers and live **lobsters**.

Road transportation

Road infrastructures are large consumers of space with the lowest level of physical **constraints** among transportation modes. Road transportation has an average operational flexibility as vehicles can serve several purposes but are rarely able to move outside roads. Road transport systems have high maintenance costs, both for the vehicles and infrastructures.[1] They are mainly linked to light industries where rapid movements of freight in small batches are the norm. Yet, with containerization, road transportation has become a crucial link in freight distribution. The first land roads took their origins from trails which were generally used to move from one hunting territory to another. Road development **accelerated** in the first half of the 20th century. All road transport modes have limited potential to achieve economies of scale. This is due to size and weight constraints imposed by governments and also by the technical and economic limits of engines.

Pipeline

The first pipelines in the United States were introduced in 1860s. Pipelines are generally the most economical way to transport large quantities of oil, refined oil products or natural gas over land. In September, 1825, the Stockton & Darlington Railroad Company began as the first railroad to carry both goods and passengers on regular schedules using locomotives designed by English inventor, George Stephenson. Stephenson's locomotive pulled six loaded coal cars and 21 passenger cars with 450 passengers over 9 miles in about one hour.

The most dependable mode of transportation is the pipeline. Twenty-four percent of intercity freight is handled by pipelines. Pipeline transport is the transportation of goods through a pipe (see Figure 3-3). Most commonly, liquid and gases are sent. Pipelines are really the energy lifelines of almost every daily activity. Pipelines play a role in everyone's lives and are essential to the nation's industries. Product flow is continuous; movement is unaffected by weather conditions, and there are few labor strikes. Crude oil and product pipelines transport petroleum through a 6-40 inch diameter pipeline at a speed of 2-4 miles an hour. Natural gas, coal in slurry, liquid fertilizer, grain, potash, and similar products lend themselves to pipeline movement. The petroleum network includes approximately ninety carriers and extends over 165,000 miles, with single minimum shipments ranging from 25,000-75,000 barrels. Pipelines are almost everywhere designed for a specific purpose only, to carry one commodity from a location to another. The routing of pipelines is largely indifferent to terrain, although environmental concerns frequently delay approval for construction. Pipeline construction costs vary according to the diameter and increase proportionally with the distance and with the **viscosity** of fluids. Move costs for these types of products are only slightly higher than water, but substantially below those of other modes. Pipelines represent a very important mode for the transport of liquid and gaseous products.

Figure 3-3　Alaska Oil Pipeline

拓展资源

Water Transportation

From its modest origins as Egyptian coastal sail ships around 3,200 BC, maritime transportation has always been the dominant support of global trade. Water transportation, similar to land and air modes, operates on its own space, which is at the same time geographical by its physical attributes, strategic by its control and commercial by its usage. [2]

Water carriage by nature is particularly suited for movements of heavy, bulky, low-value-per-unit commodities that can be loaded and unloaded efficiently by mechanical means in situations where speed is not of primary importance, where the commodities shipped are not particularly susceptible to shipping damage or theft, and where accompanying land movements are unnecessary. [3]

Water transportation can be broken down into several distinct categories: (1) inland water way such as rivers and canals; (2) lakes; (3) coastal and intercoastal ocean; and (4) international deep sea. Water carriage competes primarily with rail and pipeline, since the majority of commodities carried by water are semi-processed or raw materials transported in bulk.

But because of the inherent limitations of water carriers, it is unlikely that water transport will gain a larger role in domestic and international commerce, although international developments have made marine shipping increasingly important. [4]

Some of the most outstanding technological development in transportation has occurred in the preceding 200 years. Each of them plays an important role in logistics by contributing to the movement of goods as well as providing additional transport-related services to shippers. All of the legal forms of transportation are woven into the modern forms, thereby complicating transport choice. To present the composition and characteristics of each mode is the objective of the section (see Table 3-2).

Table 3-2   Modern Transportation Characteristics

Mode	Service features
rail	Mass movement, long distances, low unit cost High capabilities Extensive coverage and large number of accessorial services
motor	Accommodates all types of goods Door-to-door service Intensive geographical coverage Speed, flexibility, and frequency
water	Mass movement of bulk commodities at the lowest cost High capabilities Advanced technology of loading and unloading
pipeline	Mass movement of liquid and gaseous materials at very low cost High capabilities Greatest dependability Pricing flexiblity
air	Premium service Reduced packaging and handling requirements Reduced costs for other logistics components

New Words

1. alternative   n.选择的余地;可供选择的事物;取舍,非传统生活方式的追随者(或鼓吹者)

2. substantially   adv.本质上,实质上;大体上;充分地;相当多地

3. dominant   *adj.*占主导地位的

4. consolidation   *n.*巩固;联合;合并;变坚固

5. illustrative   *adj.*用作说明的,解说性的

6. precondition   *n.*前提;先决条件;*vt.*预先处理;事先准备

7. administrative   *adj.*管理的,行政的;行政职位的;非战斗性行政勤务的

8. breakthrough   *n.*突破;穿透;重要技术成就

9. faltering   *adj.*犹豫的,支吾的,蹒跚的;*v.*(嗓音)颤抖(falter 的现在分词);支吾其词;蹒跚;摇晃

10. literally   *adv.*逐字地;照字面地;确实地,真正地;[口语]差不多,简直(用于加强语意)

11. capacity   *n.*容量;才能;性能;生产能力;

12. perishable   *adj.*易腐烂的;易腐败的;易毁灭的;易消亡的;*n.*容易腐坏的东西(尤指食品)

13. lobster   *n.*龙虾;龙虾肉

14. constraint   *n.*约束

15. accelerated   *adj.*加速的;*v.*(使)加快,(使)增速(accelerate 的过去式和过去分词);促使……早日发生,促进;[教育学]使(学生)跳级;提早学完(课程等)

16. viscosity   *n.*<术>黏稠;黏性;黏质

Phrases

1. connect up   接通,连接在一起

2. be borne aloft   被高擎

3. crucial to   至关重要的

4. be dwarfed by   相形见绌

5. light industry   轻工业

6. play an important role in   起着重要的作用

7. contribute to   有助于

8. air freight   空运的货物

Notes

1. Road transport systems have high maintenance costs, both for the vehicles and infrastructures.

公路运输系统中,无论是对车辆还是对基础设施的维护,其成本都很高。

2. Water transportation, similar to land and air modes, operates on its own space, which is at the same time geographical by its physical attributes, strategic by its control and commercial by its usage.

与陆地和空中的运输模式类似,水上运输在自己的空间内进行,同时在物理特性方面有地域性、在控制方面有策略性、在使用方面有商业性。

3. Water carriage by nature is particularly suited for movements of heavy, bulky, low-value-per-unit commodities that can be loaded and unloaded efficiently by mechanical means in situations where speed is not of primary importance, where the commodities shipped are not particularly susceptible to shipping damage or theft, and where accompanying land movements are unnecessary.

水上运输就其性质来说,尤其适合于承运大宗低值的商品,而且可采用机械装卸。其适应状况包括:速度对产品的运输影响不大,而且所运商品不易被损坏或偷窃,也不需要有路上运输。

4. But because of the inherent limitations of water carriers, it is unlikely that water transport will gain a larger role in domestic and international commerce, although international developments have made marine shipping increasingly important.

但是,由于水上运输的固有限制,尽管水上运输在国际贸易中的地位日益重要,但它不可能在国内与国际贸易中发挥更大作用。

Section D   Classification of Carriers   承运人分类

Transportation companies are classified into four basic types: common carriers, contract carriers, private carriers, and freight forwarders. [1] A common carrier offers to perform services within a particular line of business for the general public. Economically, the common carrier is the most highly **regulated** of all the legal carrier types. The economic regulation imposed upon these carriers (railroads and pipelines) acts to protect the shipping public and to ensure sufficient transport service within normal limits. One example is a truck line operating in an area where general merchandise is handled. The truck line is available to serve all the people in the area who offer it general merchandise to haul. However, it may decline to handle such items as liquid petroleum gas or **aviation** gas. Examples of common carriers are United Airlines. Common carriers are liable for all goods lost, damaged, or delayed unless caused by an act of God, an act of a public enemy, an act of public authority, an act of the shipper, or some defect within the good itself.

Contract carrier is for-hire carrier that does not hold itself out to serve the general public, rather it serves a limited number of shipper under specific contractual arrangement. [2] Contract carriers transport goods for hire by individual contract or agreement. They do not offer to perform services for the general public; instead, they usually offer services that meet the special needs of their customers. Contract carriers are most frequently engaged in business as owner/operator motor carriers. Usually they **solicit** large shipments from a particular shipper to a particular recipient. They have no legal service obligation. They often provide a specialized service and usually have lower rates than common or regulated carriers.

Private carriers transport their own property or deliver their services in their own vehicles. A private carrier's crucial legal distinction is that transportation must not be the controlling firm's primary business: stated differently, the carrier owner's primary business must be some commercial endeavor other than transportation. Private motor carriers may charge 100% owned **subsidiaries** and inter-corporate hauling fee. Amoco(American oil company) has its own fleet of oceangoing crude oil carriers. Federal Express has a ground fleet of more than 17, 000 vehicles and 145 airplanes to ensure fast, on-time delivery for its package service. The Federal Express trucks, painted with the company name and logo, also serve as advertisements. A private carrier is distinguished from a common carrier whose primary business is the transport of goods, and which is in business to serve any customers that hire them, such as buses, railroads, trucking companies, airlines and taxi. [3]

Freight forwarders differ from the other carriers in that they do not own any of the equipment used in intercity carriage of freight. They are common carriers that lease or contract bulk space from other carriers such as the airlines and railroads and resell this space to small-volume shippers. The freight forwarder picks up the merchandise from the shipper, loads it into the equipment of whatever carrier is being used, delivers it to its destination, and takes care of all the billing involved.

Freight forwarders provide shippers the advantage of better, less-expensive service, and the carriers do not have to handle many small shipments and the billing for them. [4] A further advantage of freight forwarding is that the forwarder knows at all times where each piece of freight is while it is in **transit**. This intermediary saves money for everyone and makes for improved service.

New Words

1. regulated　*v.*控制(regulate 的过去式和过去分词);管理;调整;调节
2. aviation　*n.*航空;飞行术,航空学;飞机制造业;[集合词]飞机
3. solicit　*vt.& vi.*恳求;征求;提起
4. subsidiary　*n.*附属事物,附属机构,子公司
5. transit　*n.*通过;搬运;转变;运输线;*vt.*通过;横越;运送;使(望远镜)水平横轴回转;*vi.*通过,经过

Phrases

1. classify into　分为
2. impose upon　强加
3. be engaged in　从事
4. commercial endeavor　商业行为
5. United Airlines　联合航空公司
6. Amoco　美国石油公司
7. on-time delivery　交货及时
8. bulk space　大容量空间

Notes

1. Transportation companies are classified into four basic types: common carriers, contract carriers, private carriers, and freight forwarders.

运输公司被分为四种基本类型：普通承运人、契约承运人、私人承运人和货运承运人。

2. Contract carrier is for-hire carrier that does not hold itself out to serve the general public, rather it serves a limited number of shipper under specific contractual arrangement.

契约承运人是待租承运人的一种，他们按照特定的合同向数量有限的托运人提供服务而不是向公众提供服务。

3. A private carrier is distinguished from a common carrier whose primary business is the transport of goods, and which is in business to serve any customers that hire them, such as buses, railroads, trucking companies, airlines and taxi.

私营承运人和普通承运人的区别在于，公共承运人的主营业务是货运运输，并对所有客户提供运输服务，如公路公司、铁路公司、卡车公司、航空公司和出租公司。

4. Freight forwarders provide shippers the advantage of better, less-expensive service, and the carriers do not have to handle many small shipments and the billing for them.

货运代理公司为货主提供更出色、更便宜的服务，因而运营商不必为他们处理出货量小和计费等问题。

Section E   Solving International Transportation Problems
解决国际运输中的问题

The recent **resurgence** in international trade has provided U. S. firms with a major opportunity to expand sales through exporting. This is particularly true for small and medium sized firms which have traditionally limited their marketing efforts to **domestic markets**. However, in order to **take advantage of** expanding foreign trade, infrequent and small volume producers must first **dispel** a major myth **associated with** distributing products to foreign customers. [1] This myth is that the complexities of international distribution make it very difficult for smaller firms to take advantage of expanding exports. So it seems that making arrangements for inland and port-to-port movements, combined with a **myriad** of documents, terms of sale, and government requirements is a **formidable** barrier to developing export sales. [2]

One solution to the problem of distribution complexities is to develop an external partnership with a third-party facilitator specializing in small volume movements and international documentation. Most firms entering world markets begin on a limited scale and cannot afford to invest heavily in a separate internal department with the required expertise to handle transportation arrangements and documentation associated with exporting. Even firms projecting large volume movements can encounter serious problems in organizing for foreign distribution. However, understanding what is involved with international movements and in partnership with a third- party intermediary, most companies can effectively develop export capabilities.

The following first examines the segments or components of an international movement along with the documentation required to complete the move. Second, the roles played by two external third parties, international freight forwarders and non-vessel-owning common carriers, in international distribution are examined. By understanding the requirements associated with an export movement, an appreciation can be developed for how a partnership with a third- party intermediary can make exporting a reality.

International distribution is **complicated** by the fact that transportation from a point of origin to **ultimate destination** involves decisions or **components** not associated with a domestic move. The basic components of an international movement include:

1) Port Selection—Domestic and foreign ports are selected based on **proximity** to origin and destination, land routing, ocean and air carrier services **available**, port costs (e.g. wharfage and handling), and any delays which may occur at the port. [3]

2) Inland Movement (Domestic origin to port)—A transportation mode and carrier must be selected and the routing from plant to a predetermined port established.

3) Port to Port Carrier Selection—For movements other than to Canada or Mexico, the choice of overseas modes is limited to ocean carriage and **air freight**. Selection of a mode is basically a function of rates, time in transit, and needs of the customer.

4) Delivery Movement (Foreign port to destination)—Upon arrival at the foreign port, arrangements must be made for delivery to the final destination.

5) Packing/Packaging—International and carrier requirements often dictate a necessity for a change in the way a product is packaged. This can be particularly true for ocean transportation.

6) Transit Insurance—Ocean carriers accept minimal liability, **necessitating** the purchase of additional insurance. [4] The type and scope of coverage must be determined.

7) Terms of Sale—A wide variety of sale terms are available which assign responsibility for method of payment, insurance, claims, and freight charges.

8) Import Duties—Duties are normally a function of the designed use of the product and product configuration.

9) Handling/Loading—Containerized **cargo** must be loaded at the plant, port, or by a third party. [5] **Break-bulk** movements often require additional handling and packaging.

10) Method of Financing—The costs and risks associated with the different methods of financing must be considered.

A complete description of all the alternatives related to each of these considerations is beyond the scope of this case. However, the above elements do provide the potential exporter with an appreciation for the variety of decisions that must be made.

New Words

1. resurgence　*n.* 复活;再现;再起
2. dispel　*v.* 驱散,驱逐;消除(烦恼等)
3. myriad　*n.* 无数,极大数量;无数的人或物　*adj.* 无数的;种种的
4. formidable　*adj.* 强大的;可怕的;令人敬畏的;艰难的
5. complicated　*adj.* 难懂的,复杂的
6. component　*n.* 部件;组件;成分
7. proximity　*n.* 接近;接近度,距离;亲近
8. available　*adj.* 可获得的;可购得的;可找到的;有空的
9. necessitating　*v.* 迫使(necessitate 的现在分词)
10. cargo　*n.* 货物,船货
11. break-bulk　*n.* 拆装;开舱卸货

Phrases

1. domestic markets　国内市场
2. take advantage of　利用
3. associated with　与……有关系;与……相联系
4. ultimate destination　最终目的地
5. air freight　航空运费;空运的货物

Notes

1. However, in order to take advantage of expanding foreign trade, infrequent and small volume producers must first dispel a major myth associated with distributing products to foreign customers.

然而,为了扩大对外贸易的优势,少数和小批量生产商必须首先消除向国外客户分销产品有关的这一主要幻想。

2. So it seems that making arrangements for inland and port-to-port movements, combined with a myriad of documents, terms of sale, and government requirements is a formidable barrier to developing export sales.

因此,为内陆和港口之间的运输做出安排,再加上大量的文件、销售条款和政府要求,似乎是发展出口销售的一个巨大障碍。

3. Port Selection—Domestic and foreign ports are selected based on proximity to origin and destination, land routing, ocean and air carrier services available, port costs (e.g. wharf-age and handling), and any delays which may occur at the port.

港口选择——选择国内和国外港口的依据是离出发地和目的地的远近、陆路路线、可用的海运和航空运输服务、港口成本(例如码头装卸)以及港口可能发生的任何延误。

4. Transit Insurance—Ocean carriers accept minimal liability, necessitating the purchase of additional insurance.

运输保险——海运承运人承担最少的责任,因此需要购买额外的保险。

5. Handling/Loading—Containerized cargo must be loaded at the plant, port, or by a third party.

装卸——集装箱货物必须在工厂、港口或由第三方进行装卸。

🎯 Core Concepts   核心概念

1. Liner transport has three specific components: fixed ports, fixed routes and announcing shipping time in advice.

班轮运输有三个专门要素:固定的港口,固定的航线和预定的船期表。

2. Shipping by chartering is used for transporting low value goods.

租船运输用来运输低值货物。

3. The broker company in ocean transportation is called shipping agency.

从事海洋运输的经纪公司被称为船务代理。

4. Air freight costs 5 times more than transportation by trucks and 20 times more than by rail. But it is more reliable, punctual and predictable under normal operating condition.

航空运输的费用是公路运输的5倍,铁路运输的20倍之多,但是它在通常情况下更加准时、可靠和可预测。

5. Bulk container is used to load bulk cargo.

散货集装箱用来装载散货。

6. Cargo is freight carried by a ship, an aircraft, or another vehicle, upon the agreement for the delivery of goods.

货物通过货物运送协议被装载于轮船、飞机,或者其他交通工具。

7. Tanker container is mainly used to transport oil and gas.

罐式集装箱主要用来运输石油和天然气。

8. Deadhead means a vehicle, such as an aircraft and truck that transports no passengers or freight during a single trip.

"空车"意味着交通工具如:飞机,卡车等在某次运输中无乘客或货物。

9. Back haul is the distance traveled from the delivery destination point back to the departure point.

回程运输是指从交货目的地到出发点的反向运输。

10. Shipper and carrier are two parties in a shipping contract.

托运人和承运人是海运合同的两个当事人。

11. Usually, the buyer in the trading contract is consignee.

通常贸易合同的买方是收货人。

12. Liner sails in the fixed route between fixed ports and sends sailing information in

advance.

班轮运输在固定港口之间有固定的航线而且事先公布航运信息。

13. Brokers are agents who coordinate shippers and carriers by providing timely information about rates, routes and service capabilities.

经纪人是协调托运人和承运人关系的代理人,他能及时提供关于费率,航线和服务能力的相关信息。

14. TEU and FEU both are containers which are used in ocean transportation frequently.

20 英尺集装箱和 40 英尺集装箱都是在海运中经常使用的集装箱。

15.Transport agencies include air and surface freight forwarders, shippers associations and transport brokers.

运输代理包括航空和水陆货运代理、托运人协会和运输经纪人。

16. Freight forwarders purchase long distance service from water, rail, air even and truck carriers.

货运代理人从水运,铁路运输,航空甚至公路运输中购买长距离运送服务。

17. International Railway Bill can be used in land bridge transport.

国际铁路货运单可以用于大陆桥运输。

18. Transportation using multiple transportation means is also called combined transport.

采用多种运输方式的运输也叫多式联运。

19. Transportation creates location value in logistics.

在物流中运输创造了地点价值。

20. Door-to-door delivery refers to carriers picking up the goods from the shipper's warehouse and delivering it to consignee's warehouse.

门到门运输是指从托运人的仓库提取货物送到收货人的仓库。

21. Containerization can speed up the logistics process, such as handling, loading and unloading, storing and transport.

集装箱化可以加速物流过程如:处理、装载、卸载、存储及运输过程。

22. Transport does not need to change packages of goods or stop in any place between the departure point and destination location.

运输不需要改变货物的包装或停在出发点和目的地之间的任何地方。

23. Domestic intercity truck is the motor carrier service between the different cities domestically.

国内城市间的卡车运输提供国内不同城市之间的汽车运输服务。

24. A fleet is group of vehicles or ships owned or operated as a unit.

运输队是指拥有一队汽车或轮船的单位。

25. Transportation is usually the biggest logistic costs for most companies.

运输费通常是大多数公司最大的一块物流费用。

26. There are three kinds of freight in transport: Full-car load, Less-than-truck load and container.

运输中存在三种装载方式:整车装载、拼箱装载和集装箱。

27. Water transport can carry the greatest amount of goods for the longest distance with the lowest cost.

水上运输可以用最低的成本装载最多的货物、航运最远的距离。

28. Air transport has the distinct advantage in the terms of fast delivery and enjoy the lowest ratio of loss and damage.

空运在交货快和低破损率方面有独特的优势。

29. The most economic feasible products transported by pipeline are crude oil, natural gas and refined petroleum one.

通过管道运输最经济可行的产品有石油,天然气和炼油。

30. Grouping small shipment into large ones is the primary method to lower cost per unit of weight in transportation.

将小批量货物组成大批量货物运送是降低运输单位货运成本的主要方法。

31. Transportation decision is referred to the transportation models and carriers selected for delivery, vehicle routing, scheduling, and freight grouping.

运输决策是根据运输模型由承运人选择运送方式,运输路线,时间表和货物分组。

32. Container logistics management is becoming a core strategy for large shipping company for its fast loading and unloading process, safe transportation and goods storage.

集装箱物流管理是大型运输公司实现快速装卸过程,安全运输和货物仓储的核心战略。

33. The primary factor to influent transport cost is distance and competition.

影响运输成本的基本因素是距离和竞争。

34. Containerization ensures quick transit between ships and other transport vehicles such as trucks and freight rail cars.

集装箱化确保在轮船和其他运输工具如:卡车、货运铁路车辆之间实现快速中转。

Exercises　练习

I. Answer the follow questions in English.

1. Try to describe the history of transportation in your own words.

2. What does transportation mean in the eyes of an economist?

3. What does transportation mean in the eyes of a consumer?

4. What principles must the movement organization operate on in order to be effective?

5. What are the strengths and weaknesses of transportation?

6. What are the five modes of modern transportation?

7. What is the fastest method of transport among the five modes?

8. Why do the road transport modes have limited potential to achieve economies of scale?

9. What is the most dependable mode of transportation?

10. How are the transportation companies classified?

II. Choose the best word or phrase that fits the sentence.

1. Tax paid on goods brought into or taken out of a country is called _____.

    A. fees   B. costs   C. payment   D. customs duty

2. Leaving the port is also called _____.

    A. arrival   B. export   C. departure   D. port entry

3. The time limit for loading the goods on board of the vessel at port of shipment is called _____.

    A. time of shipment   B. terms of shipment

    C. shipment limit   D. terms of delivery

4. _____ is the person, usually the exporter, who sends the goods.

    A. Shipper   B. Carrier   C. Agent   D. Operator

5. Please make sure that our order will be executed to the entire _____ of our customers.

    A. satisfactory   B. satisfaction   C. satisfy   D. satisfied

6. If you were the purchasing manager, what would you _____ consideration in buying raw materials.

    A. go to   B. make to   C. take into   D. have to

7. Your explanation on EOQ is _____, and few of us can follow you.

    A. unattractive   B. clear   C. vague   D. prospective

8. If you don't have the raw material, you won't make a _____.

    A. work   B. product   C. margin   D. revenue

9. I have to make telephone calls to _____ the movement of my cargo.

    A. check in   B. check at   C. check on   D. check to

10. Can you check the _____ for me again, I want to know the details of tomorrow's meeting, thanks!

    A. schedule   B. room   C. bar   D. bike

11. _____ oil and product pipelines transport petroleum through 6-40 inch diameter pipeline at speeds of 2-4 miles an hour.

    A. Raw   B. Crude   C. Original   D. Mineral

12. Pipeline construction costs vary _____ the diameter and increase proportionally with the distance and with the viscosity of fluids.

    A. due to   B. because of   C. thanks to   D. according to

13. Transportation companies are classified _____ four basic types.

    A. to   B. in   C. for   D. into

14. However, it may decline to handle _____ items as liquid petroleum gas or aviation

gas.

    A. so   B. that   C. such   D. whose

15. Freight forwarders _____ the other carriers in that they do not own any of the equipment used in intercity carriage of freight.

    A. differ from   B. result from   C. result in   D. differ in

Ⅲ. Match each word on the left with its corresponding meaning on the right.

A.	B.
1. domestication	(a) the basic structure or features of a system or organization
2. infrastructure	(b) the largest possible quantity
3. utility	(c) the property of being flexible; easily bent or shaped
4. packaging	(d) combining into a solid mass
5. consumption	(e) accommodation to domestic life
6. flexibility	(f) the service provided by a public utility
7. maximum	(g) a storehouse for goods and merchandise
8. warehouse	(h) the process of taking food into the body through mouth
9. consolidation	(i) of or relating to or responsible for administration
10. administrative	(j) the business of packing

Ⅳ. Fill in the blanks with words or phrases from the list below.

destination	suitable for	derived from
take advantage of	communications-based	distinguished
find out lack	purpose	construction

1. There is evidence that many cultures in many geographic areas used simple log roller technology. Pyramid _____ has involved complex organization of labor and the physical movement of large stone blocks from their quarries to the pyramid sites.

2. ITS encompasses a broad range of wireless and wire line _____ information and electronics technologies.

3. This satisfaction is _____ the safe delivery of hundreds of thousands of goods into the hands of millions of people everywhere.

4. Movement refers to the planning, monitoring and controlling of the movement through all the stages of the journey between origin and ultimate _____.

5. An order-management methodology that encourages maximum consolidation of shipments between common points enables a company to give larger shipments to its carriers and _____ volume discounts.

6. A _____ of infrastructure makes it difficult to transport.

7. All modes are _____ transporting goods, and most are suitable for transporting

people.

8. The railroads are _____ by their ability to move mass quantities of goods over long distances in an economical manner.

9. Comparing rail traffic with other traffic modes, we _____ the rail traffic is undoubtedly the most reliable traffic mode.

10. Pipelines are almost everywhere designed for a specific _____ only, to carry one commodity from a location to another.

Ⅴ. Translate the following sentences into Chinese.

1. It has become a global trend for TPL to apply technology to achieve an integrated process.

2. Supply chain management of TPL company has large potentiality for further development, but it has a long way to go before reaping a greater success.

3. A considerable amount of cargo is shipped by huge container ships running off fixed lines around the world.

4. The capability to efficiently transport large tonnage over long distances is the main reason railroads continue to handle significant inter-city tonnage and revenue.

5. Coal slurry lines require massive quantities of water, which is a significant concern of environmentalists, particularly in selected areas where water is scarce and large coal reserves are located.

Ⅵ. Translate the following sentences into English.

1. 可以说第三方物流所提供的增值服务之一是它的信息系统。
2. 海上运输是国际物流中的一个重要环节。
3. 就厂商出口到外国的产品而言,集装箱船通常是使用频率最高的。
4. 如果采用国内的出发地或目的地长途运输,出口率可以使总费用下降。
5. 在发生短缺、破损或延误时,装货清单是索赔的基础。

Ⅶ. Fill in the blanks with words from the list below and each word can be used once.

The global markets continue to expand, leading to more intense international transport. With the global ___1___ of international markets ___2___ like meeting the transit time, dividing the ___3___ when carrying out international transport services for ___4___ stores, consolidation of many goods; changes in ___5___ , taxes; transportation of ___6___ equipment, raise problems that need to be solved by modern transport companies from the European logistics network IFA (International Funkausstellung Berlin,柏林国际电子消费品展览会) that deal with specialized international transport services.

For the timely implementation of the international transport services, it's necessary to meet the planned transit time. For that __7__ , conditions on the route must be __8__ , the eventual emergence of problems __9__ deviations from the route in certain sections, changes in weather __10__ .

A) oversized	B) purpose	C) chain
D) chains	E) expansion	F) enlarge
G) sectors	H) sections	I) regulations
J) controlling	K) monitored	L) conditions
M) requiring	N) challenges	O) opportunity

Chapter 4

Warehousing Management
仓 库 管 理

Section A   Nature of A Warehouse   仓库的本质

Warehousing in the 2000s has a different focus than in the recent past. Traditionally, warehousing served the strategic role of long-term storage for raw materials and finished goods. Manufacturers produced for inventory and sold out of inventory stored in the warehouse. Warehouses had to support inventory levels of sixty to ninety days supply. [1]

We continue to eat a variety of food in our daily life. Some of us may take rice, while others may take bread as their main food. But have you ever thought about where the paddy or wheat is from. We know that these food grains are not produced throughout the year without any break. But we need to eat them every day. So how are the farmers able to supply these continuously to us? You might be thinking that they store the grains in food **storage** and supply them at the time of need. We may keep limited **stock** for our own consumption in our house. But there are certain places or stores, where these items are stored in huge quantities in a proper and **systematic** way. [2] We have many conversations about how to store grains in food storage, how much grain we should store, and what the best methods are. Storage involves proper arrangement for preserving goods from the time of their production or purchase till the actual use. When this storage is done on a large scale and in a specified manner it is called warehousing.

A warehouse, also known as a go-down in Indian English, is a commercial building for storage of goods. Warehouses are used by manufacturers, importers, exporters, wholesalers, retailers, transport businesses, customs, etc. They are usually large plain buildings in industrial areas of cities and towns. They usually have loading **docks** to load and unload goods from trucks. Sometimes warehouses load and unload goods directly from railways, airports, or seaports. They often have **cranes** and **forklifts** for moving goods, which are usually placed on ISO standard pallets loaded into pallet racks.

As a channel of distribution, the warehouse can play a key role in integrated logistics strategy and in building and maintaining good relationships between supply chain partners. [3] Warehousing becomes a support unit for numerous retail outlets; it affects customer service, stock-out rates, and a firm's sales and marketing success. Warehousing supports production by consolidating **inbound** materials and distributing them to the production facility at the appropriate time; it creates time utility by bridging the time gap between production and consumption of goods. Warehousing plays a vital role in providing a desired level of customer service at the lowest possible total cost. It takes 10 percent or more of total integrated logistics costs for most companies. Towards the latter decades of the 20th century economic activities management began to question the need for so many warehouses.

New Words

1. storage   *n.*贮存;贮藏;储藏处,仓库;贮存器,蓄电(瓶)

2. stock   *n.*股份,股票;库存;树干;家畜;*adj.*常备的,存货的;陈旧的;*vt.*提供货物;备有;*vi.*出新芽;囤积

3. systematic   *adj.*有系统的,有规则的;有条不紊的;有步骤的;一贯的,惯常的

4. dock   *n.*码头;被告席;(供运货汽车或铁路货车装卸货物的)月台;港区;*v.*(使)船停靠码头;(使宇宙飞船在外层空间)对接;减少;扣除

5. crane   *n.*起重机

6. forklift   *n.*叉车

7. inbound   *adj.*回内地的;归本国的;到达的;入境的

Phrases

1. supply to   提供,供应给

2. in huge quantities   大量

3. on a large scale   大规模地

4. in a specified manner   以特定的方式

5. stock-out rate   缺货率

6. ISO standard   国际标准化组织标准

Notes

1. Warehousing in the 2000s has a different focus than in the recent past. Traditionally, warehousing served the strategic role of long-term storage for raw materials and finished goods. Manufacturers produced for inventory and sold out of inventory stored in the warehouse. Warehouses had to support inventory levels of sixty to ninety days supply.

21 世纪以来,仓储比以往更受重视。传统上,仓储对原材料和产品的长期存储起到了战略性作用。制造商为维持一定库存而生产,然后卖掉存储在仓库里的存货。仓库必须提供 60~90 天的库存。

2. But there are certain places or stores, where these items are stored in huge quantities in a proper and systematic way.

但也有某些地方或卖场,其商品以一个适当和系统化的方式大量存储起来。

3. As a channel of distribution, the warehouse can play a key role in integrated logistics strategy and in building and maintaining good relationships between supply chain partners.

作为一个分销渠道,仓库可以在综合物流战略,以及建立和维护良好的供应链合作伙伴之间的关系发挥关键作用。

Section B Purpose of A Warehouse 仓库的目的

With the arrival of just-in-time, strategic alliances, and logistics supply chain philosophies in the 1990s, the warehouse has taken on a strategic role of attaining the logistics goal of shorter cycle times, lower inventories, lower costs, and better customer service. [1]

Warehousing is not a new concept, but it has gained new function in modern logistics. Warehousing has three basic functions, movement, storage and information transfer. It is necessary due to the following reasons:

- Seasonal Production. Crop cropper is harvested during certain seasons, but their consumption takes place throughout the year. [2] Therefore, there is a need for warehousing for these **commodities**, from where they can be supplied as and when required.

- To cope with seasonal fluctuations. There are certain goods, which are demanded seasonally, like down jacket in winters or raincoat in the rainy season. The production of these goods takes place throughout the year to meet the seasonal demand. So there is a need to store these goods in a warehouse to make them available at the time of need.

- Large-scale Production. Today most goods are mass-produced; mass production is the production of large amounts of standardized products, especially on assembly lines. [3] Manufacturers produce goods in huge quantity to enjoy the benefits of large-scale production, which is more economical. So the finished products, which are produced on a large scale, need to be stored properly till they are sold.

- To provide products in a centralized location. A variety of products are produced at some specific places but consumed throughout the country. Therefore, it is essential to stock these goods near the place of consumption, so that without making any delay these goods are made available to the consumers needs.

- Continuous Production. Continuous production is a method used to manufacture, produce, or process materials without **interruption**. This process is followed in most oil and gas industries and petrochemical plant, process manufacturing. Continuous production of goods in factories requires adequate supply of raw materials. So there is a need to keep sufficient quantity of raw material in the warehouse to ensure continuous production.

- Price **Stabilization**. To maintain a reasonable level of the price of the goods in the market there is a need to keep sufficient stock in the warehouses. **Scarcity** in supply of goods may increase their price in the market. Again, excess production and supply may also lead to fall in prices of the product. By maintaining a balance of supply of goods, warehousing leads to price stabilization.

The use of warehousing enables management to select the transport modes and inventory levels that when combined with communication and order processing systems and produciton alternatives, minimize total cost while providing a desired level of customer service. [4]

New Words

1. commodity   *n.* 商品;农产品;有价值的物品;有用的东西
2. interruption   *n.* 中断;打断;障碍物;打岔的事
3. stabilization   *n.* 稳定性;稳定化;安定面
4. scarcity   *n.* 不足,缺乏;稀少;萧条

Phrases

1. throughout the year   一年到头;整年
2. cope with   对付……;支应
3. assembly line   组装线
4. petrochemical plant   石油化工装置,石油化学工厂
5. take place   发生,举行
6. a variety of   种种;各种各样的
7. lead to   导致
8. raw material   原材料
9. seasonal fluctuation   季节性波动

Notes

1. With the arrival of just-in-time, strategic alliances, and logistics supply chain philosophies in the 1990s, the warehouse had taken on a strategic role of attaining the logistics goal of shorter cycle times, lower inventories, lower costs, and better customer service.

20 世纪 90 年代,随着准时制、战略联盟、物流供应链概念的出现,仓库在实现短周期时间、减少库存、降低成本及提供更好的客户服务等物流目标方面起到了战略性的作用。

2. Crop cropper is harvested during certain seasons, but their consumption takes place throughout the year.

某些农作物只在某一特定季节收获,但人们一年四季却都在吃这些农作物。

3. Today most goods are mass-produced; mass production is the production of large amounts of standardized products, especially on assembly lines.

今天,大多数商品都是大规模生产。大规模生产是指在装配线上,大量生产出标准化的产品。

4. The use of warehousing enables management to select the transport modes and inventory

levels that when combined with communication and order processing systems and production alternatives, minimize total cost while providing a desired level of customer service.

运用仓储可使管理部门在保持既定的顾客服务水平下,通过结合信息及订单处理系统与生产要素,选取一定的运输方式及库存水平,以使总成本降至最低。

Section C   Types of Warehouse   仓库的类型

Warehouses for storage are of several types. It can be classified into private warehouse, public warehouse and contract warehouse.

Private warehouse

The warehouses which are owned and managed by the manufacturers or traders to store, **exclusively**, their own stock of goods are known as private warehouses. Generally these warehouses are constructed by the farmers near their fields, by wholesalers and retailers near their business centers and by manufacturers near their factories. The design and the facilities provided therein are according to the nature of products to be stored. The decision as to which strategy best fits an individual firm is essentially financial. The major benefits of private warehousing include control, flexibility, cost, and other **intangible** benefits.

Public warehouse

The warehouses which are run to store goods of the general public are known as public warehouses. Any one can store his goods in these warehouses on payment of rent. An individual, a partnership firm or a company may own these warehouses. To start such warehouses a license from the government is required. The government also regulates the functions and operations of these warehouses. Mostly these warehouses are used by manufacturers, wholesalers, exporters, importers, government agencies, etc. A classification of public warehouses has been developed. On the basis of a range of specialized operations performed, they are classified as general merchandise, refrigerated, special commodity, bonded, and household goods and furniture. There are many benefits of using the services of public warehouses. Public warehouses can help a business in many facets including recall inventory, distribution, packaging, labeling, transportation, and marketing resources, among others. It provides financial flexibility and scale economy benefits as well. Drawback of public warehouses is the lack of space available, especially during the peak times of the year, such as holiday seasons. The temperature within the warehouse is another aspect to consider. Very often the temperature, within the public warehouse, is not sufficiently monitored. In relation to many goods, this incorrect temperature can create a problem.

Contract warehouse

Warehousing might be public, private or contracted. Contract warehousing (also referred to as third-party warehousing) has emerged as another warehousing alternative. Contract warehouses can provide unique and specially tailored warehousing service to the customers.

A private warehouse facility is owned or operated and manned by the owner of the products it contains. A public warehouse rents space, typically by the square foot or pallet, and could charge for some other services, such as accepting or perhaps loading goods. [1] Contract warehousing is becoming a preferred choice for many organizations because it allows a company to focus on its **competencies**, with warehousing providing a great deal of **expertise** for logistics demands.

Distribution center

A distribution center for a set of products is a warehouse or other specialized building, often with refrigeration or air conditioning, which is stocked with products (goods) to be redistributed to retailers, to wholesalers, or directly to consumers [2] (see Figure 4-1). A distribution center is a principal part, the order processing element, of the entire order **fulfillment** process. Distribution centers (DC) are usually thought of as being demand driven. A distribution center can also be called a warehouse, a DC, a fulfillment center, a cross-dock facility, a bulk break center, and a package handling center. The name by which the distribution center is known is commonly based on the purpose of the operation.

Figure 4-1　Wal-Mart Distribution Center

In each of these warehouses, adequate arrangements are made to keep the goods in proper conditions.

- Warehouse should be located at a convenient place near highways, railway stations, airports and seaports where goods can be loaded and unloaded easily.

- Mechanical appliances should be there to load and unload the goods. This reduces the wastages in handling and also minimizes handling costs.
- Adequate space should be available inside the building to keep the goods in proper order.
- Warehouses are meant for preservation of perishable items like fruits, vegetables, eggs, butter, etc. It should have cold storage facilities.
- Proper arrangement should be there to protect the goods from sunlight, rain, wind, dust, **moisture** and pests.
- Sufficient parking space should be there inside the **premises** to facilitate easy and quick loading and unloading of goods.
- Round the clock, security arrangement should be there to avoid theft of goods.
- The building should be fitted with latest fire-fighting equipments to avoid loss of goods due to fire.

New Words

1. exclusively   *adv.*唯一地;专门地,特定地;专有地;排外地
2. intangible   *adj.*触不到的;难以理解的;无法确定的;*n.*<商>(指企业资产)无形的
3. competency   *n.* 能力
4. expertise   *n.*专门知识或技能;专家的意见;专家评价,鉴定
5. fulfillment   *n.*完成;实现;满足(感);实施过程
6. moisture   *n.*水分;湿气;潮湿;降雨量
7. premise   *n.*(包括附属建筑、土地等在内的)房屋或其他建筑物;<律>(契约)前言;契据的缘起部分(记述财产的详情、当事人姓名等);(企业的)房屋建筑及附属场地;前提

Phrases

1. of several types   有几种类型
2. be classified into   被分类成……
3. be known as   被认为;被认为是;以……著称
4. as well   也, 同样地
5. peak time   高峰时间
6. in relation to   关于,涉及
7. focus on   集中于
8. protect ... from ...   保护……不受……
9. cross-dock facility   跨码头设施

Notes

1. A public warehouse rents space, typically by the square foot or pallet, and could charge for some other services, such as accepting or perhaps loading goods.

公共仓库租用空间,通常以平方英尺或货盘来计算,也能提供其他服务并收取费用,比如接收或装载货物。

2. A distribution center for a set of products is a warehouse or other specialized building, often with refrigeration or air conditioning, which is stocked with products (goods) to be redistributed to retailers, to wholesalers, or directly to consumers.

一组产品的集散地必须是一个仓库或其他拥有空调或制冷设备的专用建筑物,用来存储产品并把它们重新分配给零售商、批发商,或直接卖给消费者。

Section D　Basic Regulations in Warehouse
仓库的基本原则

1. Regulation of personnel in and out

Warehouse is the place storing the products and property of the company. No one is allowed to enter without working issues.

1) No one is allowed to take materials or property from warehouse or **wander** in warehouse except warehouse personnel. [1] Personnel without working issue are not allowed to stay in warehouse.

2) Any personnel need to enter warehouse for maintaining house, air-conditioner, or material handling products (see Figure 4-2). The relevant person in charge should inform logistic **supervisor** about the construct area and the influence to the warehouse. Warehouse staff should take relevant protect action according the situation to ensure the safety of the stocks of warehouse.

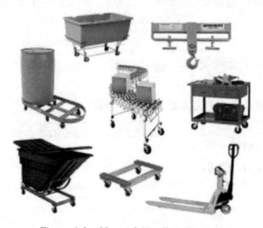

Figure 4-2　Material Handling Products

3) **Forwarder** should take goods from appointed area with the company of warehouse staff.

4) Forwarder should deliver goods in appointed area with the company of warehouse staff.

5) All stock in and out should be handled by warehouse staff according to the stock in or stock out list. Other staff should wait outside the warehouse.

6) Visitor is not allowed to enter warehouse without **approval** of management team.

7) Taking photos is not allowed in warehouse without approval of management team.

2. Warehouse design and layout

Warehouse design must consider product movement characteristics. Three factors to be determined during the design process are the number of floors to include in the facility, a cube utilization plan, and product flow. [2]

The ideal warehouse design is one-floor building that eliminates the need to move product vertically. The use of vertical handling devices, such as elevators and conveyors, to move product from one floor to the next requires time, energy, and typically creates handling bottlenecks. So, while it is not always possible, particularly in centural business dsitricts where land is restricted or expensive, as a gengeral rule, warehouses should be designed as an one-floor operation to facilitate materials handling. [3]

A good warehouse layout can increase output, improve product flow, reduce costs, improve service to customers, and provide better employee working conditions. The optimal warehouse layout and design for a firm will vary by the type of product being stored, the company's finacial resources, the competitive environment, and the needs of customers. Irrespective of the preceding factors, however, it is imperative that the firm develop an optimal warehousing system for itself using a logical and constistent decision strategy. [4]

3. Requirement of warehouse environment and firefighting facility maintenance

In order to ensure a good storing environment, warehouse should be clean and tidy all the time. [5]

1) Smoking is strictly forbidden in warehouse.

2) Eating and drinking is not allowed in warehouse.

3) All stocks should be stored in the main warehouse with well-controlled temperature and **humidity**.

4) All chemicals shall be stored in appointed safety cabinet in chemical warehouse.

5) All package material shall be stocked in the place far away from direct sunshine, dry and no oil stains.

6) In order to ensure the safety and firefighting of warehouse, firefighting facility should be prepared in the fixed area. It shall be ensured that all of the warehouse staff can use the firefighting equipments correctly.

7) Storage plan shall be clear. Goods shall be put tidily. All goods are not allowed to occupy the way for goods or person, let alone block the **hydrant** and firefighting equipment.

8) Packaging material and waste for throwing away shall be put into the garbage or

appointed recycling area.

　　9) Shelf in warehouse shall be cleaned by appointed cleaner every week.

　　10) Not allowed to be placed near sockets, naked flame or heats.

Source：A Berliner Glas Company

New Words

　　1. regulation　　*n.*管理;控制;规章;规则;*adj.*规定的,必须穿戴的,必须使用的

　　2. personnel　　*n.*全体员工;(与复数动词连用)人员,员工;人事部门

　　3. wander　　*vt.*漫步,漫游;*vi.*游荡,漫游,闲逛,慢走,漫步;离开原路,离群,失散;(道路或河流)蜿蜒曲折;(人的思想等)走神,胡思乱想;*n.*游荡;溜达;闲逛;失散

　　4. supervisor　　*n.*监督者,管理者;镇长

　　5. forwarder　　*n.*代运人;运输业者;转运公司;促进者

　　6. approval　　*n.*同意;批准;赞成

　　7. humidity　　*n.*(空气中的)湿度;潮湿,高温潮湿;湿热;[物]湿度

　　8. hydrant　　*n.*给水栓,消防龙头

Phrases

　　1. regulation of personnel in and out　　进出人员管理

　　2. without working issue　　没有工作的问题

　　3. be allowed to　　被允许做某事

　　4. person in charge　　负责人

　　5. far away from　　远离

Notes

　　1. No one is allowed to take materials or property from warehouse or wander in warehouse except warehouse personnel.

　　除了仓库工作人员之外,任何人不得拿取仓库的物资或财产,或在仓库内闲逛。

　　2. Warehouse design must consider product movement characteristics. Three factors to be determined during the design process are the number of floors to include in the facility, a cube utilization plan, and product flow.

　　仓库的设计必须考虑产品移动的特性。在设计时,需要确定三个因素:仓库的层数、空间使用方案和产品流动。

　　3. The use of vertical handling devices, such as elevators and conveyors, to move product from one floor to the next requires time, energy, and typically creates handling bottlenecks. So, while it is not always possible, particularly in centural business dsitricts where land is restricted or expensive, as a gengeral rule, warehouses should be designed as an one-floor operation to facilitate materials handling.

　　因为使用电梯、传送带等垂直搬运设施将货物从一层送到另一层需要时间、精力,而

且还会在搬运方面存在瓶颈问题,仓库一般建造一层作业区以方便物料搬运,但在土地紧张时或在昂贵的中心商务区,有时很难实现。

4. The optimal warehouse layout and design for a firm will vary by the type of product being stored, the company's finacial resources, the competitive environment, and the needs of customers. Irrespective of the preceding factors, however, it is imperative that the firm develop an optimal warehousing system for itself using a logical and constistent decision strategy.

最优的仓库布局和设计是随着存储商品的种类、企业的财务资源、竞争环境和客户需求而变化的。然而,除了上述因素,重要的是企业在开发自己的最优仓库系统时,要使用有逻辑的、连贯的决策战略。

5. In order to ensure a good storing environment, warehouse should be clean and tidy all the time.

为了确保一个良好的存储环境,仓库应时刻保持清洁整齐。

Section E Warehousing Security 仓库安全

It is **estimated** that the theft and **pilferage** of products stored in warehousing facilities cause losses in the range of four to five times the products' value. Theft and pilferage can result in lost sales opportunities (both present and in the future), customer dissatisfaction, additional costs to prevent theft and pilferage, and the administrative time and costs associated with filing claims, and more. [1]

The terrorist attacks of September 11, 2001, have profoundly affected warehousing security. **Cold-storage facilities**, for instance, have **enacted** more stringent security procedures because these facilities often contain large quantities of ammonia, a key ingredient for making a bomb. [2] In addition, food distributors have experienced a dramatic increase in theft because, in an age of terrorism, food theft is not a high priority for local, state, or federal law enforcement. [3]

In general, warehousing security can be enhanced by focusing on people, facilities, and processes. In terms of people, one area of focus should be the hiring process for warehousing workers; a starting point might be determining whether an individual facility even has a formal hiring process. **In terms of** a facilities focus, a number of different low-tech (e.g., fences) and high-tech (e.g., **closed-circuit** video cameras) devices can help to enhance warehousing security; an obvious **trade-off** is the cost of the various devices. [4] In terms of processes to improve warehousing security, the more times a shipment is handled, the greater the opportunities for loss or damage. Thus, logisticians would do well to reduce the number of times an individual shipment is handled. Table 4-1 highlights some possible shortcomings in warehousing security.

Table 4-1 Possible Shortcomings in Warehousing Security

Shortcoming

Making it too easy for dock personnel to work in **collusion** with truck drivers

Relying on safeguards that simply don't work

Approach to theft is too reactive

Not weeding out **on-the-job substance abusers** or dealers

Not checking your checkers on a frequent basis

Not making it easy to report theft and substance abuse

Hiring high-risk employees

Comment

Fewer than 5% who **commit crimes** are **prosecuted**

Security cameras aren't always turned on

Don't wait until theft reaches an "unacceptable" level

Approximately 90% of **drug users** either steal or deal to support their habit

They may become **complacent**

Outsourcing the reporting may be more effective

An ounce of prevention is worth a pound of cure

New Words

1. estimated   *adj.* 估计的;预计的;估算的

2. pilferage   *n.* 偷盗,行窃;赃物

3. enacted   *v.* 制定,颁布(enact 的过去式)

4. outsourcing   *n.* 外包;外购;外部采办

5. collusion   *n.* 勾结;共谋

6. prosecuted   *v.* 起诉(prosecute 的过去分词);经营;贯彻   *adj.* 被起诉的

7. approximately   *adv.* 大约,近似地;近于

8. complacent   *adj.* 自满的;得意的;满足的

9. trade-off   *n.* 交换,交易;权衡;协定

Phrases

1. the terrorist attacks of September 11, 2001:"9·11恐怖袭击事件",是2001年9月11日发生在美国纽约世界贸易中心的一起恐怖袭击事件。两架被恐怖分子劫持的民航客机分别撞向美国纽约世界贸易中心一号楼和世界贸易中心二号楼,两座建筑在遭到攻击后相继倒塌,世界贸易中心其余5座建筑物也受震而坍塌损毁;同日,另一架被劫持的客机撞向位于美国华盛顿的美国国防部五角大楼,五角大楼局部结构损坏并坍塌。此次事件对美国民众造成的心理影响极为深远,美国民众对经济及政治上的安全感均被严重削弱。

2. cold-storage facility   冷藏设施

3. in terms of   依据;按照;在……方面;以……措辞

4. closed-circuit　闭路式的

5. on-the-job substance abuser　在职的精神药物滥用者

6. commit crime　犯罪

7. drug user　吸毒者

Notes

1. Theft and pilferage can result in lost sales opportunities (both present and in the future), customer dissatisfaction, additional costs to prevent theft and pilferage, and the administrative time and costs associated with filing claims, and more.

偷窃和偷盗会造成销售机会的损失(不仅是现在的而且包括未来的)、顾客不满、预防偷窃和偷盗的额外成本,以及与申请索赔相关的管理时间和成本,等等。

2. Cold-storage facilities, for instance, have enacted more stringent security procedures because these facilities often contain large quantities of ammonia, a key ingredient for making a bomb.

例如,冷藏设施已制定了更加严格的安全措施,因为这些设施通常含有大量的氨,而它是制造炸弹的一个主要成分。

3. In addition, food distributors have experienced a dramatic increase in theft because, in an age of terrorism, food theft is not a high priority for local, state, or federal law enforcement.

另外,食品分销商也遭遇了显著上升的失窃问题,因为在恐怖主义时代,食品失窃对于地方、州或联邦法律执行来说都不是高优先级的。

4. In terms of a facilities focus, a number of different low-tech (e.g., fences) and high-tech (e.g., closed-circuit video cameras) devices can help to enhance warehousing security; an obvious trade-off is the cost of the various devices.

在设施关注方面,很多不同的低技术(如围墙)和高技术(如闭路录像)设备都能够帮助加强仓储安全;其中一个很显然的权衡是各种设备的成本。

🎯 Core Concepts　核心概念

1. Automated warehouse must be managed by information system.

自动化(智能)仓库需由信息系统管理。

2. Warehouse rental represents a very significant proportion of total warehouse cost.

仓库租金占仓库总费用的大部分支出。

3. The size of warehouses are determined by the needs of the customer groups, such as their inventory level planning.

仓库的大小取决于客户群的需求,例如他们的计划存货水平。

4. Goods that are stored in warehouses for distribution and sales are called inventory.

为了配送和销售而在仓库中存储的货物叫存货.

5. Goods handling may account for only 50% of the direct labor cost in warehouse and

70% in distribution center.

货物处理成本占仓库直接劳动成本的50%,配送中心成本的70%。

6. Boned warehouse is the place to store the goods imported or in transit, without paying duty under custom's supervision.

保税仓库是用来存储进口或转运货物的处所,并不用支付关税。

7. Data warehouse is a consolidated database maintained separately from different organizations' production system databases.

数据仓库是独立于不同企业产品系统数据库的联合数据库。

Exercises 练习

Ⅰ. Answer the follow questions in English.

1. What is the definition of warehousing?

2. What are the three basic functions of warehousing?

3. What are the reasons for the necessity of warehousing?

4. What are the types for warehouses for storage?

5. What does private warehouse refer to?

6. What are the benefits of using the services of public warehouses?

7. What can contract warehouses provide?

8. What are the basic regulations in warehouse?

Ⅱ. Choose the best word or phrase that fits the sentence.

1. If the ship had sailed along the recommended _____ , it would have to avoid the heavy weather.

    A. route   B. rout   C. road   D. way

2. What is the labor party's _____ on immigration?

    A. policy   B. police   C. polite   D. polity

3. By the accurate demand forecast , a manager can determine whether to _____ more chips from Intel.

    A. order   B. book   C. spread   D. produce

4. The _____ action would lead to a great loss.

    A. perfect   B. bold   C. blind   D. wonderful

5. —Do you hear that _____ has become a hot career?

    —It sounds too good to true.

    A. logical   B. logistics   C. logic   D. logistic

6. With the help of logistics expert, the company has made a _____ rise in profits.

    A. increased   B. decreased   C. significant   D. slightly

7. Ford decided to invest in railroads,trucks and both Great Lakes and ocean _____.

    A. vessels   B. vehicles   C. equipment   D. shipments

8. The _____ usually leads to ineffective decision.

    A. bureau   B. bureaucy   C. bureaucracy   D. bureaucrat

9. He _____ in physics and then he teaches it in college.

    A. studied   B. learned   C. specialized   D. read

10. The supermarket has to _____ 400 TEU of cargo from China every year.

    A. purchased   B. purchasing   C. bought   D. purchase

11. We continue to eat a _____ of food in our daily life.

    A. variety   B. variable   C. vary   D. various

12. When this storage is done _____ and in a specified manner it is called warehousing.

    A. on a small scale   B. on a large scale

    C. on balance   D. quickly

13. Crop cropper is harvested during certain seasons, but their consumption _____ throughout the year.

    A. takes place   B. take the place

    C. take the place of   D. change

14. There are certain goods which are demanded seasonally, like down jacket in winters or raincoat in the _____ season.

    A. snowy   B. windy   C. rainy   D. foggy

15. The decision _____ which strategy best fits an individual firm is essentially financial.

    A. as for   B. for   C. as   D. as to

Ⅲ. Match each word on the left with its corresponding meaning on the right.

A.	B.
1. warehouse	(a) a wave motion organization
2. storage	(b) the act of stabilizing something or making it more stable
3. commodity	(c) the act of storing something
4. fluctuation	(d) a device or control that is very useful for a particular job
5. stabilization	(e) the process of cooling for preservative purposes
6. merchandise	(f) a bony hollow into which a structure fits
7. expertise	(g) a storehouse for goods and merchandise
8. appliance	(h) commodities offered for sale
9. socket	(i) articles of commerce
10. refrigeration	(j) skillfulness by virtue of possessing special knowledge

Ⅳ. Fill in the blanks with words or phrases from the list below.

processing	in charge	storage	functions	available
industries	assembly	according to	quantities	preserving

1. But there are certain places or stores, where these items are stored in huge _____ in a proper and systematic way.

2. Storage involves proper arrangement for _____ goods from the time of their production or purchase till the actual use.

3. A warehouse, also known as a go-down in Indian English, is a commercial building for _____ of goods.

4. Warehousing has three basic _____, movement, storage and information transfer.

5. So there is a need to store these goods in a warehouse to make them _____ at the time of need.

6. Mass production is the production of large amounts of standardized products, especially on _____ lines.

7. This process is followed in most oil and gas _____ and petrochemical plant, process manufacturing.

8. The design and the facilities provided therein are _____ the nature of products to be stored.

9. A distribution center is a principal part, the order _____ element, of the entire order fulfillment process.

10. The relevant person _____ should inform logistic supervisor about the construct area and the influence to the warehouse.

Ⅴ. Translate the following sentences into Chinese.

1. This fine line between keeping too much inventory and not enough is not the manager's only concern.

2. When choosing the site for a warehouse, it is important to consider its availability and accessibility to your customers.

3. In the beginning, companies that could afford inventory were able to satisfy customer demand.

4. It's key to understand your distribution centers, plants, 3PL and vendors/customers and how each component works together.

5. A strong project team consists of warehouse and operations personnel, sales, IT, customer service and finance.

Ⅵ. Translate the following sentences into English.

1. 物流对国内经济和全球经济有巨大的影响。

2. 为了保证物流的及时性，就要求一定的库存存在。

3. 这并不意味着以库存的形式存放的货物越多，你就越富。

4. 仓储管理包括仓储的管理体制、治理结构、管理组织、管理方法和管理目标等几个方面。

5. 作为一种经济活动，向社会提供服务的商业仓储业如其他经济活动主体一样，只有在充分市场化的条件下，才能充分发展其经济价值。

Ⅶ. Fill in the blanks with words from the list below and each word can be used once.

Cambridge Security has years of experience in warehouse, merchandise, and pharmaceutical distribution centers. From emergency services in the event of a natural __1__ to a security during.

__2__ labor job actions and strikes, Cambridge Security Services is your trusted partner that keeps your supply __3__ moving.

Cambridge Security Services is __4__ capable of satisfying your warehouse security and supply chain needs, including: Armed and Unarmed Security Personnel. Cambridge Security tailors training to each individual __5__ and site with a thorough training __6__ that exceeds state __7__ . From terrorism __8__ and active shooter training to courses on great customer service and __9__ resolution, Cambridge officers are equipped to handle all your security needs with __10__ and skill.

A) client	B) chain	C) disaster
D) only	E) uniquely	F) conflict
G) professionalism	H) requirements	I) process
J) method	K) presence	L) present
M) danger	N) conscious	O) awareness

Chapter 5

Protective Packaging and Materials Handling
包装与物料处理

Section A　History of Packaging　包装的历史

Most goods require protection as they move through the **integrated** logistics system. Package is best described as a **coordinated** system of preparing goods for transport, distribution, storage, retailing, and use of the goods. It is considered as "the art, science, and technology of preparing goods for transport and sale" by British Standards Institution. Packing is a complex, **dynamic**, scientific, artistic, and controversial business function; it is a means of ensuring the safe delivery of a product to the consumer in sound condition and at minimum cost.[1] Packaging is also considered as an important part of the supply chain, and the very proper design and use of packaging not only facilitate on storage, handling in transportation but also on other functions such as production, selling and purchasing.

Packaging is not a recent **phenomenon**. **Primitive** people needed containment and carrying devices. The first packages used the natural materials available at the time: a wrap of leaves, an animal skin, the shell of a nut or gourd, wooden boxes, **pottery** vases, woven bags, etc. Processed materials were used to form packages as they were developed: for example, early bronze and glass vessels (see Figure 5-1). Packaging is an activity closely associated with the **evolution** of society and can be traced back to human beginning.

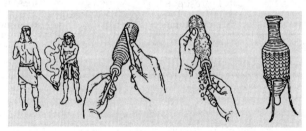

Figure 5-1　Forming a Hollow Glass Vessel around A Core

In China, Cai Lun[2] is credited with inventing paper circa 104AD. The invention is directed to packaging product for a variety of goods. Iron and tin plated steel were used to make cans in the 19th century, meanwhile paperboard cartons and fiberboard boxes were introduced.

Packaging advancements in the early 20th century included Bakelite closures on bottles, transparent cellophane over wraps and panels on cartons, increased processing efficiency and improved food safety. [3] As additional materials such as several types of plastic were developed, they were incorporated into packages to improve performance and functionality since the 1980s.

There are various types of materials used in packaging now. The common ones are:

Paper and paper-made materials: brown paper, cellophane paper, vegetable **parchment**, asphalted paper, paperboard, corrugated paperboard, etc.

Plastic and plastic-made materials: polythene, polypropylene, polystyrene, PVC

Timber and wood-made materials.

Metal: tin-coated sheet, dopend iron, aluminum alloy.

Glass, ceramics, composite material.

Packing goods to minimize volume and weight while reinforcing them may save money, as well as ensure that the goods are properly packed. Packaging can not only help prevent theft and damage but also help promote goods and inform the customer. A professional firm is hired to pack the products if the supplier is not equipped to do so. AEC Packaging America is part of AEC Group that specializes in product packaging which operated worldwide. Products include packaging box, customized box, non-woven reusable bag, paper bag and PP products.

The environmental impacts of product packaging and its waste are an issue of growing importance and concern worldwide. [4] Green packing, namely pollution-free or environment-friendly packing, refers to packing which is non-pollutive to the environment, unharmful to human body, recyclable or reusable, and can promote the strategy of sustainable development. It is possessed of two features: eco-environment protection and resources recycling.

Package development involves considerations for sustainability, environmental responsibility, and applicable environmental and recycling regulations. It is necessary to know the relevant regulatory requirements for point of manufacture, sale, and use. The "three R's" principle is involved in product and package development.

- Reducing—The mass and volume of packaging can be measured and used as one of the **criteria** to minimize costs during the package design process. Usually "reduced" packaging also helps minimize costs.

拓展资源

- Reuse—The reuse of a package or component for other purposes is encouraged.

- Recycling— Recycling is the collection and reprocessing of manufactured materials for reuse either in the same form or as part of a different product. [5] Collecting, and separating products, preparing them to buyers' specifications, sale to markets, processing, and eventual reuse of materials are part of the recycling loop. Emphasis is focused on recycling the largest primary components of a package: steel, aluminum, papers, plastics, etc.

Wal-mart started the "packaging scorecard" and expected a decrease of 5% of packaging waste before year 2013. Development of sustainable packaging is an area of considerable interest by standards organizations, government, consumers, packagers, and retailers.

New Words

1. integrated　*adj.*完整的;整体的;结合的;(各组成部分)和谐的;*v.*使一体化(integrate 的过去式和过去分词);使整合;使完整;使结合成为整体

2. coordinated　*adj.*协调的;*v.*使协调,使调和(coordinate 的过去式和过去分词);协调;协同;成为同等

3. dynamic　*adj.*动态的;动力的,动力学的;充满活力的,精力充沛的;不断变化的,充满变数的;*n.*动态;动力,推动变化的力量;动力学;活力

4. phenomenon　*n.*现象,事件;奇迹;非凡的人

5. primitive　*adj.*原始的;发展水平低的;落后的;[生物学]原生的;*n.*原始人;早期的艺术家(作品);单纯的人,不世故的人;自学的艺术家

6. pottery　*n.*陶器;陶器厂[作坊];<集合词>陶器类;陶器制造(术)

7. evolution　*n.*演变,发生;进化论;(天体的)形成;(气体等的)放出

8. parchment　*n.*羊皮纸;文凭;上等纸;羊皮纸古文稿

9. criteria　*n.*(批评、判断等的)标准,准则(criterion 的名词复数);(criterion 的复数)

Phrases

1. minimum cost　最低成本
2. be necessary to　对……来说是有必要的
3. woven bag　编织袋
4. transparent cellophane　透明的玻璃纸
5. asphalted paper　沥青纸
6. corrugated paperboard　瓦楞纸板

Notes

1. Packing is a complex, dynamic, scientific, artistic, and controversial business function; it is a means of ensuring the safe delivery of a product to the consumer in sound condition and at minimum cost.

包装是一个拥有复杂的、动态的、科学的、艺术的且有争议的业务功能,它能确保产品处于良好安全的状态,以最低的成本卖给消费者。

2. Cai Lun
蔡伦(61?—121),字敬仲,汉族,东汉桂阳郡人。我国四大发明中造纸术的发明者。

3. Packaging advancements in the early 20th century included Bakelite closures on bottles, transparent cellophane over wraps and panels on cartons, increased processing

efficiency and improved food safety.

包装在 20 世纪初的进步包括胶木瓶盖、透明玻璃纸包裹和纸盒板，这大大提高了加工效率、改善了食品安全。

4. The environmental impacts of product packaging and its waste are an issue of growing importance and concern worldwide.

产品包装及其废弃物对环境的影响已成为一个日益被重视的全球问题。

5. Recycling is the collection and reprocessing of manufactured materials for reuse either in the same form or as part of a different product.

回收是指以相同的形式或作为不同产品的一部分，对已使用过的材料进行收集和再加工的过程。

▧ Section B　Package Functions　包装的功能

No matter what environment conditions are encountered, the package is expected to protect the product, keeping it in the condition intended for use until the product is delivered to the ultimate consumer. [1]

The various functions of packaging are divided into primary, secondary and **tertiary** functions. In contrast with the primary functions, which primarily concern the technical nature of the packaging, secondary functions relate to communications.

Primary, secondary and tertiary functions are divided into the following sub-functions:

Protective function

The protective function of packaging essentially involves protecting the contents from the environment and vice versa. [2] The inward protective function is intended to ensure full **retention** of the utility value of the packaged goods. The packaging is thus intended to protect the goods from loss, damage and theft.

In addition, packaging must also reliably be able to withstand the many different static and **dynamic** forces to which it is subjected during transport, handling and storage operations. The goods frequently also require protection from **climatic** conditions, such as temperature, humidity, **precipitation** and solar radiation.

Storage function

The packaging materials and packaging containers required for producing packages must be stored in many different locations both before packaging of the goods and once the package contents have been used. [3] Packaging must thus also fulfill a storage function.

Loading and transport function

Convenient goods handling **entails** designing transport packaging in such a manner that it may be held, lifted, moved, set down and stowed easily, efficiently and safely. Packaging thus has a crucial impact on the efficiency of transport, handling and storage of goods. Packaging should therefore be designed to be easily handled and to permit space-saving storage and stowage. The shape and strength of packages should be such that they may not only be stowed side by side leaving virtually no **voids** but may also be stowed safely one above the other.

Sales function

The purpose of the sales function of a package is to enable or promote the sales process and to make it more efficient.

Promotional function

Promotional material placed on the packaging is intended to attract the potential purchaser's attention and to have a positive impact upon the purchasing decision. Promotional material on packaging plays a particularly important role on sales packaging as it is directly addressed to the consumer. This function is of **subordinate** significance in transport packaging. While product awareness is indeed generated along the transport chain, excessive promotion also increases the risk of theft.

Service function

The various items of information printed on packaging provide the consumer with details about the contents and use of the particular product. Examples are the **nutritional** details on yogurt pots or dosage information on medicines.

Guarantee function

By supplying an undamaged and **unblemished** package, the manufacturer guarantees that the details on the packaging correspond to the contents. The packaging is therefore the basis for branded goods, consumer protection and product liability. There are legislative requirements which demand that goods be clearly marked with details indicating their nature, composition, weight, and quantity and storage life.

Additional function

The additional function in particular relates to the extent to which the packaging materials or packaging containers may be reused once the package contents have been used. [4] The most significant example is the recycling of paper, paperboard and cardboard packaging as waste paper.

New Words

1. tertiary   *adj.*第三的;<医>第三期的;(T-)<地>第三纪的;<化>叔的;*n.*(T-)<地>

第三纪;第三系;三期梅毒病害;<宗>第三级教士

  2. retention　*n.*保留;记忆力,保持力;滞留,扣留;闭尿

  3. dynamic　*adj.*动态的;动力的,动力学的;充满活力的,精力充沛的;不断变化的,充满变数的;*n.*动态;动力,推动变化的力量;动力学;活力

  4. climatic　*adj.*气候的;风土的;受气候影响的

  5. precipitation　*n.*匆促;沉淀;(雨等)降落;某地区降雨等的量

  6. entail　*v.*使……成为必要(entail 的第三人称单数);需要;限定继承;使必需

  7. void　*n.*太空;宇宙空间;空隙;空虚感;*v.*使无效;宣布……作废;取消;排泄

  8. subordinate　*adj.*级别或职位较低的;下级的;次要的;附属的;*n.*部属;部下,下级;*vt.*使……居下位,使……在次级;使服从;使从属

  9. nutritional　*adj.*营养的;滋养的;营养品的

  10. unblemished　*adj.*(人的名声、记录或性格)无污点的,完美无缺的;无瑕疵的

Phrases

  1. be divided into　被分成
  2. be intended to　打算……;意图是
  3. in addition　此外,另外
  4. be able to　会;能够
  5. set down　放下
  6. side by side　一起;并肩;一个挨一个
  7. correspond to　符合于;相当于
  8. in particular　尤其;特别
  9. relate to　涉及,有关
  10. and vice versa　反之亦然
  11. dosage information　剂量信息

Notes

1. No matter what environment conditions are encountered, the package is expected to protect the product, keeping it in the condition intended for use until the product is delivered to the ultimate consumer.

不论遇到什么样的环境,包装是用来保护产品的,它保护产品在完好状态下被送至消费者手中。

2. The protective function of packaging essentially involves protecting the contents from the environment and vice versa.

包装的保护功能主要涉及保护产品不受环境的破坏,反之亦然。

3. The packaging materials and packaging containers required for producing packages must be stored in many different locations both before packaging of the goods and once the package contents have been used.

产品进行包装之前以及包装内容被使用之后,生产包装所需的包装材料和容器必须存放在不同位置。

4. The additional function in particular relates to the extent to which the packaging materials or packaging containers may be reused once the package contents have been used.

附加功能尤其与包装内容被使用后,包装材料或包装容器再利用的程度有关。

Section C　Types of Container　集装箱的类型

The **exterior dimensions** of all containers conforming to ISO standards are 20 feet long×8 feet wide×8 feet 6 inches high or 9 feet 6 inches high for high cube containers (see Table 5-1).

Table 5-1　The High Cube Containers

	VENTILATED CONTAINER 20′	Ideal for cargo requiring ventilation
	BULK CONTAINER 20′	For bulk cargoes
	TANK CONTAINER 20′	For transportation of liquid chemicals and food stuffs
	DRY FREIGHT CONTAINER 20′ and 40′	General purpose container
	HIGH CUBE CONTAINER 40′ and 45′	9′6″High—For over height and voluminous cargo
	OPEN TOP CONTAINER 20′ and 40′	Removable tarpaulin for top loading of over height cargo
	FLAT RACK 20′ and 40′	For over width and heavy cargo
	PLATFORM 20′ and 40′	For extra length and heavy cargo
	INSULATED CONTAINER 20′ and 40′	For additional insulation of sensitive cargo
	REEFER CONTAINER 20′ and 40′	For cooling, freezing or heating of foods or chemicals
	HIGH CUBE REEFER CONTAIINER 40′ and 45′	9′6″High—For over height and voluminous cargo requiring cooling or freezing

Rigid containers are simply thicker **gauges** of **foil** that have been formed into **semi-rigid** containers to bring the convenience of modern food technology into our homes, schools, and restaurants.

Rigid containers, like foil sheets, provide an ideal barrier to moisture, light, and air. Rigid containers are perfect for holding leftovers and catered food items because, unlike other types of containers, rigid containers do not get **soggy** or wet—and they can be easily recycled.[1]

The use of containers handled and transported by special equipment and ships is common practice in air and water transport. In domestic distribution, containerization offers substantial transport efficiency and reduces product handling.

As the name implies, flexible containers don't protect a product by complete enclosure. To the contrary, the most common type of flexible container is stacked master cartons on rather pallets or slipsheets (see Figure 5-2).

Figure 5-2　Flexible Containers (Master Cartons)

New Words

1. exterior　*n.*外部,外面,表面,外形,外观;外貌;[影视]外景,[戏,影视]户外布景; *adj.*外面的,外部的,外表上的,表面的

2. dimension　*vi.*按规格尺寸切割;*vt.*在……上标尺寸;*n.*面积;特点;(长、宽、厚、高等的)尺寸;重要性;尺寸;方面;(长、宽、高的)量度;规模

3. gauge　*n.*规格(gauge 的名词复数);厚度;宽度;标准尺寸;*v.*(用仪器)测量;估计;计量;划分

4. foil　*n.*箔,金属薄片;陪衬,陪衬物;(镜底的)银箔,(宝石等的)衬底;(船)翼;*vt.*用……陪衬,衬托;铺箔于;[建]给……加上叶形饰;挫败,使受挫折

5. semi-rigid　*adj.*半刚性

6. soggy　*adj.*湿透的,浸透的;沉闷的,乏味的

Phrases

1. form into 使成为;变成
2. common practice 惯例;习惯做法
3. to the contrary 相反
4. rigid container 硬包装容器

Notes

1. Rigid containers are perfect for holding leftovers and catered food items because, unlike other types of containers, rigid containers do not get soggy or wet—and they can be easily recycled.

硬包装容器最适合用于装剩菜和食品,因为不像其他类型的容器,硬包装容器不易浸水或潮湿,而且可以很容易地回收。

Section D Package Labeling 包装标签

Once the material being packaged is placed into the box and the cover is closed, the contents are hidden. At this point, it becomes necessary to label the box. Labeling is any written, electronic, or **graphic** communications on the packaging or on a separate but associated entity. [1] Whether words or code numbers are used depends on the nature of the product and its **vulnerability** to **pilferage.** Reflective labels, also often referred to as **retro-reflective** labels are manufactured of a special material which can allow for the **infra-red** beam of a scanner to be returned to the scanner at greater strength, thus allowing the operator to scan from further away.

Barcodes are widely used in labeling, and they are read by scanners, or sensors, (See Figure 5-3). A barcode is an optical machine-readable representation of data, which shows data about the object to which it attaches. Originally, barcodes represented data by varying the widths and spacing of parallel lines, and might be referred to as linear or 1 **dimensional** (1D). Later they evolved into **rectangles**, dots, **hexagons** and other **geometric** patterns in 2 dimensions (2D). Although 2D systems use a variety of symbols, they are generally referred to as barcodes as well. Barcodes originally were scanned by special optical scanners called barcode readers. Scanners and **interpretive** software are available on devices including desktop printers and smartphones.

Not all labels are visible to the naked eyes; some are tiny chips that are embedded into the product and can be read using various electronic devices. [2] These RFID labels allow information contained in the chips to be updated as they move through the supply chain (See Figure 5-4).

RFID Tag: A microchip attached to an **antenna** that is packaged in a way that it can be

Figure 5-3   Bar Codes in Carrefour Food Labeling

applied to an object. The RFID tag picks up signals from and sends signals to a reader. The tag contains a unique serial number, but may have other information, such as a customers' account number. RFID tags can be active, passive or semi passive.

Antenna: The microchip antenna is the conductive element that enables the microchip to send and receive data. Readers also have antennas which are used to emit and receive radio waves.

Recently, the big box retailers like Wal-Mart have introduced initiatives to ultimately place an RFID label on every item they sell (see Figure 5-4).

Packaging needs both appropriate materials to protect the product and proper labels to guide the handling and storage thereof. There are various types of packaging labels and below is a list of the most commonly used logistics labels (see Figure 5-5).

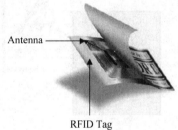

Figure 5-4   RFID Label

Brand labeling plays an increasingly important role in consumer purchasing decisions.

In an increasingly global economy, it is important to recognize that labeling regulations differ from country to country. As a general rule, labeling requirements and enforcement tend to be more stringent in economically developed countries than in economically developing ones. There are Golden rules in Carrefour store to have a good labeling, as follows:

- Adequate labeling of the packaged products
- All packaged products must have a label
- Respect the chart of limit consumption date, time in display

New Words

1. graphic   *adj.*图解的,用图表示的;用文字表示的;形象的,生动的
2. vulnerability   *n.*弱点,攻击;易伤性;致命性;脆弱性
3. pilferage   *n.*行窃,偷盗;小偷小摸

Figure 5-5　Types of Packaging Labels

4. retro-reflective　*adj.*反光的

5. infra-red　*adj.*红外线的

6. dimensional　*adj.*尺寸的;<物>量纲的;<数>因次的;维的

7. rectangle　*n.*<数>长方形,矩形

8. hexagon　*n.*六边形,六角形

9. geometric　*adj.*几何学的;成几何级数增减的;几何装饰的

10. interpretive　*adj.*作为说明的,解释的

11. antenna　*n.*天线

Phrases

1. global economy　全球经济

2. differ from　与……不同;区别于……

3. as a general rule　一般地;照例

4. be embedded into　嵌入

Notes

1. Labeling is any written, electronic, or graphic communications on the packaging or on a

separate but associated entity.

标签指的是在包装上或独立但关联的实体上所标注的书面、电子、图形信息。

2. Not all labels are visible to the naked eyes; some are tiny chips that are embedded into the product and can be read using various electronic devices.

并非所有的标签都是肉眼可见的。一些标签就是嵌入到产品中的微小芯片，可以通过各种电子设备读取。

Section E　Materials Handling Principles　物料处理原则

As a **supply chain** is linked together, one of the concerns of those involved with logistics is the physical transfer of the product from one party to another: How will it be handled? In what form will it be? In what quantities? What kind of equipment is needed to handle or to store it? **Materials handling processes** generally receive little public attention. An exception to this was the new luggage-handling system at the Denver airport, which was **initially** so defective that it delayed the airport's opening by many months.

The College-Industry Council on Material Handling Education, which is sponsored by the **Material Handling Institute**, has developed a list of 10 materials handling **principles**. The principles are more important when laying out the intended design or when troubleshooting to learn why a system is not performing well. [1] The Material Handling Institute suggests that these principles, which are listed following, are "the key to greater productivity, customer service, and profitability."

1) The planning principle. All material handling should be the result of a deliberate plan where the needs, performance, objectives and functional specification of the proposed methods are completely defined at the outset. [2]

2) The **standardization** principle. Material handling methods, equipment, controls, and software should be standardized within the limits of achieving overall performance objectives and without sacrificing needed flexibility, modularity, and throughput.

3) The work principle. Material handling work should be minimized without sacrificing productivity or the level of service required of the operation.

4) The ergonomic principle. **Ergonomics** refers to the science that seeks to adapt work or working conditions to suit the abilities of the worker. With this principle, human capabilities and limitations must be recognized and respected in the design of material handling tasks and equipment to ensure safe and effective operations.

5) The unit load principle. Unit loads shall be appropriately sized and configured in a way that achieves the material flow and inventory objectives at each stage in the supply chain. [3]

6) The **space utilization principle**. Effective and efficient use must be made of all available space.

7) The system principle. Material movement and storage activities should be fully

integrated to form a coordinated, operational system that spans receiving, inspection, storage, production, assembly, packaging, unitizing, order selection, shipping, transportation, and the handling of returns. [4]

8）The **automation** principle. Material handling operations should be mechanized or automated where **feasible** to improve operational efficiency, increase responsiveness, and improve **consistency** and predictability.

9）The environmental principle. Environmental impact and energy consumption should be considered as a criteria when designing or selecting alternative equipment and material handling systems.

10）The life cycle cost principle. A thorough economic analysis should account for the entire life cycle of all material handling equipment and resulting systems.

These 10 principles are accompanied by varying numbers of key points to consider when **implementing** the principles. With respect to the planning principle, for example, one key point is that the material handling plan should be in line with the **strategic objectives** of the organization. In a similar fashion, the work principle reminds us of a lesson that many of us learned in geometry class: The shortest distance between two points is a straight line. One key point associated with the environmental principle reinforces our earlier discussion in the sense that material handling and packaging products should be chosen with reusability or biodegradability in mind. [5]

New Words

1. initially　*adv.* 最初,首先;开头
2. principle　*n.* 原则;法则;信念(principle 的复数);本源　*v.* 向……灌输原则
3. standardization　*n.* 标准化;规格化;校准
4. ergonomics　*n.* 工效学;人类工程学
5. automation　*n.* 自动化;自动操作
6. feasible　*adj.* 可行的;可能的;可实行的
7. consistency　*n.* 一致性;稠度;相容性
8. implementing　*v.* 贯彻,实行(implement 的现在分词)

Phrases

1. supply chain　供应链;供给链;供需链
2. materials handling processe　物料处理流程
3. The College-Industry Council on Material Handling Education　物料搬运教育-工业审议会
4. Material Handling Institute　物料搬运协会
5. space utilization principle　空间利用原则
6. strategic objective　战略目标

Notes

1. The principles are more important when laying out the intended design or when troubleshooting to learn why a system is not performing well.

这些原则对方案设计或在发现运作问题排除故障时是非常重要的。

2. All material handling should be the result of a deliberate plan where the needs, performance, objectives and functional specification of the proposed methods are completely defined at the outset.

所有物料搬运都应该是详细计划的结果。具体的需求、运作、目标、建议方法的功能说明都必须完全界定。

3. Unit loads shall be appropriately sized and configured in a way that achieves the material flow and inventory objectives at each stage in the supply chain.

一个单位装载的尺寸和构造需要正确选择,以达成供应链每个阶段的物料流和库存的目标。

4. Material movement and storage activities should be fully integrated to form a coordinated, operational system that spans receiving, inspection, storage, production, assembly, packaging, unitizing, order selection, shipping, transportation, and the handling of returns.

物料的移动和储存活动应当充分集成,以形成一个协调的运作系统,包括从收货、检查、储存、生产、装配、包装、单元化、订货选择、装运、运输和回收等一系列活动。

5. One key point associated with the environmental principle reinforces our earlier discussion in the sense that material handling and packaging products should be chosen with reusability or biodegradability in mind.

与环境原则相关的一个关键点则加强了我们前面的讨论:在选择物料搬运和包装产品时要考虑到物料的可重复使用性或生物分解性。

🎯 Core Concepts   核心概念

1. Packaging performs two basic functions, marketing and delivery in logistics.

包装有两个物流基本功能:销售和运送。

2. The purpose of sales package is for sales and convenient use.

销售包装的目的是为了销售和方便使用。

3. In logistic and transportation process, it is very important to package the goods appropriately for protection and safety purposes.

在物流和运输过程中,对物品进行妥善包装非常重要,以达到防护和安全的目的。

4. Vacuum packaging is used to protect goods from deterioration or contamination, like food and medicine.

真空包装用于保护物品免于变质或污染,例如:食品或药品。

5. Palletizing refers to the process of loading goods in pallet.

托盘装运指将货物装载到托盘的过程。

6. Palletizing is to load goods onto a pallet and wrap to form a handling and loading unit.

托盘装运是指将货物装载到托盘并且打包成搬运货件。

7. The No.1 function of packaging is to protect goods.

包装的首要功能是保护货物。

8. In marketing, the package also aims for promoting and advertising the attractiveness of goods to be sold.

在销售市场上,包装也是为了促销和宣传商品的吸引力。

 Exercises 练习

Ⅰ. Answer the follow questions in English.

1. What is package best described as?

2. Try to describe the history of package in your own words.

3. How many types of materials are used in packaging now? What are they?

4. What are the "three R's" principle involved in product and package development?

5. How are the various functions of packaging divided?

6. What sub-functions are the primary, secondary and tertiary functions divided into?

7. What is the purpose of the sales function of a package?

8. What are the ISO standards of the exterior dimensions of all containers ?

Ⅱ. Choose the best word or phrase that fits the sentence.

1. The bags can be _____ on pallets to facilitate handling.

    A. stacked   B. put   C. carried   D. measured

2. Barrels, hogsheads and drums are used for the conveyance of liquid or _____ cargoes.

    A. light   B. heavy   C. greasy   D. important

3. This concerns the characteristics of the goods concerned and their _____ to various loss/damage.

    A. consideration   B. emotion   C. features   D. susceptibility

4. If packing is _____, bearing in mind transit and declared cargo valuation, problems could be experienced in carriers' liability, acceptance and adequate cargo insurance coverage.

    A. adequate   B. inadequate   C. good   D. thick

5. Overall, this type of packing gives complete protection and _____ the risk of pilferage and it is an aid to handling.

    A. lessens   B. increases   C. improves   D. avoids

6. Constructed of aluminium, they are lightweight and can be both stacked and _____.

    A. interstacked   B. packed   C. carried   D. taken

7. Many goods have little or no form of packing and are carried _____.

    A. quickly   B. bare   C. faster   D. loose

8. In the main, the _____ the cargo becomes, the greater the degree of packaging is required.

    A. more fragile   B. smaller   C. bigger   D. lighter

9. Baling is a form of packing _____ of a canvas cover often cross-looped by metal or rope binding.

    A. including   B. consisting   C. providing   D. offering

10. Packing, therefore, is not only designed as a form of protection to reduce the risk of goods being damaged in transit, but also to _____ pilferage and aid marketing.

    A. cause   B. enhance   C. lead to   D. prevent

11. Packaging is an activity closely associ ated with the evolution of society and, can be _____ to human beginning.

    A. traced back   B. come back   C. tracked back   D. gone back

12. Packing goods to _____ volume and weight while reinforcing them may save money, as well as ensure that the goods are properly packed.

    A. maximize   B. minimize   C. minimum   D. maximum

13. The goods frequently also require _____ from climatic conditions, such as temperature, humidity, precipitation and solar radiation.

    A. protection   B. protest   C. preserve   D. prevention

14. Promotional material placed on the packaging is _____ attract the potential purchaser's attention and to have a positive impact upon the purchasing decision.

    A. tend to   B. intended to   C. aimed at   D. intend to

15. The additional function in particular relates to the extent _____ the packaging materials or packaging containers may be reused once the package contents have been used.

    A. for which   B. to that   C. which   D. to which

Ⅲ. Match each word on the left with its corresponding meaning on the right.

A.	B.
1. packaging	(a) coming next after the second and just before the fourth
2. recycling	(b) lower in rank or importance
3. tertiary	(c) a written assurance that some product or service will be provided or will meet certain specifications
4. dynamic	(d) the act of processing used or abandoned materials for use in creating new products
5. loading	(e) not fully rigid

6. subordinate （f）characterized by action or forcefulness of personality

7. guarantee （g）the state of being vulnerable or exposed

8. semi-rigid （h）of or relating to dimensions

9. vulnerability （i）the business of packing

10. dimensional （j）a quantity that can be processed at one time

Ⅳ. Fill in the blanks with words or phrases from the list below.

recycling	barrier to	a variety of	focused on	primitive
considerable	efficient	impact	described	visible to

1. Package is best _____ as a coordinated system of preparing goods for transport, distribution, storage, retailing, and use of the goods.

2. Packaging is not a recent phenomenon; _____ people needed containment and carrying devices.

3. The invention is directed to packaging product for _____ goods.

4. Emphasis is _____ recycling the largest primary components of a package: steel, aluminum, papers, plastics, etc..

5. Development of sustainable packaging is an area of _____ interest by standards organizations, government, consumers, packagers, and retailers.

6. Packaging thus has a crucial _____ on the efficiency of transport, handling and storage of goods.

7. The purpose of the sales function of a package is to enable or promote the sales process and to make it more _____.

8. The most significant example is the _____ of paper, paperboard and cardboard packaging as waste paper.

9. Rigid containers, like foil sheets, provide an ideal _____ moisture, light, and air.

10. Not all labels are _____ the naked eyes; some are tiny chips that are embedded into the product and can be read using various electronic devices.

Ⅴ. Translate the following sentences into Chinese.

1. This form of packing is particularly prominent in surface transport and is used for much machinery and other items of expensive equipment.

2. Crates or skeleton cases are a form of container halfway between a bale and a case.

3. The more handling goods must endure, the stouter the packaging is required; furthermore, the greater the degree of overstowage that the goods must endure, then the stronger the packaging needs to be.

4. The same industry that led the way in the adoption of warehouse management and labor management systems, wireless bar code scanning and voice technology is now adopting

automated materials handling in a big way.

5. The system uses a separate mini-load system for buffer storage, a customer-designed palletizer to place the cartons on the right spot on the pallet, and an automatic stretch wrapper.

Ⅵ. Translate the following sentences into English.

1. 包装不仅影响生产和销售，而且也影响综合物流活动。

2. 许多公司在努力创造自己的特色品牌，以引导消费者的偏好。

3. 越来越多的全球运输方提供各种各样的包装服务。

4. 中国的生产流通企业为原料和产成品的运输支付了高昂的费用。

5. 调研显示，有 75% 的企业的物流信息管理技术主要集中在互联网，39.1% 的企业建立了相关的条码识别，14.6% 的企业使用了地理信息系统，使用自送分拣系统的企业则更少，只占 7.3%。

Ⅶ. Fill in the blanks with words from the list below and each word can be used once.

Raw materials form a critical part of manufacturing as well as service organization. In any ___1___ , a considerable amount of material handling is done in one form or the ___2___ . This movement is either done ___3___ or through an ___4___ process. Throughout material, handling processes significant.

___5___ and health; challenges are ___6___ to workers as well as management. Therefore, manual material handing is of prime concern for health and safety professional, and they must determine practical ways of reducing health ___7___ to the workers.

Manual material handling ranges from movement of raw material, work in progress, finished goods, rejected, scraps, packing material, etc. These materials are of different shapes and sizes as well as weight. Material handling is a systematic and scientific method of moving, packing and ___8___ of material in ___9___ and suitable location. The main ___10___ of material handling are as follows.

A) another	B) other	C) appropriate
D) presented	E) manually	F) automated
G) organizing	H) organization	I) automating
J) objectives	K) safety	L) storing
M) store	N) risk	O) benefit

Chapter 6

How Supply Chain Works
供应链如何运行

📚 Section A   Definition of Supply Chain   供应链的概念

With reference to supply chain management that can be traced to the 1980s, it is safe to say that it was not until the 1990s that the term supply chain management captured the attention of senior level managemnet in numerous organizations. [1] They recognized the power and political impact of a supply chain approach to making organizations more globally competitive and helping to increase their market share with consequent improvements in shareholder value.

Various definitions of a supply chain have been offered in the past several years as the concept has gained popularity. The APICS Dictionary [2] describes the supply chain as:

1. The processes from the initial raw materials to the ultimate consumption of the finished product linking across supplier-user companies; and

2. The functions within and outside a company that enable the value chain to make products and provide services to the customer.

Another source defines supply chain as the network of entities through which material flows. Those entities may include **suppliers**, **carriers**, manufacturing sites, distribution centers, retailers, and customers. [3] The Supply Chain Council (1997) uses the definition: "The supply chain—a term increasingly used by logistics professionals—encompasses every effort involved in producing and delivering a final product, from the supplier's supplier to the customer's customer. Four basic processes—plan, source, make, deliver —broadly define these efforts, which include managing supply and demand, sourcing raw materials and parts, manufacturing and assembly, warehousing and inventory tracking, order entry and order management, distribution across all channels, and delivery to the customer. [4]" Quinn (1997) defines the supply chain as " ... all of those activities associated with moving goods from the raw-materials stage through to the end user. This includes sourcing and procurement, production scheduling, order processing, inventory management, transportation, warehousing, and customer service. Importantly, it also embodies the information systems so necessary to monitor all of those activities."

In addition to defining the supply chain, several authors have further defined the concept of supply chain management. As defined by Ellram and Cooper (1993), supply chain management is "an integrating philosophy to manage the total flow of a distribution channel from supplier to ultimate customer". Monczka and Morgan (1997) state that "integrated supply chain management is about going from the external customer and then managing all the processes that are needed to provide the customer with value in a horizontal way." They believe that supply chains, not firms, compete and that those who will be the strongest competitors are those that "can provide management and leadership to the fully integrated supply chain including external customer as well as prime suppliers, their suppliers, and their suppliers' suppliers." [5]

From these definitions, a summary definition of the supply chain can be stated as: all the activities involved in delivering a product from raw material through to the customer including sourcing raw materials and parts, manufacturing and assembly, warehousing and inventory tracking, order entry and order management, distribution across all channels, delivery to the customer, and the information systems necessary to **monitor** all of these activities. [6] Supply chain management coordinates and integrates all of these activities into a seamless process. It links all of the partners in the chain including departments within an organization and the external partners including suppliers, carriers, third-party companies, and information systems providers. Managers in companies across the supply chain take an interest in the success of other companies. They work together to make the whole supply chain competitive. They have the facts about the market; they know a lot about competition; and they coordinate their activities with those of their trading partners. It encompasses the processes necessary to create, source, make to, and to deliver to demand. They use technology to gather information on market demands and exchange information between organizations. A key point in supply chain management is that the entire process must be viewed as one system. Any **inefficiencies** incurred across the supply chain (suppliers, manufacturing plants, warehouses, customers, etc.) must be assessed to determine the true capabilities of the process.

New Words

1. supplier   *n.* 供应商
2. carrier   *n.* 承运商
3. monitor   *n.*显示屏,屏幕;[计]显示器;监测仪;监控人员,班长 *vt.*监控,监听;搜集,记录;测定;监督 *vi.*监视
4. inefficiency   *n.*无效率,无能;无效率事例

拓展资源

Phrases

1. APICS:American production and Inventory Control Society   美国生产与库存管理学会
2. raw material   原材料

3. finished product　产成品

4. value chain　价值链

5. distribution center　分销中心

6. sourcing and procurement　外购

7. inventory tracking　库存跟踪

8. order entry　订单输入

9. order processing　订单处理

10. inventory management　库存管理

11. customer service　顾客服务

12. order management　订单管理

Notes

1. With reference to supply chain management that can be traced to the 1980s, it is safe to say that it was not until the 1990s that the term supply chain management captured the attention of senior level management in numerous organizations.

虽然供应链管理的历史可以追溯到 20 世纪 80 年代,但可以说,直到 90 年代它才引起许多组织中高层管理者的关注。

2. The APICS Dictionary is the standard for defining terms used in the operations management field. This powerful tool can expand the professional vocabulary and ensure that everyone is speaking the same language. The newly updated 11th edition contains more than 3 500 important industry terms.

APICS 字典是定义操作管理领域中使用的术语的标准。这个强大的工具可以扩展专业词汇,确保每个人都说同一种语言。最新更新的第 11 版包含超过 3 500 个重要的行业术语。

3. Those entities may include suppliers, carriers, manufacturing sites, distribution centers, retailers, and customers.

这些实体包括供应商、运营商、生产基地、配送中心、零售商和客户。

4. Four basic processes—plan, source, make, deliver—broadly define these efforts, which include managing supply and demand, sourcing raw materials and parts, manufacturing and assembly, warehousing and inventory tracking, order entry and order management, distribution across all channels, and delivery to the customer.

四个基本流程——计划、货源、制造、运送——大致包括如下行为: 供求管理,采购原材料和零部件,制造和装配,仓储和库存跟踪,订单输入,订单管理,通过各种渠道配送,并交付给客户。

5. They believe that supply chains, not firms, compete and that those who will be the strongest competitors are those that "can provide management and leadership to the fully integrated supply chain including external customer as well as prime suppliers, their suppliers, and their suppliers' suppliers."

他们认为,是供应链之间,而不是企业之间相互竞争。而且在竞争中处于优势地位的是那些"能够管理和领导整个供应链的人,包括外部客户、主要供应商、他们的供应商和供应商的供应商"。

6. All the activities involved in delivering a product from raw material through to the customer including sourcing raw materials and parts, manufacturing and assembly, warehousing and inventory tracking, order entry and order management, distribution across all channels, delivery to the customer, and the information systems necessary to monitor all of these activities.

供应链涉及把产品从原材料配送到客户的整个过程,包括采购原材料和零部件、制造和装配、仓储和库存跟踪、订单输入和订单管理、通过各种渠道配送、把产品交付给客户,以及用来监控所有活动的信息系统。

Section B   Structure of the Supply Chain   供应链结构

A supply chain consists of a series of activities and organizations where materials move through on their journey from **initial** suppliers to final customers. Figure 6-1 shows the major elements in a firm's supply chain and presents **illustrations** of several types of supply chains. The simplest view of a supply chain is a single product moving through a series of organizations, each of which somehow adds value to the product. [1]

Taking one organization's point of view, activities in front of it—moving materials inwards—are called upstream; those after the organization—moving materials outwards—are called downstream.

The upstream activities are divided into tiers of suppliers. A supplier that sends materials directly to the operations is a first-tier supplier; one that send materials to a first-tier supplier is a second-tier supplier; one that sends materials to a second-tier supplier is a third-tier supplier, and so on back to the original sources. Customers are also divided into tiers. One that gets a product directly from the operations is a first-tier customer; one that gets a product from a first-tier customer is a second-tier customer; one that gets a product from a second-tier customer is a third-tier customer, and so on to final customers (see Figure 6-1).

In practice, most organizations get materials from many different channels. Moreover, the structure of the supply chain can vary dramatically for different companies, even within the same industry; complex supply chains may include third-party logistics providers, to facilitate coordination among various supply chain parties.

Many companies are using the terms logistics and supply chain **interchangeably**, but this is not correct. Supply chain management integrates product, information, and cash flows among organizations from the point of origin to the point of consumption, with the goal of maximizing consumption satisfaction and minimizing organization costs. [2] Logistics has traditionally been responsible for managing the physical slow of products among organizations. Activities such as transportation and warehousing were used to ensure that the movement of goods was continuous

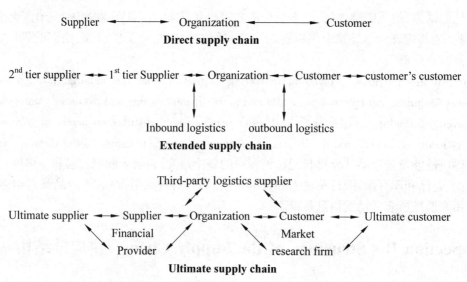

Figure 6-1 Different Supply Chain Configurations

and reliable. Marketing and sales have been responsible for providing information to customers before and after the transaction. Information technology has allowed logistics to take on additional responsibility for managing information flow among organization. Bar coding and EDI have allowed logistics to provide information on product flows before they occur, during movement, and after delivery. Finally, finance and accounting have been responsible for cash flows among organization in a channel by controlling **invoicing** and collections.

Some logistics organization, like Welch's foods, have taken on these additional cash-flow activities. Even if logistic does not have control over a firm's cash flow, it certainly has influence over it. For example, many firms will invoice a customer upon receipt of an order. The customer will not process payment until proof of delivery is received, so faster and more reliable transportation can begin this customer payment process sooner as well as offer the ability to generate a proof of delivery document through EDI. Thus, logistics management is part of supply chain management. In some organizations logistics controls all three flows: product, information, and cash; in other organizations logistics controls product flow, manages additional information flows, and influences cash flows. This integral involvement of logistics in supply chain management might be one explanation for the two terms being used **interchangeably**.

New Words

1. initial   *adj.*最初的;开始的;首字母的;*n.*首字母;[语音学]声母;特大的大写字母; *vt.*用姓名的首字母签名

2. illustration   *n.*说明;例证;图解;插图

3. interchangeably   *adv.*可交换地;可交替地;可互换地

4. invoicing   *n.*货品计价

Phrases

1. consist of 由……组成;包括
2. tiers of suppliers 供应商的层次
3. point of view 观点;见地;立场
4. in pratice 在实践中;实际上,事实上
5. in essence 其实;本质上;大体上
6. cash flow 资金流动;现金流动量

Notes

1. The simplest view of a supply chain is a single product moving through a series of organizations, each of which somehow adds value to the product.

供应链最简单的说法是,某个产品从多个组织中通过,每一个组织都在某种程度上增加了产品的价值。

2. Supply chain management integrates product, information, and cash flows among organizations from the point of origin to the point of consumption, with the goal of maximizing consumption satisfaction and minimizing organization costs.

供应链管理是指整合从起源地到消费的整个过程中的产品、信息、现金流,最大化地满足消费、降低组织成本。

Section C Interest in Supply Chains 供应链利益

Why has **supply** chain management become increasingly popular? The answer lies in the fact that few companies continue to be **vertically** integrated. Companies have become more specialized and search for suppliers who can provide low cost, quality materials rather than own their source of supply .[1] It becomes critical for companies to manage the entire network of supply to **optimize** overall performance. These organizations have realized that whenever a company deals with another company that performs the next phase of the supply chain, both stand to benefit from the other's success.

A second reason partially stems from increased national and international competition. Customers have **multiple** sources from which to choose to satisfy demand; locating product throughout the distribution channel for maximum customer accessibility at a minimum cost becomes crucial. Previously, companies looked at solving the distribution problem through maintaining inventory at various locations throughout the chain. However, the dynamic nature of the marketplace makes holding inventory a risky and potentially unprofitable business. Customers' buying habits are constantly changing, and competitors are continually adding and deleting products. Demand changes make it almost a sure bet that the company will have the wrong inventory. The cost of holding any inventory also means most companies cannot provide a low cost product when funds are tied up in inventory.

A third reason for the shift in emphasis to the supply chain is due to a realization by most companies that maximizing performance of one department or function may lead to less optimal performance for the whole company. Purchasing may negotiate a lower price on a component and receive a favorable purchase price variance, but the cost to produce the finished product may go up due to inefficiencies in the plant. Companies must look across the entire supply chain to gauge the impact of decisions in any area.

Advanced Manufacturing Research, a Boston-based consulting firm, developed a supply chain model which emphasizes material and information flow between manufacturers and their trading partners. [2] They believe the changes required by management are due to the following changes in how manufacturers are doing business:

- Greater sharing of information between vendors and customers.
- Horizontal business processes replacing vertical departmental functions.
- Shift from mass production to customized products.
- Increased reliance on purchased materials and outside processing with a **simultaneous reduction** in the number of suppliers.
- Greater emphasis on organizational and process flexibility.
- Necessity to **coordinate** processes across many sites.

Employee **empowerment** and the need for rules-based real time decision support systems. Competitiveness pressures to introduce new products more quickly. For these reasons, expertly managing the supply chain has become critical for most companies.

Ultimately, effectively integrated supply management results in lower costs, higher quality, better customer service, and higher profits for the organization, its suppliers, and its distributors. Supply chains are integrated by having various parties enter into and carry out long-term **mutually beneficial** agreements. These agreements are known by several names, including partnerships, strategic alliances, third-party arrangements, and contract logistics. Whatever they are called, these agreements should be designed to reward all participants when **collaborative** ventures are successful, and they should also provide **incentives** for all parties to work toward success. In a similar fashion, the participants should share the consequences when cooperative ventures are less successful than desired.

When an organization enters into a long-term agreement with a source or customer, the organization must keep in mind how this arrangement could affect the rest of the supply chain. Ideally, all participants in the supply chain will meet at one time and work out whatever agreements are necessary to ensure that the entire supply chain functions in the most **desirable** manner.

To integrate a particular supply chain, the various organizations must recognize the shortcomings of the present systems and examine channel arrangements as they currently exist and as they might be. All this is done within the framework of the organization's overall strategy, as well as any logistic strategies necessary to support the goals and objectives of the form's top management.

Broadly speaking, organizations can **pursue** three primary methods when attempting to integrate their supply chains. One method is through vertical integration.

A second possible method of supply chain coordination involves the use of formal contracts among various participants.

A third method of supply chain coordination involves informal agreements among the various organizations to pursue common goals and objectives, with control being exerted by the largest organization in the supply chain.

New Words

1. vertically　*adv.*垂直地;直立地;陡峭地;在顶点

2. optimize　*vt.*使最优化,使尽可能有效

3. multiple　*adj.*多重的;多个的;复杂的;多功能的;*n.*<数>倍数;[电工学]并联;连锁商店;下有多个分社的旅行社

4. simultaneous　*adj.*同时发生的,同时存在的;同时的;联立的;*n.*同声译员

5. reduction　*n.*减少;降低;[数学]约简;[摄影术]减薄

6. coordinate　*vt.*使协调,使调和;整合;使(身体各部分)动作协调;(衣服、布料等)搭配;*vi.*协调;协同;成为同等;被归入同一类别

7. empowerment　*n.*授权;许可

8. mutually　*adv.*互相地,互助

9. beneficial　*adj.*有利的,有益的;[法]可享受利益的

10. collaborative　*adj.*合作的;协作的

11. incentive　*n.*激励某人做某事的事物;刺激;诱因;动机

12. desirable　*adj.*令人满意的;值得拥有的;可取的;性感的;*n.*称心如意的人[东西]

13. pursue　*vt.*继续;追求;进行;追捕;*vi.*追,追赶;继续进行

Phrases

1. lie in　在于

2. continue to　继续,延续

3. search for　寻找;搜索

4. benefit from　得益于;得利于;因……而得到好处

5. distribution channel　分销渠道;销售渠道

6. be tied up　被占用;很忙的

7. due to　由于;取决于

8. purchase price　买价;进货价格

9. finished product　成品

10. shift from　从……转换

11. enter into   进入;讨论;参加;开始从事
12. carry out   执行,实行;贯彻;实现;完成
13. be designed to   目的是;被设计用于做
14. broadly speaking   一般地说;广义地说;泛泛地说

Notes

1. Companies have become more specialized and search for suppliers who can provide low cost, quality materials rather than own their source of supply.

公司变得更加专业化,它们寻找能够提供低成本、高质量材料的供应商,而不是由自己提供货源。

2. Advanced Manufacturing Research, a Boston-based consulting firm, developed a supply chain model which emphasizes material and information flow between manufacturers and their trading partners.

总部位于波士顿的高等制造研究咨询公司,开发了一种供应链模式,强调制造商和其贸易伙伴之间的信息交流。

Section D   Barriers to Supply Chain Management
供应链管理障碍

A supply chain may have hundreds, even thousands of **interconnected** components and **contributors**. To keep them all running smoothly, managers need to see what's going on, what's most critical, what decisions they need to make, and the impact these decisions will have on the extended supply chain. [1] There are many barriers to building a high-performance supply chain.

Regulatory and political consideration

Decades ago, many of the supply chain managements used today would have been considered illegal under certain regulatory statues. Long-term **commitments**, which are one of the **bedrocks** of supply management, may **stifle** competition to the extent that they make it more difficult for others to enter the market.

Political reasons, such as war and governmental stability can also act as a barrier to supply chain management. Political uncertainties might cause some organizations to shy away from joining or developing supply chains.

Lack of top management commitment

Top management commitment is regularly cited as an important component when individual companies attempt to **initiate** and implement new initiatives, programs, and products. Because of supply chain management's inter-organizational focus, top management commitment is absolutely essential if supply chain efforts are to have any chance of success. Unfortunately, recent research presents a **vague** of sorts with respect to top management commitment to supply chain management.

Reluctance to share, or use relevant information

One tenets of supply chain management is that well-run supply chains are characterized by information sharing among their participants. Nevertheless, some organizations are reluctant to share information, particularly information that might be considered **proprietary** in nature. [2] However, this reluctance can contribute to supply chain problems because members may be making decisions based on **erroneous** data or assumptions. For example, one cause of the bullwhip effect is asymmetrical information among supply chain participants.

The Bullwhip Effect (or Whiplash Effect) is an observed phenomenon in forecast-driven distribution channels (see Figure 6-2). The concept has its roots in J. Forrester's Industrial Dynamics and thus it is also known as the Forrester Effect. Since the **oscillating** demand magnification upstream a supply chain reminds someone of a cracking whip it became famous as the Bullwhip Effect. The bullwhip effect is a dynamical phenomenon in supply chains. It refers to the tendency of the variability of orders rates to increase as they pass through the **echelons** of a supply chain towards producers and raw material suppliers.

The Bullwhip Effect

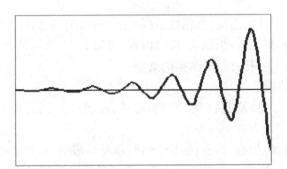

Consumer Demand ————▶ Manufacturer Predictions

Figure 6-2　The Bullwhip Effect

Furthermore, advances in computer hardware now permit **copious** amounts of information to be processed and analyzed relatively quickly. However, some companies are reluctant to fully utilize the information that comes from this data. For example, some companies may be uncomfortable with the concept of customer power in supply chains. Alternatively, other companies may be hesitant to enter into long-term relationships because such relationships might be perceived as limiting their operational flexibility.

Incompatible corporate cultures

Because supply chain management emphasizes a long-term orientation and partnerships between various participants, it is important that the participants are comfortable with the companies they will be working with. Corporation Culture is the result of the commodity economy and the market economy, which representing the method the company is using for the achievement of its unique purpose, is a company's managing philosophy of arts. In a word, corporation culture leads to the concept value of the company, the physical and psychical appearance of the whole staff-the spiritual backbone of the whole company.

Globalization

Although much of the discussion so far focused on domestic supply chains, one should recognize that supply chains are becoming increasingly global in nature. Reasons for the increased globalization of supply chain include lower-priced materials and labor, the global perspective of companies in supply chains, and the development of global competition, among others. Supply chain integration can be challenging in a domestic setting, but integration challenges are even greater in global supply chains due to cultural, economic, technological, political, spatial, and logistical differences.

New Words

1. interconnect　*v.*互相连接,互相联系(interconnect 的过去式和过去分词)

2. contributor　*n.*捐款人;捐助人;促成因素;投稿者

3. commitment　*n.*委托;任务;承担的义务

4. bedrock　*n.*基岩

5. stifle　*vt.& vi.*(使)窒息;(使)室闷;扼杀;*vt.*镇压;遏制;扼杀;藏匿;*n.*后腿膝关节;后膝关节病

6. initiate　*vt.*开始,发起;传授;创始,开辟;接纳新成员;*n.*新加入某组织(或机构、宗教)的人,新入会的人;被传授初步知识的人;*adj.*被传授初步知识的;新入会的

7. vague　*adj.*模糊的;(思想上)不清楚的;(表达或感知)含糊的;暧昧的;*n.*模糊不定状态

8. reluctance　*n.*不愿意,勉强;[电]磁阻;反应式

9. proprietary　*adj.*专有的,专利的;所有(人)的;(商品)专卖的;*n.*所有权,所有物;所有人;专卖药品;独家制造(及销售)的产品

10. erroneous　*adj.*错误的;不正确的;纰缪;讹

11. oscillating　*v.*(使)摆动(oscillate 的现在分词);振荡

12. echelon　*n.*(机构中的)等级,阶层;梯形,梯形编队;*vi.vt.*排成梯队

13. copious　*adj.*丰富的;大量的;多产的;冗长的

Phrases

1. high-performance　高效能,高性能的,高指标
2. shy away from　回避,退缩;躲避;羞于
3. respect to　关于;考虑
4. reluctant to　不心甘情愿做
5. in nature　本质上;事实上;实际上
6. contribute to　有助于;促成;捐献
7. be reluctant to　不愿意,不情愿
8. be hesitant to　犹豫,犹豫不决
9. in a word　总之,简言之
10. Bullwhip Effect　牛鞭效应

Notes

1. To keep them all running smoothly, managers need to see what's going on, what's most critical, what decisions they need to make, and the impact these decisions will have on the extended supply chain.

为了让它们都平稳运行,管理者需要看看会发生什么,什么是最关键的,需要做出什么样的决定,这些决定对延伸的供应链会有什么样的影响。

2. Nevertheless, some organizations are reluctant to share information, particularly information that might be considered proprietary in nature.

尽管如此,一些组织不愿意分享信息,特别是那些可能被视为性质专有的信息。

Section E　Green Logistics　绿色物流

As know well, each activities of tradition logistics has huge impact to the environment, such as the **exhaust gas** in transportation; dust pollution in loading and unloading. [1] The new concept, green logistics, comes from the requirement of the **sustainable development** of economic, in order to change the one-way relationship between economic developing and logistics; and to **restrain** the impact of logistics for the environment. [2]

Green logistics means: using the advanced logistics technology and operating the transportation, storage, packaging, loading & unloading, and **distribution process**, in order to reduce the pollution to the environment, and the **consumption** of natural resource. [3]

Green logistics is meaningful: firstly, it is the requirement of the sustainable development of economic and the globalization; secondly, it is the **inevitable** road to reduce the operate cost maximally; and the last but not the least, it can help an enterprise to gain the competitive advantage.

To build a green logistics system needs to integrate six parts of logistics activities.

1）green transportation

Green transportation is referred to reduce the pollution of exhaust gas, noise, tries to save the building and maintains fee of transportation. [4]

2）**green warehousing** and storage

Green warehousing and storage means to use scientific warehousing and storage **strategy** and methods, in order to avoid the damage of goods and reduce the pollution to the environment.

3）green loading and unloading

Green loading and unloading is to use modern equipment and methods and try to reduce the dust, mist pollution when loading and unloading.

4）**green packaging**

Green packaging requires an **appropriate** package which is recycle, reused and without any harmfulness and damage to the human being and environment. [5]

New Words

1. restrain   *vt.* 抑制,控制;约束;制止
2. consumption   *n.* 消费;消耗
3. inevitable   *adj.* 必然的,不可避免的
4. strategy   *n.* 战略,策略
5. appropriate   *adj.* 适当的;恰当的;合适的   *vt.* 占用,拨出

Phrases

1. exhaust gas   废气
2. sustainable development   可持续发展
3. distribution process   配送流程;分销过程;流通过程
4. green warehousing   绿色仓储
5. green packaging   绿色包装

Notes

1. As know well, each activity of tradition logistics has huge impact to the environment, such as the exhaust gas in transportation; dust pollution in loading and unloading.

众所周知,传统物流的每一项活动都会对环境产生巨大的影响,比如运输过程中的废气排放;装卸过程中粉尘污染等。

2. The new concept, green logistics, comes from the requirement of the sustainable development of economic, in order to change the one-way relationship between economic developing and logistics; and to restrain the impact of logistics for the environment.

绿色物流,作为一个新的概念,来自于经济可持续发展的要求,是为了改变经济发展与物流的单边关系,并抑制物流对环境的影响。

3. Green logistics means: using the advanced logistics technology and operating the transportation, storage, packaging, loading & unloading, and distribution process, in order to reduce the pollution to the environment, and the consumption of natural resource.

绿色物流是指利用先进的物流技术,实施运输、仓储、包装、装卸、配送等过程,以减少对环境的污染,减少对自然资源的消耗。

4. Green transportation is referred to reduce the pollution of exhaust gas, noise, tries to save the building and maintains fee of transportation.

绿色交通是指减少废气排放、噪声污染,努力节约运输的建设和维护费用。

5. Green packaging requires an appropriate package which is recycle, reused and without any harmfulness and damage to the human being and environment.

绿色包装需要适当的包装,该包装可以回收利用,重复使用,并且对人类和环境没有任何危害和损害。

Core Concepts　核心概念

1. Supply Chain Management (SCM) is a system applied to maximize profits for all parties in the whole logistic system and other economic systems.

供应链管理(SCM)是用来实现利润最大化的系统,它可以用于物流系统的各个部分以及其他经济系统。

2. Supply Chain is the relationship between suppliers and customers. In the supply chain, suppliers rank before buyer, seller and customers.

供应链是供应者和客户之间联系的桥梁,在供应链中供应者位居买方、卖方及客户之前。

3. Supply logistics is the procedure in which orders are taken from customers and purchases are delivered to the warehouse belonged of the customers.

供应物流是按照客户的定单将其购买的货物送到客户仓库的过程。

4. Supply chain links all suppliers and customers along a system in which products and services are delivered.

供应链通过产品服务递送系统连接供应商和客户。

Exercises　练习

Ⅰ. Answer the follow questions in English.

1. How does the APICS Dictionary describe the supply chain?

2. How is supply chain defined by Ellram and Cooper?

3. What is the summary definition of the supply chain ?

4. What does a supply chain consist of?

5. Why has supply chain management become more popular?

6. What are the barriers to supply chain management?

Ⅱ. Choose the best word or phrase that fits the sentence.

1. According to INCOTERMS 2000, _____ means that the sellers deliver the goods passing the ship's rail at the named port of shipment.

    A. FCA   B. FOB   C. CFR   D. CPT

2. According to UCP 600, the terms "middle" of a month in the L/C shall be construed as _____.

    A. from the 10th to the 20th of the month

    B. from the 11th to the 20th of the month

    C. from the 11th to the 21st of the month

    D. from the 10th to the 21st of the month

3. The movement of finished product to customers is _____.

    A. market distribution   B. procurement

    C. manufacturing support   D. inventory

4. For a supply chain to realize the maximum strategic benefit logistics, the full range of functional works must be _____.

    A. managed   B. integrated   C. transported   D. supplied

5. _____ is a letter from a bank to a foreign bank authorizing the payment of a specified sum to the person or company named.

    A. Letter of Delivery   B. Letter of Credit

    C. Letter of Indemnity   D. Letter of Guarantee

6. Warehousing and storage systems play a _____ role in international logistics.

    A. possible   B. better   C. key   D. understanding

7. One of the objective of logistics is to _____ distribution costs.

    A. maximize   B. minimize   C. maximum   D. minimum

8. Well organized logistics will cut _____ times and fasten flow of cargos.

    A. logistic   B. responding   C. lead   D. order

9. _____ strategy ensures that while minimizing inventory levels, materials are made available for production.

    A. Logistics   B. Just-at-time   C. Just-in-time   D. Just-on-time

10. Setting inventory levels requires _____ information from customers; _____ information from suppliers and information on current inventory levels.

    A. downstream, upstream   B. upstream, downstream

    C. onward, backward   D. backward, onward

11. A supply chain _____ the series of activities and organizations that materials move through on their journey from initial suppliers to final customers.

A. consists of　　　B. including　　　C. makes up　　　D. composed of

12. Logistics has traditionally been responsible _____ managing the physical flow of products among organizations.

A. to　　　　　B. in　　　　　C. for　　　　　D. on

13. The answer _____ the fact that few companies continue to be vertically integrated.

A. lies on　　　B. lies in　　　C. leads to　　　D. consist of

14. However, some companies are reluctant to fully _____ the information that comes from this data.

A. utilizing　　B. utilization　　C. utilize　　　D. utilized

15. Supply chain integration can be challenging in a domestic setting, but integration challenges are even greater in _____ supply chains due to cultural, economic, technological, political, spatial, and logistical differences.

A. international　　B. national　　C. global　　　D. local

Ⅲ. Match each word on the left with its corresponding meaning on the right.

1. producer　　　　（a）someone who manufactures something

2. retailer　　　　（b）a merchant who sells goods at retail

3. carrier　　　　（c）someone confined to an exclusive group

4. insider　　　　（d）someone who supplies services or commodities

5. partner　　　　（e）someone who works with others for a common goal

6. consultant　　　（f）someone who delivers something

7. distributor　　　（g）an expert who gives advice

8. supplier　　　　（h）someone who markets merchandise

Ⅳ. Fill in the blanks with words or phrases from the list below.

on top of this	outsourcing	lean	transactional-based	client
re-engineer	dynamics	track	distribution	minutiae

1. These trends resulted in increased demands on firms and possibilities for companies to operate more competitive and _____.

2. 3PL is evolving from predominately _____ to more strategic in nature.

3. _____, also Value Added Services can be provided, such as: repackaging, assembling and return logistics.

4. _____ the Logistics function can free up resources to focus on core competencies.

5. At least a mid-sized corporation such as the logistics cost is substantial enough to justify the engagement of the _____ services.

6. A Fourth Party Logistics provider is a supply chain services provider that searches the best logistical solutions for its _____, typically without using own assets and resources.

7. In the period from Go-Live through Stabilization, there can arise some behavioral _____ which will challenge the project leadership and threaten the effectiveness of your investment.

8. These characteristics commonly reside along the entire supply chain and they are more profound, more visible and more greatly exaggerated at the _____ center.

9. In a WMS project, the team and the project sponsors identify, _____ and react to issues and attempt to resolve them in a timely and effective manner.

10. They find themselves unable to differentiate the minor from the major. Their sense of scale on issues has gone myopic and they have honed a keen eye for _____. They have become the nano' manager.

Ⅴ. Translate the following sentences into Chinese.

1. Quite a number of companies achieved success by creating value throughout domestic and global supply chains.

2. The distribution or market channel is perhaps the least understood business area.

3. Little else is significant if the customer's expectations are not fully met.

4. Understandably, no one wants to be held accountable for results that are particularly the responsibility of others, be they inside or outside of the organization.

5. If the overall supply chain goals are not universally accepted, the likelihood of agreeing on (let alone, succeeding with) joint supply chain initiative is slim.

Ⅵ. Translate the following sentences into English.

1. 然而,供应链管理概念的出现使许多管理人员从采购所起到的战略性作用中受到启发。

2. 信息技术包括了在整个供应链中收集和分析信息的软件与硬件设备。

3. 虽然物流不是一件新鲜事,供应链管理相对来说却是一个新名词。

4. 成功的供应链管理需要我们改变以前只对单个过程管理的模式,代之以对一系列过程进行管理。

5. 在组织物流的过程中发生的其他费用,如有关物流活动进行的差旅费、办公费等是供应链总成本的一个构成因素。

Ⅶ. Fill in the blanks with words from the list below and each word can be used once.

What is Green Logistics? Logistics is the __1__ management of all the activities required to move products through the __2__ chain. For a __3__ product this supply chain extends from a raw material source through the production and distribution system to the point of __4__ and the associated reverse logistics.

Green logistics describes all __5__ to measure and minimize the ecological impact of logistics activities. This includes all activities of the forward and reverse flows of products, information and services between the point of origin and the point of consumption. It is the aim to create a __6__ company value using a balance of economic and environmental __7__ . Green logistics has its __8__ in the mid- 1980s and was a __9__ to characterize logistics systems and __10__ .

A) attempts	B) typical	C) tropical
D) origin	E) integrated	F) intensive
G) consumption	H) efficiency	I) sustainable
J) method	K) approaches	L) provided
M) supply	N) apply	O) concept

Chapter 7

Distribution Channel
配 送 渠 道

Section A   Definition of Distribution Channel
配送渠道的概念

A channel of distribution can be defined as the **collection** of organization units, either **internal** or **external** to the **manufacturer**, which performs the functions involved in product marketing. [1] The marketing functions are **pervasive**: they include buying, selling, transporting, storing, grading, financing, **bearing** market risk, and providing marketing information. Any organizational unit, **institution**, or agency that performs one or more of the marketing functions is a member of the channel of distribution.

Managing distribution **channels** requires firms to **coordinate** and **integrate** logistics and marketing activities in a manner **consistent** with overall corporate strategy. [2] Two channels, the logistical channel and the marketing channel, are highly related. The logistical channel refers to the means by which products flow physically from where they are available to where they are needed. The marketing channel refers to the means by which necessary **transactional** elements are managed (e.g. customer orders, billing, accounts receivable, etc.).

The Importance of Distribution Channel

Due to the **dynamic** nature of the business environment, management must **monitor** and **evaluate** the performance of the distribution channel regularly and frequently. [3] When performance goals are not met, management must evaluate possible channel **alternatives** and **implement** changes. Channel management is particularly important in nature and in declining markets and during periods of economic slowdown when market growth cannot **conceal** inefficient practices. Nevertheless, the distribution channel has been recognized as "one of the least managed areas of marketing." [4]

Management cannot determine a channel of distribution without carefully considering logistics, since logistics costs influence the ultimate profitability of a particular channel strategy. [5] For example, a manufacturer's decision to sell through wholesalers rather than directly to retail accounts can lead to: (1) lower transportation costs, because larger volumes will be shipped; (2) lower inventory carrying costs, because a portion of the inventory

investment will be shifted to the wholesaler; (3) lower order processing and handling costs as a result of receiving fewer orders for larger qualities; (4) reduced field warehousing costs; and (5) fewer bad debts. Management must compare these savings to the difference in **revenue** created by selling to wholesalers rather than directly to retailers.

New Words

1. collection   *n.*收集;收取,托收;聚集;收藏品;募捐
2. internal   *adj.*国内的;内部的;身内的
3. external   *adj.*外来的;外部的;外面的;表面的   *n.*外观;外部;外界事物
4. manufacturer   *n.*制造商
5. pervasive   *adj.*普遍的;渗透的;遍布的
6. bear   *v.*忍受;负荷
7. institution   *n.*制定;制度;机构
8. channel   *n.*频道;海峡;方法;通道;(消息)渠道
9. integrate   *v.*整合;结合;取消隔离;求积分   *adj.*完整的;组合的
10. coordinate   *v.*(使)协调;(使)一致;(使)同等
11. consistent   *adj.*始终如一的;持续的;一致的
12. transactional   *adj.*交易型的;事务性的,事务处理的
13. dynamic   *adj.*动力的;动态的;有活力的;[音]力度变化的   *n.*动力;动力学
14. monitor   *v.*监视;监督;监听
15. evaluate   *vt.*评价;评估
16. alternative   *n.*其他选择;备选方案
17. implement   *vt.*实施,执行;实现,使生效;*n.*工具;器具;当工具的物品
18. conceal   *vt.*隐藏;隐瞒;掩盖
19. investment   *n.*投资;投资额;投入
20. revenue   *n.*税收;收入;税务局

Phrases

1. distribution channel   分销渠道
2. bearing market risk   分担市场风险
3. logistical channel   物流渠道
4. marketing channel   营销渠道
5. economic slowdown   经济萧条
6. transportation cost   运输成本
7. inventory carrying cost   库存保管费
8. order processing and handling cost   订单处理成本
9. field warehousing cost   产地仓储成本
10. bad debt   呆账

Notes

1. A channel of distribution can be defined as the collection of organization units, either internal or external to the manufacturer, which performs the functions involved in product marketing.

分销渠道可以定义为一系列组织单位的集合,不管是制造商内部的还是外部的,凡是完成产品营销职能的单位都包括在内。

2. Managing distribution channels requires firms to coordinate and integrate logistics and marketing activities in a manner consistent with overall corporate strategy.

公司需要在贯彻公司整体战略的前提下对物流和营销活动进行协调和整合,以实现对分销渠道的管理。

Be consistent with: 与……一致。

3. Due to the dynamic nature of the business environment, management must monitor and evaluate the performance of the distribution channel regularly and frequently.

由于企业环境具有能动性,管理部门必须定期地对分销渠道的功能进行检查和评估。

4. Nevertheless, the distribution channel has been recognized as "one of the least managed areas of marketing".

尽管如此,分销渠道仍然是营销领域中被忽略的管理活动之一。

5. Management cannot determine a channel of distribution without carefully considering logistics, since logistics costs influence the ultimate profitability of a particular channel strategy.

管理者必须在仔细考虑物流的基础上确定分销渠道,因为物流成本最终影响特定渠道的盈利能力。

📚 Section B   Structure of Distribution Channel   配送渠道结构

The **extent** to which a channel of **distribution** creates an **efficient** flow of products from the producer to the consumer is a **major** concern of management. [1] For example, **manufacturers** depend on the distribution channel for such functions as selling, **transportation**, warehousing, and physical handling. Consequently, the manufacture's objective is to **obtain optimum** performance of these functions at minimum total cost. In order to successfully market its products, a manufacturer must: (1) select the **appropriate** channel structure; (2) choose the **intermediaries** to be used and establish policies regarding channel members; and (3) devise information and control systems to ensure that performance objectives are met. Likewise **wholesalers** and **retailers** must select manufacturers' products in a way that will provide the best assortment for their customers and lead to the desired **profitability** for themselves. [2]

The structure of a distribution channel is determined by which marketing functions are performed by specific **organizations**. Some channel members perform single market function—

carriers transport products, and public warehouse holders store them. Others, such as wholesalers, perform multiple functions. In order to successfully market their products, the companies should first select the appropriate channel structure, because it may affect: (1) control over the performance of functions; (2) the speed of **delivery** and communication; and (3) the cost of operations. While a direct manufacturer-to-user channel usually gives management greater control over the performance of marketing functions, distribution costs normally are higher, making it necessary for the firm to have **substantial** sales volume or market concentration. [3] With indirect channels, the external institutions or agencies (warehouse holders, wholesalers, retailers) assume much of the cost burden and risk, but the manufacturer receives less revenue per unit. Figure 7-1 shows the channel structures and levels.

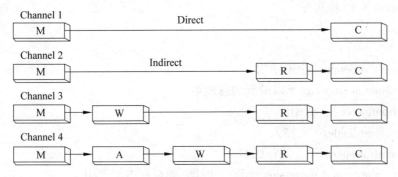

Figure 7-1   Customer Goods Channel & Levels

Nowadays, many firms choose to use intermediaries because they can increase the efficiency of the process by creating time, place, and possession utility. While channel intermediaries enable the adjustment of the discrepancy of assortments by performing the functions of sorting and assorting, marketing agencies form channel arrangements to make possible the routinization of **transactions**. [4] Finally, channels **facilitate** the searching process by consumers.

Most distribution channels are loosely structured networks of vertically aligned firms. The specific structure depends to a large extent on the nature of product and the firm's target market.

New Words

1. extent   *n.*广度;宽度;长度;大小;范围;程度
2. distribution   *n.*分布;分发;分配;散布;销售量
3. efficient   *adj.*效率高的;胜任的
4. major   *adj.*较多的;主要的;严重的;(音乐)大调的   *n.*成年人;主修(科目);陆军少校;举足轻重者   *v.*主修
5. manufacturer   *n.*制造商
6. transportation   *n.*运输;运输工具;运输系统
7. obtain   *vt.*获得;得到   *vi.*流行;通用;存在

8. optimum   *adj.*最佳的;最适宜的   *n.*最适宜

9. appropriate   *adj.*适当的;相称的   *vt.*占用;拨出(款项)

10. intermediary   *n.*仲裁者;调解者;中介   *adj.*中间的;媒介的[计算机]

11. profitability   *n.*收益性;盈利能力

12. organization   *n.*组织机构

13. delivery   *n.*传递;交付;递送;分娩;转让;演讲姿态;投球

14. substantial   *adj.*大量的;坚固的;实质的;可观的   *n.*本质;重要部分

15. facilitate   *vt.*促进;帮助;使……容易

16. wholesaler   *n.*批发商

17. retailer   *n.*零售商

18. transaction   *n.*交易

Phrases

1. channel structure   渠道结构

2. at minimum total cost   以最低的总成本

3. distribution cost   分销成本

4. warehouse holder   仓储人

5. the cost of operation   经营成本

6. time, place, and possession utility   时间,地点和占用效用

Notes

1. The extent to which a channel of distribution creates an efficient flow of products from the producer to the consumer is a major concern of management.

分销渠道能否实现货物从生产者到顾客的有效流动是管理中主要的问题。

2. Likewise wholesalers and retailers must select manufacturers' products in a way that will provide the best assortment for their customers and lead to the desired profitability for themselves.

同样,批发商和零售商也必须选择好制造商的产品,并做好搭配来满足客户需要,最终获得满意的利润。

3. While a direct manufacturer-to-user channel usually gives management greater control over the performance of marketing functions, distribution costs normally are higher, making it necessary for the firm to have substantial sales volume or market concentration.

货物由制造商直接卖给用户,管理部门能够对营销职能的完成情况做到很好的控制,但分销成本较高,因此企业只有在销售数量大或市场较集中的情况下才采用这种方式。

4. While channel intermediaries enable the adjustment of the discrepancy of assortments by performing the functions of sorting and assorting, marketing agencies form channel arrangements to make possible the routinization of transactions.

通过分类和分级,渠道中间商能够调整品种差异,营销商形成渠道配置能使交易日

常化。

Section C   Distribution Center   配送中心

Distribution center is a logistics link to fulfill physical distribution as its main function. Generally speaking, it's a large and highly automated center destined to receive goods from **various** plants and suppliers, take orders, fill them efficiently, and deliver goods to customers as quickly as possible. [1]

Unlike a warehouse, however, its **emphasis** is on the moving of goods rather than on long term storage. Practically, it's a short term storage center located close to a major market to facilitate the rapid processing of orders and shipment of goods to customers.

The differences between distribution centers and warehouses are as follows (see Table 7-1).

Table 7-1   Differences between Distribution Centers and Warehouses

Warehouses	Distribution Centers
Warehouses (W) handle most products in four cycle, e.g., receive, store, ship, and pick.	Distribution centers (DC) handle most products in two cycle, e.g., receive and ship.
Ws perform a **minimum** of value added activities (receive store ship generally in original forms).	DCs perform a great deal of value added activities, e. g., final assembly (applying the postponement strategy).
Ws collect data in batches (generally) (receive and ship goods in batches).	DCs collect data in real time (might deliver less than the batch size. The transfer batch may not, and many times should not, be equal to the process batch OPT rule). [2]
Ws store all products (slow or fast moving).	DCs hold predominantly high demand items.
Ws focus on minimizing the operating costs to meet shipping **requirements**.	DCs focus on **maximizing** the profit **impact** of fulfilling customer (external customer) delivery requirement.

There are some experts in this field that **predict** the demise of warehouses because **inventory** stocking will no longer be needed. They claim that **ECR** and **JIT** in **combination** with **POS** data will fully synchronize the company's demand chain. [3] Most other experts disagree and believe that **integrated** logistics will spur DCs to **modify** their roles, which will be based on speeding the flow of product and providing value added services. Examples of the changing role of warehouses can be seen in consolidations of shipments, **crossdocking**, and value added processes such as packaging, sub assembly, kitting, labeling, and final custom work such as providing color and style to products based on customer orders. Certainly, e-commerce has led to warehouse **expansion** in the USA and Europe and refocus by existing warehousing companies.

New Words

1. various   *adj.*各种各样的
2. emphasis   *n.*强调；重点；[语]加强语气
3. minimum   *adj.*最少的；最低程度的   *n.*最低限度；最小量
4. requirement   *n.*必要条件；要求
5. maximize   *v.*使增加至最大限度；充分利用
6. impact   *n.*影响；冲击力；撞击   *vt.*挤入；压紧；撞击；对……发生影响   *vi.*冲击；产生影响
7. predict   *v.*预言；预报；预知；预测
8. inventory   *n.*详细目录；存货（清单）；*vt.*编制（详细目录）
9. combination   *n.*结合；结合到一起的事物或人；密码
10. integrated   *adj.*综合的；整合的；融合的；动词 integrate 的过去式和过去分词
11. modify   *v.*修改；更改；缓和；修饰
12. expansion   *n.*膨胀；扩展；扩充
13. crossdocking   *n.*直接换装

Phrases

1. distribution center   配送中心
2. logistics link   物流节点
3. physical distribution   物资配送
4. final assembly   总装配
5. in batches   分批地，成批地
6. real time   实时
7. sub assembly   分装
8. ECR efficient customer response   有效客户反应
9. JIT Just-In-Time   准时生产
10. POS point of sells   电子收款机系统

Notes

1. Generally speaking, it's a large and highly automated center destined to receive goods from various plants and suppliers, take orders, fill them efficiently, and deliver goods to customers as quickly as possible.

一般而言，配送中心是一个高度自动化的大型中心，它从工厂和供应者手中接受货物、生成并有效执行订单，并将货物尽可能迅速地送给客户。

2. DCs collect data in real time (might deliver less than the batch size …).

配送中心实时收集数据（可能以小于一批的数量发送……）。

3. They claim that ECR and JIT in combination with POS data will fully synchronize the

company's demand chain.

他们声称，客户有效反应、准时生产和电子收款机系统数据能与公司的需求链完全保持同步。

Section D　Cost of Distribution　配送成本

The real costs of distribution must be **identified** when management deals with a company's cost structure. Distribution is an important aspect of a company's marketing and production effort and the costs of distribution decision can affect every cost center in the business because all costs are related to other costs.[1] Experience indicates that the following cost elements and interrelationships are the ones that are most likely to prove **critical** in evaluation of **alternative** distribution strategies and the effect on **total** costs and overall profits.[2]

Transportation costs. Both inbound and outbound transportation costs must be **considered.** [3] The most used mode of transportation is highway motor transport. It may be over-the-road equipment or specialized **short-haul** equipment. The advantages of motor transport are **flexibility**, short-haul capability, and the ability to handle variable capacities. Rail transport can be less costly than motor, but large volumes are required and there is a loss of flexibility. Water carriers are cost effective, but are slow and limited by geographic location. Air transport is expensive, but is the fastest mode over medium to long distances. Pipeline transport, which has a high **initial** cost and low operating costs, is limited by **application** and geography.

Storage costs. To provide customer service through the company's chosen channels of distribution, some warehousing is required. This requirement can range from one factory-based warehouse used to supply all customers, to a network of warehouses dispersed geographically for **regional** distribution. Service to the customer is usually higher as the number of warehouses increases. However, as the number of warehouses increases, the average size tends to **decrease**. Costs per item handled/ stored tend to rise and customer service levels can be affected by space limitations. Any change in the number, type and location of storage points will have effects on customer service levels and distribution costs.

The keeping of stocks gives rise to costs which are not directly **attributed** to distribution but which must nevertheless be borne by that function. [4] These costs include the capital tied up in stocks, **insurance** costs, warehousing costs, losses through pierage or deterioration and in many cases stock taxes. Customer service levels improve when stocks are held close to the customer's premises but this usually increases the total of stocks held. This in turn increases the costs of stockholding. These costs are closely connected to warehouse location strategies and the desired level of customer service.

The greater the total level of stocks held by a company is, the greater the risk of the products stored becoming **obsolete** is. This will involve capital **write-off**. This is a particularly important factor in those industries whose products have a short shelf life, such as fashion goods and perishables.

Costs of production vary from location to location, with the level of investment and with the volume of output. Production decisions must take account of distribution costs if the overall cost profile of the company is to be minimized.

Communications and data processing costs vary with the **complexity** of the distribution function and operation. This includes the level of customer service provided, order processing, inventory control and transport documentation.

拓展资源

Stock-outs (the fact that orders are unfulfilled because there is no stock, of a product in a warehouse), excess delivery times or unreliability of delivery can all lead to lost sales. For the company this can be far more serious than the direct losing of one sale. Stock-outs, excess delivery times or unreliability of delivery can lead to a loss of goodwill and affect repeat orders and brand **loyalty**. Any change in the distribution system which affects these factors, especially if it results in loss of goodwill, must be counted as a cost of distribution function.

New Words

1. identified *adj.*经鉴定的;动词 identify 的过去式和过去分词
2. critical *adj.*批评的;挑剔的;决定性的;危险的;[核]临界的
3. alternative *adj.*两者择一的;供选择的;非主流的 *n.*二者择一;供替代的选择
4. total *adj.*总的;全体的;完全的 *n.*总数;合计 *v.*共计;总计
5. considered *adj.*考虑过的;被尊重的
6. flexibility *n.*灵活性;弹性;适应性;柔韧性
7. initial *n.*(词)首字母 *adj.*开始的;最初的;字首的
8. application *n.*应用;申请;专心;应用程序
9. regional *adj.*地区的;局部的;当地的;方言的 *n.*分部
10. decrease *v.*减少;减小;降低 *n.*减少;降低
11. attribute *vt.*把……归于 *n.*属性;标志;象征;特征
12. insurance *n.*保险;保险费;安全保障
13. obsolete *adj.*已废弃的;过时的
14. complexity *n.*复杂;复杂性;复杂的事物
15. loyalty *n.*忠诚;忠心;忠贞

Phrases

1. costs of distribution   配送成本
2. cost structure   成本结构
3. mode of transportation   运输模式
4. short-haul   短途运输

5. rail transport   铁路运输

6. water carrier   水运

7. air transport   空运

8. pipeline transport   管道运输

9. storage cost   存储成本

10. write-off   严重损坏而值得修理的东西

11. level of investment   投资水平

12. volume of output   输出量

13. stock out   断货

Notes

1. Distribution is an important aspect of a company's marketing and production effort and the costs of distribution decision can affect every cost center in the business because all costs are related to other costs.

分销是公司营销和生产工作的一个重要方面,而且分销决策的成本会影响每一个成本中心的业务,因为所有的成本与其他成本是相互关联的。

2. Experience indicates that the following cost elements and interrelationships are the ones that are most likely to prove critical in evaluation of alternative distribution strategies and the effect on total costs and overall profits.

经验表明以下成本项目及其相互关系对各可选分销战略的评估及总成本和总利润可能非常关键。

3. Both inbound and outbound transportation costs must be considered.

必须考虑出入境的运输成本。

4. The keeping of stocks gives rise to costs which are not directly attributed to distribution but which must nevertheless be borne by that function.

保留库存会产生成本,尽管这种成本不是直接促成分销的原因,但仍然必须承担该功能。

Section E   Four Examples of Distribution Center Layout
配送中心分配案例

The phrase distribution center is applied somewhat loosely. [1] Some public warehouses refer to themselves as distribution centers, where they emphasize the distribution aspects of warehousing rather than the storage operations. [2] The emphasis is on fast turn-over of goods.[3]

Distribution centers have varying layout objectives, as the following four examples illustrate:

(1) A men's jeans manufacturer/distributor has only a few products. The main difference is in size of jeans. In laying out the facility, jeans could be arranged by size moving from the

smallest waist and pants length through all lengths with that waist, to the next waist size, through all the lengths for that waist size, and so on. [4] This is the way they are displayed in retail stores, instead, in order to minimize the time of order pickers, the jeans are arranged so that the most popular sizes are in the locations that are the easiest (i.e., least time consuming) for the order pickers to reach. The less popular sizes are placed on less accessible shelves.

(2) A difference approach is taken by an auto accessories chain for their distribution center. [5] First, they insist that all of their retail outlets have the same physical arrangement of merchandise. Goods in the warehouse are arranged in the same order. Inventory and reorder forms for use at the retail level are laid out in the same order, which is retained when they are converted to the order picker's form to be used in the warehouse. [6] The warehouse order pickers use metal carts upon which metal baskets can be stacked. The order is picked in the same sequence as it appears in retail shelves, and the baskets are delivered to the retail stores. This allows the retail clerk to rapidly place the items from the basket onto the shelves.

(3) A large food chain continually attempts to encourage its retail outlets to order the "optimum" lot size for a specific item. [7] They may require or encourage the store to order ant poison by the tube, tomato puree by the 48-can case, and paper towels by the pallet load. Forms supplied to the retail store allow for orders in only these quantities or multiples thereof. The warehouse is split into three sections: for the individual items, for the items handled in case lots, and for the items handled in pallet lots. When assembling an order for a retail store, a computer separates the three types of orders and assignments are made to order pickers who have different equipment, depending upon the section of warehouse in which they are working. [8] During the course of the year, some items move from one category of minimum lot size to another, and the computer is programmed to make the adjustment readily.

(4) Pic'n Pay's distribution center near Charlotte, North Carolina, operates on such a just-in-time pace that 70 percent of the incoming goods are placed directly for assignment to be loaded on to outgoing trucks. [9] The remaining 30 percent are placed into storage and handled in the conventional warehouse manner. This is an example of "inventories in motion," since 70 percent of the goods do not rest in the warehouse, but move continuously through it. Also, there is sufficient confidence that they will arrive on time, that they are scheduled to be loaded on outgoing deliveries before they arrive.

New Words

1. layout   *n.* 布局
2. accessible   *adj.* 易受影响的,已接近的,可进入的
3. accessory   *n.* 附件
4. merchandise   *n.* 商品
5. inventory   *n.* 库存
6. retail   *n.* 零售

7. convert   *v.* 转换；兑换

8. item   *n.* 项目

9. outlet   *n.* 批发商店，零售商店

10. optimum   *n.* 最适宜   *adj.* 最适宜的

11. tube   *n.* 管子

12. puree   *n.* 煮烂过滤或制浆的食物；浓汤

13. pallet   *n.* 托盘；集装架子

14. minimum   *adj.* 最小化的

15. conventional   *adj.* 传统的；惯例的；常规的

16. adjustment   *n.* 调节；校正；调整

17. outgoing   *adj.* 外向的；即将离职的；出发的

Phrases

1. refer to   涉及；指的是；提及；参考；适用于

2. distribution center   分销中心

3. lay out   设计；安排；陈列

4. retail store   零售商店

Notes

1. The phrase distribution center is applied somewhat loosely.
配送中心主要适用在一些比较开阔的地方。

2. Some public warehouses refer to themselves as distribution centers, where they emphasize the distribution aspects of warehousing rather than the storage operations.
有些公共仓库也称自己为配送中心，他们强调的是配送功能而不是仓储操作功能。

3. The emphasis is on fast turn-over of goods.
强调的是货物的快速周转。

4. In laying out the facility, jeans could be arranged by size moving from the smallest waist and pants length through all lengths with that waist, to the next waist size, through all the lengths for that waist size, and so on.
在布置场地时，牛仔裤可以按照尺寸来安排：从最小的腰围和对应此腰围的所有裤长，再到对应下一个腰围的所有裤长，等等。

5. A difference approach is taken by an auto accessories chain for their distribution center.
汽车配件连锁店为其配送中心采取了一个不同的方法。

6. Inventory and reorder forms for use at the retail level are laid out in the same order, which is retained when they are converted to the order picker's form to be used in the warehouse.
在零售层面使用的库存和再订购表格按照相同的顺序排列，当它们转换为要在仓库中供订单拣货员使用的表格形式时被保留。

7. A large food chain continually attempts to encourage its retail outlets to order the "optimum" lot size for a specific item.

一家大型食品连锁店不断尝试鼓励其零售店订购特定商品的"最佳"批量。

8. When assembling an order for a retail store, a computer separates the three types of orders and assignments are made to order pickers who have different equipment, depending upon the section of warehouse in which they are working.

在为零售商店组装订单时,计算机将三种类型的订单分开,并根据他们工作的仓库部分对具有不同设备的订单进行分配。

9. Pic'n Pay's distribution center near Charlotte, North Carolina, operates on such a just-in-time pace that 70 percent of the incoming goods are placed directly for assignment to be loaded on to outgoing trucks.

位于北卡罗来纳州夏洛特附近的 Pic'n Pay 的配送中心以如此及时的速度运营,70%的抵港货物进货直接被装载到外出的卡车上进行分配。

◎ Core Concepts 核心概念

1. Delivery refers to sending goods to the destination specified by buyers and collection of the transportation costs.

运送指将货物送至买方指定的目的地并收取一定运输费用。

2. Joint distribution refers to delivering goods for different shippers using the same vehicle by the most economic route.

共同配送采用同一交通工具以最经济的航线为不同的托运人运送货物。

3. Distribution is one of the functions in logistics, which deliver goods to customers directly according to the order in the most economic way.

配送是物流的一个功能,根据订单以最经济的方式将货物直接送达客户。

4. Distribution includes logistics activities related to the sales and delivery of goods.

配送包括与物品的销售和运送相关的物流活动。

5. Distribution center is a short-storage center located close to a major market to facilitate the rapid processing of orders and shipment of goods to customers.

配送中心是一个临时存储中心,位于主要市场附近以利于快速处理定单和将货物送达顾客。

6. The national distribution center is linked to the metropolitans outer expressway, providing easy access to and from key ports, roads and other distribution channels for importers.

全国配送中心与大城市的外环高速公路相连以方便进口方往返于主要港口,道路和其他配送渠道。

7. The regional distribution center provides customized solution for supply chain management, warehousing and sea, air freight transport in the international logistics market.

地区配送中心提供供应链管理的定制解决方案及国际物流市场的仓储,海空运输。

8. The distribution centers focus on maximizing the profit impact of fulfilling customer delivery requirement and distribution processing.

配送中心着眼于满足顾客配送要求和配送处理的利润影响最大化。

 # Exercises   练习

I. Answer the following questions.

1. What is a channel of distribution?

2. What does the logistical channel refer to?

3. What does the marketing channel refer to?

4. What determines the structure of a distribution channel?

5. Can you tell whether or not there is a best channel structure for all firms producing similar products? Say something to support your answer.

6. What must a manufacturer do in order to market their products successfully?

7. What is the definition of distribution center?

8. What is the main difference between DC and a warehouse?

9. What will synchronize the company's demand chain?

10. What is the use of e-commerce in warehouse?

11. What are the elements of distribution cost?

12. What are the modes of transportation?

II. Choose the best word or phrase that fits the sentence.

1. Managing distribution channels requires firms to coordinate and integrate logistics and marketing activities in a manner _____ with overall corporate strategy.

    A. consist   B. insistent   C. consistent   D. persistent

2. The logistical channel refers to the means by which products flow physically from where they are _____ to where they are needed.

    A. available   B. unavailable   C. avail   D. availability

3. Management must compare these savings to the difference in revenue created by selling to wholesalers _____ directly to retailers.

    A. other than   B. rather than   C. besides   D. beside

4. The extent _____ which a channel of distribution creates an efficient flow of products from the producer to the consumer is a major concern of management.

    A. on   B. with   C. to   D. in

5. The structure of a distribution channel is _____ by which marketing functions are performed by specific organizations.

    A. determined   B. dependent   C. caused   D. depended

6. Nowadays, many firms choose to use intermediaries _____ they can increase the efficiency of the process by creating time, place, and possession utility.

    A. when   B. while   C. because   D. that

7. Unlike a warehouse, however, its emphasis is on the moving of goods _____ on long term storage.

    A. more than   B. rather than   C. other than   D. less than

8. Warehouses generally receive and ship goods _____.

    A. in batches   B. at once   C. in no time   D. immediately

9. DCs collect data _____.

    A. in batches   B. in bundles   C. greatly   D. in real time

10. Most other experts disagree and believe that integrated logistics will _____ DCs to modify their roles.

    A. reduce   B. eliminate   C. spur   D. have

11. As the number of warehouses increases, the average size tends to _____.

    A. decrease   B. increase   C. reduce   D. lower

12. This is a particularly important factor in those industries _____ products have a short shelf life, such as fashion goods and perishables.

    A. which   B. that   C. who   D. whose

13. Air transport is expensive, but is the _____ mode over medium to long distances.

    A. slowest   B. fastest   C. complex   D. complicated

14. Production decisions must _____ distribution costs if the overall cost profile of the company is to be minimized.

    A. take account of   B. take advantage of

    C. account for   D. consideration

15. Any change in the distribution system which _____ these factors, especially if it results in loss of goodwill, must be counted as a cost of distribution function.

    A. effects   B. affects   C. influence   D. impact

Ⅲ. Match each word on the left with its corresponding meaning on the right.

A.	**B.**
1. channel of distribution	(a) the act of distributing things into classes or categories of the same type
2. manufacturer	(b) someone who manufactures something
3. carrying costs	(c) that is going out or leaving
4. operation	(d) a pipe used to transport liquids or gases
5. assortment	(e) the opportunity cost of unproductive assets
6. interrelationship	(f) the act of stealing small amounts or small articles
7. outbound	(g) process of changing to an inferior state

8. pipeline   (h) mutual or reciprocal relation or relatedness

9. pilferage   (i) the state of being in effect or being operative

10. deterioration   (j) the collection of organization units

IV. Fill in the blanks with words or phrases from the list below.

costly	distribution	assortment	related
burden	structure	transport	economic

1. Two channels, the logistical channel and the marketing channel, are highly _____ .

2. Channel management is particularly important in declining markets and during periods of _____ slowdown when market growth cannot conceal inefficient practices.

3. Management cannot determine a channel of _____ without carefully considering logistics, since logistics costs influence the ultimate profitability of a particular channel strategy.

4. Likewise wholesalers and retailers must select manufacturers' products in a way that will provide the best _____ for their customers and lead to the desired profitability for themselves.

5. With indirect channels, the external institutions or agencies (warehouse holders, wholesalers, retailers) assume much of the cost _____ and risk, but the manufacturer receives less revenue per unit.

6. The specific _____ depends to a large extent on the nature of product and the firm's target market.

7. The most used mode of transportation is highway motor _____ .

8. Rail transport can be less _____ than motor, but large volumes are required and there is a loss of flexibility.

V. Translate the following sentences into Chinese.

1. The major factors influencing locational decisions are markets and resource availability; most facilities are located near one or the other. Labor and transport services are two other key factors in facility location. Labor is of special significance because it can be considered as both a market (in the sense of demand for products) and a resource (in terms of human resources to staff a particular facility). The transportation system makes other resource factors mobile and allows a firm to combine factors of production that originate great distance apart.

2. Few firms start business on one day and have a need for large-scale production and distribution the next day. Rather, distribution and production facilities tend to be added one at a time, as needed. The need for additional distribution and production facilities often arises when an organization's service performance from existing facilities drops below "acceptable" levels. Retailers, for example, might add a distribution center when some of its stores can no longer consistently be supplied within two days by existing facilities.

Ⅵ. Translate the following sentences into English.

1. 准确的市场预测对一个成功的配送中心是必要的。在这里,产品流必须是连续的,以便能够充分地利用空间,防止无用和废旧的物品占用空间。

2. 配送是以现代生产劳动手段作为支撑,特别依赖于现代化信息系统和信息作业的高水平送货服务。离开了现代化的技术设施,很难从水平、速度、服务质量上达到一个新的高度,更难以展开社会性流通配送。

Ⅶ. Fill in the blanks with words from the list below and each word can be used once.

To facilitate the shipping and distribution operations of domestic and international ___1___ , Chinese Taiwan has instituted cargo clearance regulations for distribution centers. Goods reorganization and simple ___2___ can be performed inside distribution centers, while goods ___3___ inside the centers are treated as bonded goods. Customs clearance can be ___4___ 24 hours a day and is managed by the operators themselves, with the customs ___5___ performing occasional audits.

In recent years there has been a pronounced increase in the shipment of products from Taiwan China by air not only to the US and Europe, but also to ___6___ China. On the import side, in addition to ___7___ materials and components imported into Taiwan for research, development, and further processing, corporate headquarters, ___8___ , and customers have also seen a significant increase in demand for express delivery services due to sample verification needs.

Taiwan China is an ideal transportation hub for the Asia Pacific. In terms of shipping by either air or sea, Taiwan possesses the advantages of shortest distances, fastest speed, and lowest ___9___ . With the greater mailand China market as a whole growing rapidly, Taiwan China will need more professionally managed international logistics companies to ___10___ in the development of the Asia Pacific market.

A) costs	B) mainland	C) developing
D) stored	E) manufacturers	F) inland
G) authorities	H) vendors	I) rapidly
J) raw	K) performed	L) reprocessing
M) participate	N) story	O) professional

Chapter 8

Procurement
采　购

📚 Section A　Definition of Procurement　采购的概念

Every organization, whether it is a **manufacturer**, wholesaler, or retailer, buys **materials**, services, and supplies to support operations. Historically, purchasing has been perceived as a clerical or low-level managerial activity charged with responsibility to execute and process orders initiated elsewhere in the organization. [1] The role of purchasing was to obtain the desired resource at the lowest possible **purchase** price. This traditional view of purchasing has changed **substantially** in the past several decades. The modern focus is on total cost and the development of relationships between buyers and sellers. As a result, **procurement** has been elevated to a strategic activity.

The increasing importance of procurement can be attributed to several factors. The most basic of these factors has been the recognition of the substantial dollar spent for purchase of a typical organization and the **potential** dollar savings from viable procurement strategy. [2] The simple fact is that purchased goods and services are among the largest cost elements for most firms. In the average manufacturing firm in North America, purchased goods and services account for approximately 55 cents of every sales dollar. By way of contrast, the average expense of direct labor in the manufacturing process accounts for about 10 cents of each sales dollar. While the percentage spent on purchased inputs varies considerably across manufacturing industries, it is clear that the potential savings from strategic management of procurement can be substantial. [3]

Related to the cost of purchased inputs is a growing emphasis on **outsourcing**. The result is that the amount spent on procurement has increased **significantly** in many organizations. [4] Firms today purchase not only raw materials and basic supplies but also complex fabricated components with very high value-added content. They spin off functions to suppliers to focus internal resources on core competencies. The result is that more managerial attention must then be focused on how the organization **interfaces** and effectively manages its supply base. For example, General Motors uses its first-tier supplier network and third-party logistics providers to complete subassemblies and deliver finished components as needed to their **automotive**

<u>assembly lines.</u> [5] Many of these activities were once performed internally by the General Motors organization. Developing and **coordinating** these relationships represent critical aspects of an effective procurement strategy.

New Words

1. procurement   *n.*采购
2. materials   *n.*(pl.)原料;素材
3. purchase   *vt.*购买   *n.*购买;购买的物品
4. substantially   *adv.*大体上;实质上;非常
5. potential   *adj.*潜在的;可能的   *n.*潜力;潜能   *n.*电位;电势
6. outsourcing   *n.*外包
7. significantly   *adv.*意味深长地;意义深远地;重要地;较大地
8. fabricated   *adj.*制造好的;装配式的;动词 fabricate 的过去式和过去分词形式
9. component   *n.*零组件;成分
10. interface   *n.*界面;接口   *v.*连接;作接口
11. subassembly   *n.*部件;组件
12. coordinate   *v.*(使)协调;(使)一致;(使)同等   *n.*坐标;同等的人物;配套   *adj.*同等的;等位的;(大学)男女分院制的
13. manufacturer   *n.* 制造商

Phrases

1. fabricated component   元器件
2. automotive assembly lines   汽车组装线
3. General Motors   通用汽车

Notes

1. Historically, purchasing has been perceived as a clerical or low-level managerial activity charged with responsibility to execute and process orders initiated elsewhere in the organization.

以前,人们普遍认为采购是一种事务性的活动,属于低层次的管理活动,其职责仅仅是执行和处理公司其他部门所制定的订单。

2. The most basic of these factors has been the recognition of the substantial dollar spent for purchase of a typical organization and the potential dollar savings from viable procurement strategy.

其中,最基本的原因在于企业开始意识到采购支出的金额非常巨大,而使用可行的采购策略则可以节约大量资金。

3. While the percentage spent on purchased inputs varies considerably across manufacturing industries, it is clear that the potential savings from strategic management of procurement can be substantial.

虽然在不同制造业中,实际购买费用存在较大的差异,但是毋庸置疑的是,对采购进行战略管理将有可能节约大量资金。

4. Related to the cost of purchased inputs is a growing emphasis on outsourcing. The result is that the amount spent on procurement has increased significantly in many organizations.

与购买成本息息相关的是,外包日益受到重视。导致许多公司的采购开销大量增加。

5. For example, General Motors uses its first-tier supplier network and third-party logistics providers to complete subassemblies and deliver finished components as needed to their automotive assembly lines.

例如,通用汽车公司利用第一级供应商网络和第三方物流提供商完成组件的装配,然后根据需求将完成组装后的元器件送往对应的汽车装配线。

Section B   Procurement Perspectives   采购观点

The evolving focus on procurement as a key organizational capability has **stimulated** a new **perspective** regarding its role in supply chain management. The emphasis has **shifted** from adversarial, transaction-focused **negotiation** with suppliers to ensuring that the firm is positioned to **implement** its manufacturing and marketing strategies with support from its supply base. In particular, **considerable** focus is placed on ensuring continuous supply, inventory minimization, **quality** improvement, supplier development, and lowest total cost of **ownership**.

Continuous Supply

Stockouts of raw materials or component parts can shut down or force a change in production plans, resulting in unexpected cost. Downtime due to production stoppage increases operating costs and may result in an inability to provide finished goods as promised to customers. [1] Imagine the chaos that would occur if an automobile assembly line had all parts available but tires. Assembly of automobiles would have to be halted until tires become available. Thus, one of the core objectives of procurement is to ensure that a continuous supply of materials, parts, and components is available to certain manufacturing operations. [2]

Minimize Inventory Investment

In the past, downtime due to material shortages was minimized by maintaining large inventories of materials and components to protect against potential disruption in supply. However, maintaining inventory is expensive and requires scarce capital. One goal of procurement is to **maintain** supply continuity with the minimum inventory **investment** possible. This requires balancing the costs of carrying material against the possibility of a production stoppage. The ideal, of course, is to have needed materials arrive just at the moment they are **scheduled** to be used in the production process, in other words, just-in-time (JIT). [3]

Quality Improvement

Procurement is critical to the quality requirements. The quality of finished goods and services is dependent upon the quality of the materials and components used. If poor-quality components and materials are used, then the final product likely will not meet customer quality standards. Thus, both a firm and its suppliers need to be jointly **committed** to a continuous quality improvement initiative.

Supplier Development

In the final **analysis**, successful procurement depends on locating or developing suppliers, analyzing their capabilities, and selecting and working with those suppliers to achieve continuous improvement. [4] Developing good supply relationships with firms that are committed to the buying organization's success is critical in supplier development. It is important to develop close relationships with those suppliers in order to share information and resources to achieve better results. For example, a manufacturer might share a production schedule with key suppliers, which in turn allows them to better meet the buyer's delivery requirements. A retailer might share point-of-sale information and promotional plans to help suppliers meet **quantity** requirements at specific times. This **perspective** on effective procurement stands in stark **contrast** to the traditional focus on price alone, which has inherently created adversarial relationships between a firm and its suppliers. [5]

Lowest Total Cost of Ownership

Ultimately, the difference in perspective between a traditional adversarial and more **contemporary** collaborative procurement strategy can be summarized as a focus on Total Cost of Ownership (TCO) as contrasted to a focus on purchase price. Procurement **professionals** recognize that, although the purchase price of a material or item remains important, it is only one part of the total cost for their organization. [6] Service costs and life cycle costs must also be considered.

Whether **established** through competitive bidding, buyer-seller negotiation, or simply from a seller's published price schedule, the purchase price and discounts of an item are obviously a concern in procurement. No one wants to pay a higher price than necessary. Related to the price quote is normally a schedule of one or more possible discounts a buyer may receive. For example, quantity discounts may be offered as an inducement to encourage buyers to purchase larger quantities or cash discounts may be offered for prompt payment of invoices. [7]

Consideration of supplier's discounts immediately takes the buyer beyond simple quoted purchase price. Other costs associated with purchasing must be considered. For the benefits of quantity discounts to be factored into the total cost, the buyer must quantify inventory holding costs. Larger purchase quantities increase average inventory of materials or supplies. Size of purchase also impacts **administrative** costs associated with purchasing. Lot-size techniques such as Economic Order Quantity (EOQ) can help quantify these cost trade-offs.

Supplier terms of sale and cash discount structures also impact the total cost of ownership. A supplier offering more favorable credit terms is, in effect, impacting the purchase price from the buyer's perspective. For example, a discount for prompt payment of an invoice offered by one supplier must be compared with the offers of other suppliers.

What normally is not considered in traditional purchasing practice is the impact of pricing and discount structures on logistics operations and costs. For example, while traditional EOQ does consider inventory carrying costs, it generally does not include such factors as the impact of order quantity on transportation costs or the costs associated with receiving and handling different size shipments. [8] Many of these logistical considerations are ignored or given cursory consideration as buyers attempt to achieve the lowest purchase price. Today there is increasing recognition of the importance of these logistics costs to the TCO.

Sellers typically offer a number of standard services that must be considered in procurement. Additionally, available value-added services must be evaluated as organizations seek to identify the lowest TCO. Many of these services involve logistical operations and the logistical interface between buyers and sellers.

The simplest of these services is delivery. How delivery will be accomplished, when, and at what location all impact cost structures. In many industries it is a standard practice to quote a price that includes delivery. Alternatively, the seller may offer the buyer an allowance if the item being purchased is picked up at the seller's location. The buyer may be able to reduce total costs, not only through taking advantage of such allowances, but also by more fully utilizing its own transportation equipment.

Performance of subassembly operations in a supplier's plant or at an integrated service provider warehouse represents an extension of potential value-added service. [9] The point is that each potential service has a cost to the supplier and a price to the buyer. A key aspect of determining the TCO for purchased requirements is to consider the trade-offs involved in terms of value added versus cost and price of each service. To do so, the purchase price of an item must be debundled from the price of services under consideration. Each of the related available services should be priced on an independent basis so that appropriate analysis can be performed. This practice will be referred to as menu pricing. While traditional purchasing might overlook value-added services in seeking the lowest possible price, effective procurement executives consider whether such services should be performed internally, by suppliers, or at all. Debundling allows the buyer to make the most appropriate procurement decision. [10]

The final aspect of the lowest TCO includes numerous elements known as life cycle costs. The total cost of materials, items, or other inputs extends beyond the purchase price and value-added service to include the lifetime costs of such items. Some of these costs are incurred before actual receipt of the items, some are incurred while the item is being used, and others **occur** long after the buyer has actually used the item. [11]

One aspect of life cycle costs involves the administrative expense associated with procurement. Expenses related to screening potential suppliers, negotiation, order preparation, and **transmission** are just a few procurement administrative costs. Receiving, inspecting, and payment are also important. The costs related to defective finished goods, scrap, and rework associated with poor supplier quality must also be considered, as well as related warranty administration and repair. [12] Even the costs associated with recycling or recovery of materials after the useful life of a finished product may have an impact on TCO.

Figure 8-1 presents a model of the various elements that TCO comprises. When each of these elements is considered in procurement, it is clear that **numerous** opportunities for improvement exist in most companies. Many of these opportunities arise from closer working relationships with suppliers than would be possible if adversarial price negotiation dominates the buyer-seller relationship. When buyers work cooperatively with suppliers, several strategies maybe employed to reduce both the buyers' and the sellers' costs, making the total supply chain more efficient and allowing it to more effectively meet the requirements of downstream partners.

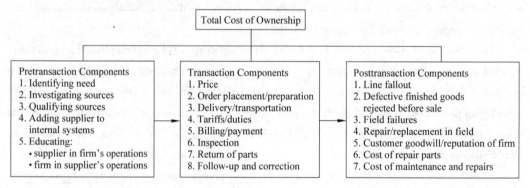

Figure 8-1 Major Categories for the Components of Total Cost of Ownership

New Words

1. stimulated   *adj.*刺激的;动词 stimulate 的过去式和过去分词

2. perspective   *n.*远景;看法;透视   *adj.*透视的

3. shift   *v.*移动;改变;换挡;字型转换   *n.*轮班;变化;移动;计谋;轮班职工

4. negotiation   *n.*谈判;协商

5. implement   *n.*工具;器具;当工具的物品   *vt.*实施;执行;向……提供工具(或手段)

6. considerable   *adj.*重要的;相当大的;可观的

7. quality   *n.*品质;才能;特质   *adj.*高品质的;<英俚>棒极了

8. ownership   *n.*所有权

9. maintain   *vt.*维持;维修;保养;坚持;断言

10. scarce *adj.*缺乏的;不足的;稀少的;罕见的 *adv.*勉强

11. capital *n.*首都;资本;大写字母;[建筑]柱顶 *adj.*资本的;大写的;一流的;首要的;极其严重的;涉及死亡的

12. investment *n.*投资;投资额;投入

13. scheduled *adj.*预定的;预先安排的;动词 schedule 的过去式和过去分词

14. committed *adj.*忠诚的;坚定的;献身于某种事业的;委托的

15. quantity *n.*量;数量;大量

16. contrast *n.*对比;差别;对照物 *v.*对比;成对照 *n.*[计算机] 反差

17. contemporary *adj.*同时代的;当代的 *n.*同时代的人;同龄人

18. professional *adj.*职业的; 专业的 *n.*专家; 内行

19. item *n.*项目;条款;一件商品(或物品);一则或一条新闻 *adv.*也

20. established *adj.*确定的;建立的;制定的;动词 establish 的过去式和过去分词

21. administrative *adj.*行政的;管理的

22. occur *vi.*发生;存在;出现;想到

23. transmission *n.*传输;传播;播送;变速器

24. numerous *adj.*为数众多的;许多

25. debundling *n.*拆分

Phrases

1. continuous supply 持续供应

2. stockout 断货

3. downtime 停产

4. production stoppage 停产

5. operating cost 运营成本

6. minimize inventory investment 最小化库存投入

7. production process 生产过程

8. just-in-time (JIT) 准时(送到)

9. quality standard 质量标准

10. point-of-sale(POS) 销售点

11. Total Cost of Ownership (TCO) 所有权总成本

12. life cycle cost 生命周期成本

13. quantity discount 数量打折

14. cash discount 现金打折

15. Economic Order Quantity (EOQ) 经济订货量

16. administrative cost 管理费用

17. standard service 标准服务

18. value-added service 增值服务

19. menu pricing 菜单定价

20. downstream partner 下游伙伴

Notes

1. Downtime due to production stoppage increases operating costs and may result in an inability to provide finished goods as promised to customers.

如果工厂出现停工,企业的运营成本就会增加,也可能导致企业不能像早先向顾客承诺的那样提供成品。

2. Thus, one of the core objectives of procurement is to ensure that a continuous supply of materials, parts, and components is available to certain manufacturing operations.

因此,采购的根本目标之一就是要确保原材料、零部件和配件持久地供应给生产运营的各个环节。

3. The ideal, of course, is to have needed materials arrive just at the moment they are scheduled to be used in the production process, in other words, just-in-time (JIT).

当然,理想的情况是,在生产的过程中,所需的原材料恰好能够按时送到。也就是说,能"准时"送到。

4. In the final analysis, successful procurement depends on locating or developing suppliers, analyzing their capabilities, and selecting and working with those suppliers to achieve continuous improvement.

采购能否成功,取决于企业是否能够有效地确定供应商,分析供应商的运作能力、选择合适的供应商,然后与之合作,实现可持续性的改善。

5. This perspective on effective procurement stands in stark contrast to the traditional focus on price alone, which has inherently created adversarial relationships between a firm and its suppliers.

这种有效采购的理念与传统的只关注价格的购买模式形成了鲜明的对比,从而造成在传统模式下企业与供应商之间的关系相互对立。

6. Procurement professionals recognize that, although the purchase price of a material or item remains important, it is only one part of the total cost for their organization.

采购人员开始意识到,尽管物料的采购价格非常重要,但是它仅仅只是企业总成本的组成部分之一。

7. For example, quantity discounts may be offered as an inducement to encourage buyers to purchase larger quantities or cash discounts may be offered for prompt payment of invoices.

例如,通过提供数量折扣促使买方增加订货量,或者通过现金折扣的方式刺激买方尽快付款。

8. For example, while traditional EOQ does consider inventory carrying costs, it generally does not include such factors as the impact of order quantity on transportation costs or the costs associated with receiving and handling different size shipments.

例如,传统的经济订货批量模型虽然考虑了库存持有成本,但是却没有考虑订货数量对运输成本的影响,以及接收并处理各种不同批量的订单所产生的成本等因素。

9. Performance of subassembly operations in a supplier's plant or at an integrated service provider warehouse represents an extension of potential value-added service.

在供应商的工厂中从事组装加工,或者在综合服务提供商的仓管中进行加工等活动也可以被视为潜在的增值服务。

10. While traditional purchasing might overlook value-added services in seeking the lowest possible price, effective procurement executives consider whether such services should be performed internally, by suppliers, or at all. Debundling allows the buyer to make the most appropriate procurement decision.

在传统的采购模式下,企业或许为了追求最低价格而忽视增值服务。而现在采购主管会判断该服务是由内部提供、由供应商提供、或不提供。对服务进行合理的拆分,有利于买方作出最明智的采购决策。

11. Some of these costs are incurred before actual receipt of the items, others are incurred while the item is being used, and some occur long after the buyer has actually used the item.

一部分成本产生于实际接收产品之前,另一部分成本在使用产品的过程中产生,还有一部分成本则是在买方实际使用产品很长时间之后才逐渐显现出来的。

12. The costs related to defective finished goods, scrap, and rework associated with poor supplier quality must also be considered, as well as related warranty administration and repair.

企业还要考虑其他成本,如供应商提供的产品或服务的质量较差,出现次品、废品和返工所导致的成本,以及为售后产品提供质量保证所带来的管理费用和维修成本。

Section C Procurement Strategies 采购策略

Effective procurement strategy to support supply chain operations requires a much closer working relationship between buyers and sellers than was traditionally practiced. Specifically, three strategies have emerged: volume consolidation, supplier operational integration, and value management. Each of these strategies requires substantial collaboration between supply chain partners and should be considered as stages of continuous improvement. [1]

Volume Consolidation

An important step in developing an effective procurement strategy is volume consolidation through reduction in the number of suppliers. Beginning in the 1980s many firms faced the reality that they dealt with a large number of suppliers for almost every material or input used. In fact, purchasing literature prior to that time emphasized that multiple sources of supply constituted best procurement practice. First, potential suppliers were continually **bidding** for a buyer's business, ensuring constant pressure to quote low prices. Second, maintaining multiple sources reduced the buyer's dependence on any one supplier. [2] This in turn served to reduce the buyer's risk should a specific supplier encounter supply disruptions such as a **strike**, a fire, or internal quality problems.

By **consolidating** volumes with a limited number of suppliers, procurement is also positioned to leverage its share of a supplier's business. At the very least, it increases the buyer's negotiating strength in relationship to the supplier. More importantly, volume consolidation with a reduced number of suppliers provides a number of advantages for those suppliers. The most obvious advantage of concentrating a larger volume of purchases with a supplier is that it allows the supplier to improve economies of scale by spreading fixed cost over a larger volume of output. [3] Additionally, assured of a volume of purchases, a supplier is more likely to make investments in capacity or processes to improve customer service. When a buyer is constantly switching suppliers, no one firm has an incentive to make such investment.

Clearly, when a single source of supply is used, risk increases. For this reason, supply base reduction programs are almost always **accompanied** by **rigorous** supplier screening, selection, and certification programs. In many instances, procurement executives work closely with others in their organization to develop preferred or **certified** suppliers. It should be noted that volume consolidation does not necessarily mean that a single source of supply is **utilized** for every, or any, purchased input. [4] It does mean that a substantially smaller number of suppliers are used than was traditionally the case in most organizations. Even when a single source is chosen, it is **essential** to have a contingency plan.

The savings potential from volume consolidation is not trivial. One consulting firm has estimated that savings in purchase price and other elements of cost can range from 5 to 15 percent of purchases. If the typical manufacturing firm spends 55 percent of its **revenue** on purchased items and can save 10 percent through volume consolidation, the potential exists to deliver a \$5.5million improvement on revenue of \$100 million to the bottom line.

Supplier Operational Integration

The next stage of development occurs when buyers and sellers begin to integrate their processes and activities in an attempt to achieve substantial performance improvement. Such integration typically involves alliances or partnerships with selected suppliers to reduce total cost and improve operational integration.

Such integration takes many different forms. For example, the buyer may allow the supplier to have access to sales and ordering information, thereby giving the supplier continuous knowledge of which products are selling. **Detailed** sales information allows the supplier to be better positioned to effectively meet buyer requirements at a reduced cost. Cost reduction occurs because the supplier has more information to plan and can reduce **reliance** on cost-inefficient practices, such as forecasting and expediting. [5]

Further operational integration can result for buyers and suppliers working together to identify processes involved in maintaining supply and searching for ways to redesign those processes. Establishing direct communication linkages to reduce order time and **eliminate** communication errors is a common benefit of such integration. More **sophisticated** integrative efforts may involve eliminating redundant activities that both parties perform. For example, in some sophisticated relationships, activities such as buyer counting and inspection of incoming deliveries have been eliminated as greater reliance and responsibility are assumed by suppliers.[6] Many firms have achieved operational integration focused on logistical arrangements, such as continuous replenishment programs and vendor-managed inventory. Such integration has considerable potential for reducing TCO.

Some of the efforts in operational integration strive to reduce total cost through two-way learning. For example, Honda of America works closely with its suppliers to improve their quality management. Honda visits supplier facilities and helps identify ways to increase quality. Such improvements ultimately benefit Honda by reducing the supplier's costs of rework and by providing Honda with higher levels of quality materials.

The **primary** objective of operational integration is to cut waste, reduce cost, and develop a relationship that allows both buyer and seller to achieve mutual improvements. **Combined** creativity across organizations can create synergy that one firm, operating in isolation, would be unable to achieve. [7] It has been estimated that operational integration with a supplier can provide incremental savings of 5 to 25 percent over and above the benefits of volume consolidation.

Value Management

Achieving operational integration with suppliers creates the opportunity for value management. Value management is an even more intense aspect of supplier integration, going beyond a focus on buyer-seller operations to a more comprehensive and sustainable relationship. Value engineering, reduced complexity, and early supplier involvement in new product design represent some of the ways a company can work with suppliers to reduce TCO.

Value engineering is a concept that involves closely examining material and component requirements at the early stage of product design to ensure that a balance of lowest total cost and quality is incorporated into new product design. [8] Figure 8-2 shows how early supplier involvement can be critical in achieving cost reductions. As a firm's new product development process proceeds from idea generation through the various stages to commercialization, the company's flexibility in making design changes decreases. Design changes are easily accommodated in the early stages, but by the time **prototypes** have been developed, a design change becomes difficult and expensive. The earlier a supplier is involved in the design process, the more likely an organization is to capitalize on that supplier's knowledge and capabilities.

An example from an automobile manufacturer demonstrates the benefit of early supplier involvement. In designing the front bumper for a new model, the design engineer was completing design of the bracket assembly for the bumper. During the process, an engineer from the assembly supplier, which had already been identified even though actual production was in

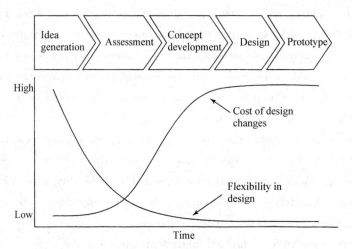

Figure 8-2   Flexibility and Cost of Design Changes

the future, asked if the bracket location could be moved by about 1/2 inch. [9] The design engineer, after some consideration, replied that it could be done with no impact on the final product. The design engineer was interested to know why the supplier requested the change. The answer was that by moving the bracket, the supplier would be able to use existing tools and die to manufacture the bracket. Under the original design, major capital investment would have been required for new tooling. The result was approximately a 25 to 30 percent reduction in cost of the bracket.

Clearly, value management extends beyond procurement in an organization and requires cooperation between numerous participants, both internal and external. Teams representing procurement, engineering, manufacturing, marketing, and logistics as well as key supplier personnel jointly seek solutions to lower total cost, improve performance, or improve accommodation of customer requirements.

Purchase Requirement Segmentation

The Pareto effect applies in procurement just as it applies in almost every facet of business activity. In procurement, it can be stated simply: A small percentage of the materials, items, and services acquired account for a large percentage of the dollars spent. The point is that all procured input are not equal. However, many organizations use the same approach and procedures for procuring small-volume items that they do for acquiring their most strategic purchases. As a result, they spend as much in acquiring a ＄10,000 order of raw materials as they do for a ＄100 order of copy paper. Since all purchased inputs are not equal, many firms have begun to pay attention to segmented purchase requirements and prioritizing resources and expertise to handle those requirements.

It would be a mistake, though, to simply use dollar expenditure as the basis for segmenting requirements. Some inputs are strategic materials. Others are not. Some inputs have potential for high impact on the business success. Others do not. Some purchases are very complex and high risk. Others are not. For example, failure to have seat assemblies delivered to an auto assembly line on time could be **catastrophic**, while failure to have cleaning supplies might constitute a nuisance. [10] Volume consolidation and supply base reduction most likely can be justified for almost every material and service. The benefits described earlier can be enjoyed for office supplies as well as raw materials. Operational integration and value management may be reserved for more strategic purchase requirements.

New Words

1. internal　*adj.*国内的;内部的;身内的

2. consolidating　*v.*合并;统一;巩固

3. accompany　*vt.*陪伴;伴随……发生;补充;给……伴奏　*vi.*伴奏

4. rigorous　*adj.*严格的;严厉的;严峻的;细致的

5. certified　*adj.*经证明的;经认证的;有保证的,保证合格的

6. essential　*adj.*本质的;必要的;重要的　*n.*要素;必需品

7. revenue　*n.*税收;收入;税务局

8. detailed　*adj.*详细的

9. reliance　*n.*信赖;所信赖的人或物

10. eliminate　*v.*除去;剔除;忽略;淘汰

11. sophisticated　*adj.*老练的;精密的;复杂的;久经世故的

12. primary　*adj.*首要的;主要的;初级的;初等教育的;根本的;初期的　*n.*第一位;初选的主要者;要素;原色;初级线圈

13. combined　*adj.*组合的;结合的

14. catastrophic　*adj.*灾难的;灾难性的

15. bidding　*n.* 投标

16. prototype　*n.*原型产品

Phrases

1. volume consolidation　批量合并

2. supplier operational integration　供应商运作一体化

3. value management　价值管理

4. purchasing literature　采购文献

5. continuous replenishment program　持续补货计划

6. vendor-managed inventory　供应商库存

7. value engineering　价值工程

8. idea generation　产品构思

9. concept development　概念开发

Notes

1. Each of these strategies requires substantial collaboration between supply chain partners and should be considered as stages of continuous improvement.

供应链伙伴之间的紧密合作是制定各种采购策略的基础,而这些策略则代表了采购策略发展的不同阶段。

2. First, potential suppliers were continually bidding for a buyer's business, ensuring constant pressure to quote low prices. Second, maintaining multiple sources reduced the buyer's dependence on any one supplier.

首先,潜在的供应商会不断针对买家的业务进行投标,这样可以确保持续施加压力,以降低采购价格。其次,保持与多个供应商的关系,能够在一定程度上降低买方对某一特定供应商的依赖程度。

3. The most obvious advantage of concentrating a larger volume of purchases with a supplier is that it allows the supplier to improve economies of scale by spreading fixed cost over a larger volume of output.

从单一供应商处进行大批量的采购,最明显的好处就是供应商可以将固定成本分摊到更大的采购量中,从而获得极大的规模经济效应。

4. It should be noted that volume consolidation does not necessarily mean that a single source of supply is utilized for every, or any, purchased input.

必须注意的一点是:批量合并并不意味着任何一种采购物品都只有唯一的供应来源。

5. Cost reduction occurs because the supplier has more information to plan and can reduce reliance on cost-inefficient practices, such as forecasting and expediting.

之所以能够降低成本,是因为供应商获得了明确的需求信息,减少了成本效应极低的运作,如预测或者加急运输等。

6. For example, in some sophisticated relationships, activities such as buyer counting and inspection of incoming deliveries have been eliminated as greater reliance and responsibility are assumed by suppliers.

例如,在某些复杂的情况下,买方对供应商有很强的依赖性,同时对供应商的运作能力比较信任,因此它可以取消一些活动,如买方对交付产品进行的清点和检查等活动。

7. Combined creativity across organizations can create synergy that one firm, operating in isolation, would be unable to achieve.

只有将各个企业的创新能力综合起来,才能形成协同优势,任何企业都无法通过独立运营实现这种优势。

8. Value engineering is a concept that involves closely examining material and component requirements at the early stage of product design to ensure that a balance of lowest total cost and quality is incorporated into new product design.

价值工程是指企业在产品设计初期就对原材料和部件的需求情况进行仔细审查,以确保在产品设计时能够实现质量与总成本最小化之间的均衡。

9. During the process, an engineer from the assembly supplier, which had already been identified even though actual production was in the future, asked if the bracket location could be moved by about 1/2 inch.

在设计过程中,配件供应商派来了一位工程师(尽管新产品距离实际投产还有好几年时间,但是企业早已确定了使用配件供应商),他询问托架的安装位置是否可以移动1/2英寸。

10. For example, failure to have seat assemblies delivered to an auto assembly line on time could be catastrophic, while failure to have cleaning supplies might constitute a nuisance.

举例来说,无法按时将坐椅等配件送到自动装配线上,将给汽车制造带来相当严重的后果。

Section D　E-commerce Procurement　电子商务采购

The **explosion** in technology and information systems is having a major impact on the procurement activity of most organizations. Much of the actual day-to-day work in procurement has traditionally been accomplished manually with significant amounts of paperwork, resulting in slow processes subject to **considerable** human error. [1] Applying technology to procurement has considerable potential to speed the process, reduce errors, and lower acquisition cost.

Probably the most common technology used in procurement is Electronic Data Interchange (EDI). EDI involves the electronic transmission of data between a firm and its suppliers. This allows two or more companies to obtain and provide timely and accurate information. Using EDI there are many types of data being directly transmitted, including purchase requisitions, purchase orders, purchase order acknowledgment, order status, advanced shipment notification, and tracking and tracing information. The explosion in EDI usage is a direct recognition of associated benefits, including **standardization** of data, more accurate information, shortening of lead times with associated reductions in inventories, and reduced TCOs.

Another procurement application of electronic commerce is the development of electronic catalogs. In fact, making information available about products and the suppliers is a natural application for Internet-based communications. Electronic catalogs allow buyers to gain rapid access to product information, **specifications**, and pricing, allowing buyers to quickly identify products and place orders. Many companies have developed their own online electronic catalogs and efforts have also been devoted to developing catalogs **containing** products from multiple suppliers, which permits buyers to rapidly compare features, specifications, and prices. [2]

Buying exchanges is another technology-based purchasing development. Typically, buying exchanges allows users to look for sellers or buyers of specific goods or services. Depending on the approach, a buyer may post a request for proposal and quotation, or invite bids for specified products and services. Transactions can be initiated and completed electronically.

The potential volume of procurement activity through buying exchanges is **enormous**. Exchanges have been developed in the **aircraft** parts industry, chemicals, steel building products, food distribution, and even retailing. However, there is a potential downside. Many suppliers fear that the exchanges will become a **mechanism** that **ultimately** will reinforce past practice of buyers to focus strictly on purchase price. If buyers post their requirements and needs on the Internet primarily for the purpose of soliciting bids from alternative suppliers, or use the technology to have suppliers enter into an auctioning process, some fear many of the advances in supplier integration and value management will suffer.[3]

In a supply chain management context, the link between a company and its external suppliers is critical. It provides for the integration of materials and resources from outside the organization into internal operations. Procurement is charged with the responsibility of ensuring that this transition is accomplished as efficiently and as effectively as possible. Much of the concern in procurement is focused on the logistical interface between the organization and its supply base. Ultimately, the purpose of procurement is to integrate material flow in accordance with requirements. It's the job of logistics to efficiently move purchases to the desired location.

New Words

1. explosion　*n.*爆炸;爆炸声;激增;爆发
2. considerable　*adj.*重要的;相当大的;可观的
3. standardization　*n.*标准化;用标准校验
4. containing　*n.*包含;包括　*v.*容纳;包含;抑制;克制(动词 contain 的现在分词)
5. enormous　*adj.*巨大的;庞大的
6. aircraft　*n.*飞机
7. ultimately　*adv.*最后;最终
8. mechanism　*n.*机制;原理　*n.*结构;机构;机械装置
9. specification　*n.*规格说明

Phrases

1. Electronic Data Interchange (EDI)　电子数据交换
2. purchase requisitions　采购需求
3. purchase order　采购订单
4. purchase order acknowledgment　采购订单确认
5. order status　订单状态
6. advanced shipment notification　提前交换通知
7. tracking and tracing information　信息的跟踪和查询
8. Internet-based communication　计算机网络技术
9. electronic catalog　电子目录
10. external supplier　外部供应商

Notes

1. Much of the actual day-to-day work in procurement has traditionally been accomplished manually with significant amounts of paperwork, resulting in slow processes subject to considerable human error.

在传统方式下,许多日常性的采购工作都是通过大量笔头工作完成的,这会造成处理效率低下,容易发生人为失误。

2. Many companies have developed their own online electronic catalogs and efforts have also been devoted to developing catalogs containing products from multiple suppliers, which permits buyers to rapidly compare features, specifications, and prices.

许多企业都建立了自己的在线电子目录,并且不遗余力地为许多供应商建立各自的电子目录,这样,买方就可以方便快捷地对多种产品的特性、规格和价格进行比较了。

3. If buyers post their requirements and needs on the Internet primarily for the purpose of soliciting bids from alternative suppliers, or use the technology to have suppliers enter into an auctioning process, some fear many of the advances in supplier integration and value management will suffer.

如果买方主要通过互联网提出自己的要求,然后对可选择的供应商进行招标,或者借助于技术手段使供应商参与拍卖竞价,那么大多数供应商就会产生恐惧,担心这将损害供应商一体化和价值管理带来的收益。

Section E　Globalized Purchasing　全球采购

A distinctive characteristic of our time is the evolving trend of economic globalization.[1] Globalization involves globalized production, globalized marketing and globalized purchasing.

Globalized purchasing has taken the lead in cutting costs while costs are putting enormous pressure on purchasing departments of many international companies.[2] Sourcing from low-cost countries will reduce production cost dramatically. Take South Asia for example. It has been the most important production base for its relatively rich resources and cheap labor.[3]

The trend of globalized purchasing leads international manufacturers to change their traditional manufacturers to change their traditional purchase strategy in 3 aspects.

Firstly, manufacturers should build up an international supply network and be able to make global decisions. To minimize risks, avoid supply bottlenecks and ensure favorable trading conditions, manufacturers should be familiar with suppliers and develop a global supplier footprint strategy with a decision-making framework for purchasing.[4] Different ways of investment and cooperation should be followed in light of the actual conditions of different suppliers that are grouped by products.

Secondly, integrated supply resources are better to acquire cost advantage.[5] Nowadays, many international manufacturers are willing to concentrate supply resources by cutting down the numbers of suppliers. Such as Palm Inc., a world-class enterprise has already reduced the numbers of suppliers to 50 during the last three years in order to maintain the cost advantage of purchasing. The suppliers choosing criteria of EMS companies is no longer limited to cost, but also includes logistics and distribution capabilities. [6]

Thirdly, manufacturers should build up their relationships with suppliers for mutual development. On the one hand, manufacturers should ensure suppliers continuing access to new technologies through technical cooperation, and also promote its innovation process by collecting ideas from suppliers. On the other hand, manufacturers should emphasize standardized modules and components. The standardization will greatly stimulate suppliers to make efforts to increase product reliability and durability.

On the whole, well positioned companies are always mindful of the changeable environment when it comes to optimizing purchasing strategy. [7] The measures taken must be correctly applied and constantly developed in practice to ensure their success.

New Words

1. globalization   *n.* 全球化
2. source   *n.* 来源 sourcing 采购;outsourcing 外包
3. South Asia   南亚
4. bottleneck   *n.* 瓶颈;发展限制
5. footprint   *n.* 脚印;覆盖范围
6. framework   *n.* 结构,构架,框架
7. innovation   *n.* 创新,革新
8. module   *n.* 模块,组件,配件
9. standardization   *n.* 标准化
10. stimulate   *vt.* 刺激,激励,鼓舞
11. distribution   *n.* 分销
12. durability   *n.* 持久性
13. mindful   *a.* 深切注意的,留神的,留心的

Phrases

1. globalized production   全球化生产
2. globalized marketing   全球化销售
3. globalized purchasing   全球化采购
4. take lead in   在……方面领先
5. in light of   来自于,源于,基于
6. EMS:Electric Manufacturing Services 的缩写,即电子制造服务,此类厂商为客户提供包含产品设计、代工生产、后勤管理、产品维修等服务。
7. standardized module   标准化模块

8. standardized capability　标准化零件

9. be mindful of　对……留意,密切注意

Notes

1. A distinctive characteristic of our time is the evolving trend of economic globalization.

我们这个时代的一个显著特征是经济全球化的趋势。

2. Globalized purchasing has taken the lead in cutting costs while costs are putting enormous pressure on purchasing departments of many international companies.

全球化采购在降低成本中起首要作用,而成本问题给很多跨国公司的采购部门带来很大压力。

3. Take South Asia for example. It has been the most important production base for its relatively rich resources and cheap labor.

以南亚为例,它已成为世界重要的生产基地,原因在于其相对丰富的资源和低廉的劳动力。

4. To minimize risks, avoid supply bottlenecks and ensure favorable trading conditions, manufacturers should be familiar with suppliers and develop a global supplier footprint strategy with a decision-making framework for purchasing.

为了使风险最小化,避免供应瓶颈并保证有利的贸易条件,厂商应熟悉供应商并建立起基于采购决策框架的供应商覆盖范围策略。

5. Secondly, integrated supply resources are better to acquire cost advantage.

其次,集成供应资源对获取成本优势更有利。

6. The suppliers choosing criteria of EMS companies is no longer limited to cost, but also includes logistics and distribution capabilities.

EMS厂商的供应商选择标准不再只局限于成本,还包括物流和分销能力。

7. On the whole, well positioned companies are always mindful of the changeable environment when it comes to optimizing purchasing strategy.

总地来说,当良好定位的公司在优化采购策略时总能考虑到多变的环境。

"when it comes to"意为"当……的时候,讲到……的时候",后跟名词。

🎯 Core Concepts　核心概念

1. Procurement is the process in which materials for production are ordered from customers.

采购是根据客户需求定购原料的过程。

2. In modern business, purchasing activity acts as the prelude of the production.

在现代商业中,采购活动扮演着生产前奏的角色。

3. Purchasing cost is one of the largest elements of total costs for many companies.

采购成本在许多企业中占总成本的很大比例。

4. procurement 和 purchasing 的区别

两者都是采购的意思。procurement 直译为"获得"和"取得"的意思,是指企业所需的产品及服务通过采购活动获得的过程,这里的采购活动特指一种基于订单或合同的日常采购行为。purchasing 则倾向于采购计划制定、采购比例分配以及谈定价格的问题。

Exercises 练习

Ⅰ. Answer the following questions.

1. What is the most basic factor for the increasing importance of procurement?

2. What is the reason for the growing emphasis on outsourcing?

3. What is procurement? What is its relevance to logistics?

4. Why does the contemporary view of procurement as a strategic activity differ from the more traditional view of "purchasing"?

5. How can strategic procurement contribute to the quality of products produced by a manufacturing organization?

6. What is the underlying rationale that explains why firms should segment their purchase requirement?

7. Explain how constrains in manufacturing are integrated with a company's decisions regarding volume and variety?

8. Why would a company's cost of manufacturing and procurement tend to increase as the firm changes from MTP to an MTO strategy? Why would inventory costs tend to decrease?

9. How does a firm's marketing strategy impact its decisions regarding the appropriate manufacturing strategy?

10. How is logistics performance crucial to JIT?

Ⅱ. Choose the best word or phrase that fits the sentence.

1. The modern focus is _____ total cost and the development of relationships between buyers and sellers.

    A. over   B. in   C. on   D. about

2. The increasing importance of procurement can be attributed _____ several factors.

    A. to   B. for   C. as   D. in

3. Developing and coordinating these relationships represent critical _____ of an effective procurement strategy.

    A. parts   B. roles   C. aspects   D. factors

4. In particular, considerable focus is placed _____ ensuring continuous supply, inventory minimization, quality improvement, supplier development, and lowest total cost of

ownership.

    A. in   B. onto   C. on   D. to

5. In the past, downtime due to material shortages was _____ by maintaining large inventories of materials and components to protect against potential disruption in supply.

    A. maximized   B. minimized   C. lowered   D. reduced

6. If poor-quality components and materials are used, then the final product likely will not _____ customer quality standards.

    A. satisfy   B. clarify   C. meet   D. qualify

7. For example, a manufacturer might share a production schedule _____ key suppliers, which in turn allows them to better meet the buyer's delivery requirements.

    A. on   B. to   C. within   D. with

8. When buyers work cooperatively with suppliers, several strategies maybe employed to reduce both the buyers' and the sellers' costs, making the total supply chain more _____ and allowing it to more effectively meet the requirements of downstream partners.

    A. efficient   B. effective   C. inefficient   D. ineffective

9. An important step in developing an effective procurement strategy is volume consolidation through reduction in the _____ of suppliers.

    A. amount   B. number   C. majority   D. minority

10. At the very least, it increases the buyer's negotiating strength in relationship _____ the supplier.

    A. with   B. to   C. within   D. on

11. As a result, they spend as much in _____ a $10,000 order of raw materials as they do for a $100 order of copy paper.

    A. requiring   B. inquiring   C. acquiring   D. accumulating

12. Typically, buying exchanges allow users to look _____ sellers or buyers of specific goods or services.

    A. into   B. after   C. for   D. up

13. Another procurement _____ of electronic commerce is the development of electronic catalogs.

    A. application   B. appliance   C. use   D. usage

14. Exchanges have been developed in the aircraft parts industry, chemicals, steel building products, food _____, and even retailing.

    A. attribution   B. distribution   C. contribution   D. purchase

15. Procurement is _____ with the responsibility of ensuring that this transition is accomplished as efficiently and as effectively as possible.

    A. charged   B. accused   C. related   D. associated

Ⅲ. Match each word on the left with its corresponding meaning on the right.

A. 　　　　　　**B.**

1. procurement 　（a）available source of wealth
2. strategy 　　　（b）an essential and distinguishing attribute of something or someone
3. outsourcing 　（c）the act of getting possession of something
4. resources 　　（d）the act of delivering or distributing something
5. capability 　　（e）an elaborate and systematic plan of action
6. automobiles 　（f）the state of relying on something
7. quality 　　　（g）obtain goods or services from an outside supplier
8. delivery 　　　（h）a motor vehicle with four wheels
9. reliance 　　　（i）the quality of being capable
10. integration 　（j）the action of incorporating a racial or religious group into a community

Ⅳ. Match the following definitions with the corresponding terms below.

related	capital	critical	share	collaboration	substantially
minimum	assembly	compared	emphasis	prior	external

1. The _____ has shifted from adversarial, transaction-focused negotiation with suppliers to ensuring that the firm is positioned to implement its manufacturing and marketing strategies with support from its supply base.

2. Imagine the chaos that would result if an automobile _____ line had all parts available but tires. Assembly of automobiles would have to be halted until tires become available.

3. However, maintaining inventory is expensive and requires scarce _____.

4. One goal of procurement is to maintain supply continuity with the _____ inventory investment possible.

5. Procurement is _____ to the quality requirements.

6. For example, a manufacturer might _____ a production schedule with key suppliers, which in turn allows them to better meet the buyer's delivery requirements.

7. _____ to the price quote is normally a schedule of one or more possible discounts a buyer, may receive.

8. For example, a discount for prompt payment of an invoice offered by one supplier must be _____ with the offers of other suppliers.

9. Each of these strategies requires substantial _____ between supply chain partners and should be considered as stages of continuous improvement.

10. In fact, purchasing literature _____ to that time emphasized that multiple sources of supply constituted best procurement practice.

11. It does mean that a _____ smaller number of suppliers are used than was

traditionally the case in most organizations.

12. Clearly, value management extends beyond procurement in an organization and requires cooperation between numerous participants, both internal and _____.

V. Translate the following sentences into Chinese.

1. Procurement, which refers to the raw materials, component parts, and supplies bought from outside organizations to support a company's operations, is an important activity and closely related to logistics because acquired goods and services must be entered into the supply chain in the exact quantities and at the precise time they are needed. Procurement is also important because its cost often ranges between 60 and 80 percent of an organization's revenues.

2. Because procurement has become more strategic in nature, its primary objective is no longer to achieve the lowest possible cost of supply. Potential procurement objectives include, but are not limited to, (1) supporting organizational goals and objectives, (2) managing the purchasing process effectively and efficiently, (3) managing the supply base, (4) developing strong relationships with other functional groups, and (5) supporting operational requirements.

VI. Translate the following sentences into English.

1. 电子商务为采购学科带来了很多变化。电子采购(electronic procurement),也称 e-采购(e-procurement),利用互联网使一个企业采购商品和服务变得更容易、更快速而且 更便宜。评价电子采购的一个方法是将其好处分为硬的、软的以及无形的三个方面。

2. 一个全球采购开发模型要包括以下组成部分: 规划、规范说明、评估、关系管理、运 输和库存持有成本、实施,以及监控和改进等,其中,规划是全球采购的第一步,包括对全 球采购的机会和挑战作一个真实的评估。

VII. Fill in the blanks with words from the list below and each word can be used once.

Government procurement is a kind of financial system that western countries have adopted for long years. The system of government procurement has brought ___1___ benefits for these developed countries in that it not only cuts down plenty of purchasing fund but also reduces purchasing time. Besides, the system has a significant impact on public confidence in government and on good ___2___. It is of considerable economic significance at both the ___3___ and the international levels, accounting for a significant proportion of national GDP (often 10% ~15% of GDP).

China's government purchasing system started developing from 1996, with some ___4___ on the pilot system later. Having practiced the reformation for a few years, the framework of the government purchasing system, the ___5___ of government procurement reached 200 billion yuan in 2004. While public procurement of goods and services ___6___ a major part of a country's market for foreign suppliers, it is also of great importance to domestic suppliers. At the end of

2007, the Chinese government issued a set of measures favoring government procurement of Chinese-made products, only allowing the procurement of __7__ products under limited circumstances through a government approval process.

Since public resources are scarce, the efficiency of the government procurement process is a primary consideration. In this respect, open, transparent and non-discriminatory procurement is generally considered to be the best tool to achieve cost-efficiency as it __8__ competition among suppliers. As a result, the first Agreement on Government Procurement was signed in 1979 and entered into force in 1981. It was __9__ in 1987, with this amended version entering into force in 1988. The Agreement on Government Procurement (1994) (GPA) that is __10__ in force was signed on 15 April, 1994 and it entered into force on 1 January, 1996, signifying that all WTO members are bound by it.

A) domestic	B) present	C) optimizes
D) international	E) enormous	F) currently
G) imported	H) alter	I) governance
J) port	K) amended	L) government
M) revenue	N) represents	O) reform

Chapter 9

Information Requirements
信息技术要求

Section A What Information Is Required?
需要什么样的信息技术

All parts of logistics rely on **ICT** for planning, organizing, production, administration and all of the management processes involved. [1] This will also include the customer interface, when using any form of electronic communication. [2]

There are different levels of information required in logistics. These different levels and functions can be identified as the strategies, tactical and operational levels. [3]

For example, information at the tactical level is mainly involved with medium to short-term planning such as forecasting, scheduling and resource planning. This level requires the following types of information, typically for the middle managers in a business:

Purchasing: e. g. information to assist with order scheduling.

Production: e. g. information to assist in deciding run lengths.

Inventory: e.g. information to assist in setting stock levels.

Warehousing: e.g. information on resource level needed.

Transport: e.g. information on routing and scheduling, and resource provision.

Marketing: e.g. information to assist in planning seasonal orders.

Information requirements in the supply chain

Information is required for every stage and at every level in the supply **chain**. It is usually the case that technology reduces costs, which, in turn, means that the **appropriate** use of ICT can effectively bring increased profits. [4]

ICT becomes a tool for integrating and coordinating logistics, supply chains and all the enterprises involved in the processes.

The following examples of ICT, once regarded as highly advanced, are now taken for granted and accepted as normal.

Purchasing—electronic data interchange (EDI) ordering, progress chasing and supplier payments. EDI refers to the exchange of information with other organizations, typically suppliers, by electronic means.

Production—materials requirements planning (MRP) systems which enable rapid ordering, **replenishment**, stock management and production planning for known product ranges.

Inventory—stock control and stock ordering systems.

Warehousing—warehousing management systems (WMS) and automated storage and **retrieval** systems (AS/AR).

Transport— fleet management, routing and scheduling system.

Marketing— order Processing systems.

ICT has brought and will continue to bring improvements wherever the following are needed:

Immediate access to information

Cost savings

Competitive advantage

Accuracy

Integration and coordination [5]

Lead time reduction [6]

Improved control

Better service.

New Words

1. chain   *n.*束缚;链条;链;(一)连串;连锁店(常用复数)   *vt.*束缚;用铁链锁住
2. appropriate   *adj.*适当的;相称的   *vt.*占用;拨出(款项)
3. retrieval   *n.*取回;恢复;挽回;[计]检索
4. competitive   *adj.*竞争的;有竞争力的;胜过或超过他人的
5. replenishment   *n.*补给,补充

Phrases

1. ICT: information and communication technology   信息及通信技术
2. short-term planning   短期计划
3. run length   运行长度,运行时间
4. stock level   库存水平,库存量
5. seasonal order   季节性订购量
6. electronic data interchange (EDI)   电子数据交换
7. stock management   库存管理
8. warehousing management system (WMS)   仓库管理系统
9. materials requirements planning (MRP)   材料需求计划
10. lead time   前置期(订货至交货的时间)

Notes

1. …and all of the management processes involved.

……以及所有涉及的管理程序。

involved 是过去分词作定语,修饰名词 processes。

2. This will also include the customer interface, when using any form of electronic communication.

在使用任何一种形式的电子通信方式时,也需要包括客户界面。

when using any form 相当于 which are involved

3. …can be identified as the strategies, tactical and operational levels.

……可以被视为战略水平、战术水平和操作水平。

be identified as … 意为"把……看成是"

4. It is usually the case that technology reduces costs, which, in turn, means that the appropriate use of ICT can effectively bring increased profits.

通常的情况是,技术降低成本,反过来,这又意味着恰当地使用 ICT 可以有效地增加利润。

It is usually the case that ：通常的情况是……(后接句子)

5. Integration and coordination：整合与协调

6. Lead time reduction：前置期减少。前置期是指"订货与交货之间的时间"。

Section B　Information Technology　信息技术

One of the distinctive features of modern logistics lies in information technology. [1] Information is critical to the efficiency of logistic management because it provides the rapidly **conveyed** information that logistics managers use to make decisions. Without information, a manager will not know what a customer wants, when the goods should be shipped and how much inventory should be kept. Bar Code, **POS** and **EDI** systems dramatically improve the effectiveness and efficiency of logistics process. Internet remains the most important mode of information transfer.

Although **two-dimensional** bar codes offer more information and safety for the goods, **one-dimensional** bar codes are still the most **comprehensively** used bar codes as they are more practical for wide scale operations. [2] There are many kinds of one-dimensional bar codes among which the **UPC** and **EAN** bar codes are the most influential ones. [3] A bar code reader is an essential tool to collect logistic data, especially in retail stores and warehouses. Adopting bar code in logistic management markedly improves the **accuracy** and efficiency of information collecting.

Nowadays, new business modes such as **EC** make **instantaneous** information **transmission** indispensable. [4] And EDI is just a good solution to meeting this **demand**. EDI technology was developed by Value Added Networks in the 1970s and firstly used in bank system. [5] Today, it is a method of electronical transmission of all types of information, including orders, invoices, B/L and even graphics, on the base of sharing a common language. [6] Internet EDI is a cheaper alternative compared with VAN EDI, allowing organizations all over the world to conduct business more quickly and efficiently.

Sometimes managers are misled by the information gathered along the downstream of a supply chain. [7] The reason lies in that information may be distorted or twisted in the process of transmission. POS system is a perfect solution to this problem. The term POS refers to the integrated software and hardware for managing the sales of retail Goods. When a customer purchasing something in a supermarket or a clothing boutique walks up to a counter or a checkout stand with the goods he or she prepares to buy, the POS system comes into action. [8] The data of the goods is gathered by a handheld reader and then stored and analyzed by the computer system. The data will then be transferred to the manufacturers on line for the use of further market forecasting and inventory replenishment. [9] POS system makes business run smoothly as less time and money will be spent in the business process.

Finally, let's come to the Internet. The Internet links thousands of computers spanning over 65 countries together. [10] Four basic blocks are needed to build the Internet, namely hosts, **routers** and clients and connections. The Internet provides a basic **platform** of communication between business partners especially when they are geographically apart. [11] Companies could advertise, disseminate information or even offer online customer service through the Internet. The Internet is not only changing the way information is transferred, but also changing our life.

New Words

1. convey　*vt.*表达；传达；运输；转移
2. comprehensively　*adv.*包括地；全面地
3. accuracy　*n.*准确（性）；精确度
4. instantaneous　*adj.*瞬间的；即刻的
5. demand　*n.*要求；需求　*v.*要求；查问；需要
6. platform　*n.*月台；讲台；平台；站台；(政党的)政纲
7. two-dimensional　*adj.*二维的
8. one-dimensional　*adj.*一维的
9. transmission　*n.*传输，传送，变速器
10. router　*n.*路由程序，路由器

Phrases

1. information technology　信息技术
2. Bar Code system　条形码
3. POS point of sale　销售点
4. EDI electronic data interchange　电子信息交换
5. UPC　通用产品代码。全称为"Universal Product Code"，是美国通用代码委员会(UCC)开发的商品代码。

6. EAN　欧洲物品编码,全称为"European Article Number",由国际物品编码协会(IAN)在 UPC 的基础上编制而成,与 UPC 兼容。EC：电子商务,为 Electronic Commerce 的简称。

7. Value Added Networks　增值网

8. handheld reader　手持式读写器

9. checkout stand　收银台,结账台

Notes

1. One of the distinctive features of modern logistics lies in information technology.

现代物流的一个重要特征是信息技术。

2. Although two-dimensional bar codes offer more information and safety for the goods, one-dimensional bar codes are still the most comprehensively used bar codes as they are more practical for wide scale operations.

虽然二维条码包含更多物品的信息,使物品更加安全,一维条码仍然是使用最为广泛的条码,因为它们在大范围运作中更加实用。

3. There are many kinds of one-dimensional bar codes among which the UPC and EAN bar codes are the most influential ones.

有很多种一维条码,其中 UPC 条码和 EAN 条码最具影响力。

4. Nowadays, new business modes such as EC make instantaneous information transmission indispensable.

如今,新的商业模式使得信息的瞬间传递不可或缺,例如电子商务。

5. EDI technology was developed by Value Added Networks in the 1970s and firstly used in bank system.

EDI 技术是在 20 世纪 70 年代由增值网发展起来的,并首先被应用在银行系统。

6. Today, it is a method of electronical transmission of all types of information, including orders, invoices, B/L and even graphics, on the base of sharing a common language.

现在,它是一种基于共享语言的电子化信息传递方式,这些信息包括订单、发票、提单甚至绘图。

7. Sometimes managers are misled by the information gathered along the downstream of a supply chain.

有时候经理人被供应链下游传递来的信息误导。

8. When a customer purchasing something in a supermarket or a clothing boutique walks up to a counter or a checkout stand with the goods he or she prepares to buy, the POS system comes into action.

当一个在超市或服装店购物的顾客携带着他或她要购买的商品走向收银台时,POS 系统开始发生作用(开始工作)。

9. The data will then be transferred to the manufacturers on line for the use of further market forecasting and inventory replenishment.

然后,这些数据将被传递给制造商,以便进一步进行市场预测以及进行库存补给。

10. Finally, let's come to the Internet.

最后,让我们讲讲互联网。

11. The Internet provides a basic platform of communication between business partners especially when they are geographically apart.

互联网为商业合作伙伴们提供了一个信息交流的平台,尤其是当他们在地理上相隔遥远时。

Section C   Communication System   通信系统

Communication systems help various stakeholders—employees, suppliers, customers—work together by interacting and sharing information in many different forms. [1] From a logistical perspective, the importance of well-defined and well-executed communication systems was highlighted by the events of September 11, 2002, especially for companies that use or provide airfreight services. Because of the total shutdown of the U.S. aviation system for several days following the terrorist attacks, many air shipments were delivered onto trucks, thus delaying many deliveries. As such, airfreight provides such as FedEx worked feverishly to inform customers when their shipments would be arriving. [2]

Many advances in telecommunication technology—such as fax machines, personal computers, electronic mail, cellular phones, and personal digital assistants (PDAs). As recently as the 1990s, some of these technologies were considered workplace "luxuries". Today, by contrast, many of these technologies are essential for enabling the contemporary logistician to perform in the workplace.

Electronic data interchange, or EDI, was viewed by many experts as the measuring stick for logistics information technology in the 1990s. By contrast, wireless communication has emerged as the measuring stick during the first decade of the twenty-first century. For our purposes, wireless communication refers to communication without cables and cords and includes infrared, microwave, and radio transmissions, among others.

Although wireless communication has many logistical applications, we'll take a look at two of the more popular types, namely, global positioning systems and voice-based order picking. Global positioning systems, or GPS, refer to a network of satellites that transmits signals that pinpoint the exact location of an object. Global positioning systems have become quite valuable to the transportation component of logistics in that, at a minimum, GPS allows carriers to keep track of their vehicles. GPS systems provide customer service benefits in the sense that carriers' customers can have real-time **visibility** in terms of shipment locations, which can be very helpful if a shipment needs to be diverted or rerouted. [3] At the same time, GPS systems benefit carriers by providing data on vehicle speeds (assuming greater importance as fuel costs continue to increase) as well as driver behavior. A sometimes ancillary benefit is that GPS systems can be helpful in locating lost or stolen transportation equipment.

Voice-based order picking refers to the use of speech to guide order-picking activities. Early voice-based picking systems were characterized by high adoption costs, poor voice quality, and systems that were easily disrupted by other noises. Contemporary voice-based systems, by contrast, are less costly, are more powerful, have better voice **quality**, and bear less cumbersome for workers to use. Companies that have adopted newer-generation voice-based technology have reported increased productivity and higher pick accuracy.

Continuing advances in hardware and software have resulted in dramatic cost reductions for wireless communication, and one implication is that the technology is no longer limited to those companies with the deepest **financial** resources. Moreover, hardware and software cost reductions have shortened the relevant investment payback period; GPS systems often pay for themselves within one year, whereas the payback period for voice-based order picking system is less than six months in some cases.[4]

New Words

1. visibility   *n.*能见度;可见性
2. quality   *n.*品质;才能;特质   *adj.*高品质的;<英俚>棒极了
3. financial   *adj.*金融的;财政的;<非正式>有钱的

Phrases

1. communication system   通信系统
2. airfreight service   空运服务
3. telecommunication   远程通信
4. personal digital assistants (PDAs)   个人数字助手
5. electronic data interchange (EDI)   电子数据交换
6. global positioning system (GPS)   全球定位系统
7. voice-based order picking   语音识别简练

Notes

1. Communication systems help various stakeholders—employees, suppliers, customers—work together by interacting and sharing information in many different forms.

通信系统有助于不同利益相关者(雇员、供应商和顾客)通过各种信息交流与共享一同工作。

2. As such, airfreight provides such as FedEx worked feverishly to inform customers when their shipments would be arriving.

因此,诸如联邦快递等空运服务提供商为通知客户货物抵达时间忙得不可开交。FedEx:Federal Express 指的是美国联邦快递。

3. GPS systems provide customer service benefits in the sense that carriers' customers can

have real-time visibility in terms of shipment locations, which can be very helpful if a shipment needs to be diverted or rerouted.

顾客通过 GPS 系统可实时获得承运信息。如果需要转移或更改线路,该系统能带来极大的便利。

4. Moreover, hardware and software cost reductions have shortened the relevant investment payback period; GPS systems often pay for themselves within one year, whereas the payback period for voice-based order picking system is less than six months in some cases.

而且,软硬件成本的降低缩短了相应的投资回报期,GPS 通常在一年之内收回投入,而有些情况下,语音识别拣选系统在 6 个月内就实现了投资回报。

Section D　Transaction Processing System（TPS）
交易处理系统

A transaction processing system collects and stores information about transactions and may also control some aspects of transactions. The primary objective of a TPS is the efficient processing of transactions, and to this end, organizations can choose to do batch or real-time processing. With batch processing, data are collected and stored for processing at a later time, with the later time **perhaps** being based on schedule (e.g., process every six hours) or volume (e.g., process once twenty-five transactions have accumulated) considerations. Real-time processing, not surprisingly, means that transactions are processed as they are received. Although batch processing might be somewhat out of step with the contemporary emphasis on speed and time reduction, it can be quite effective when real-time processing is not necessary.[1] Moreover, in **comparison** with real-time systems, batch processing tends to be less costly and easier for **employees** to learn.

A prominent example of a logistics-related TPS is electronic data interchange (EDI), the computer-to-computer transmission of business data in a structured format. Because EDI provides for the seamless transmission of data across companies (assuming technological compatibility), it can facilitate the integration of and coordination between, supply chain participants.[2] Thus, firms with strong EDI links to both suppliers and customers might have a substantial advantage over supply chain arrangements without such implementations. Common uses of EDI include **invoicing**, purchase orders, **pricing**, advanced shipment notices, electronic funds transfer, and bill payment.

EDI has a number of benefits, including reductions in document preparation and processing time, inventory carrying costs, personnel costs, information float, shipping errors, returned goods, lead times, order cycle times, and ordering costs. In **addition**, EDI may lead to increases in cash flow, billing accuracy, productivity, and customer satisfaction. Potential drawbacks to EDI include a lack of awareness of its benefits, high setup costs, lack of standard formats, and incompatibility of computer hardware and software.[3]

These drawbacks, the **dramatic** rise of the Internet, and the development of XML (extensible markup language, a fast, flexible text format that facilitates data exchange via the Internet) have resulted in speculation that EDI is an endangered technology and unlikely to be relevant to logistics and supply chain management in the future. In reality, EDI has increased in popularity during the early years of the twenty-first century; key EDI users such as Wal-Mart and J. C. Penney either continue to add new EDI partners or increase the number of EDI transactions. Moreover, the Internet appears to act as a complement to, rather than substitute for, EDI. For example, Owens Corning, a manufacturer of glass fiber and building materials, utilizes EDI with its transportation carriers. At the same time, these carriers are expected to regularly monitor their performance metrics by accessing Owens Corning's Carrier Web Portal.

Automatic identification technology, another type of logistics-related TPS, includes optical character recognition (which can read letters, words, and numbers), machine vision (which can scan, inspect, and interpret what it views), voice-data entry (which can record and interpret a human voice), radio-**frequency** identification (which can be used where there is no line of sight between scanner and label), and magnetic strips.

Automatic identification systems are an essential component in point-of-sale (POS) systems. Operationally, POS systems involve scanning Universal Product Code (UPC) labels, either by passing the product over an optical scanner or recording it with a handheld scanner. The UPC is read and recorded into a database that supplies information such as the product's price, applicable taxes, whether food stamps can be used, and so on. The specific price of each product and its **description** are also flashed on a monitor screen positioned near the counter. When all the products have been recorded, the customer receives verification that lists the products purchased, the price of each article, and the total bill.

Ultimately, the idea behind POS systems is to provide data to guide and enhance managerial decision making, as illustrated by the variety of ways that POS data can be used in the restaurant industry. [4] One restaurant with multiple dining areas, for example, uses POS data to identify potential no-shows by analyzing customers who have reserved tables in the same evening for two (or more) of the dining areas. Another restaurant implemented a POS system that resulted in a substantial improvement in order fulfillment; the POS system virtually eliminated the largest cause of mistakes: handwritten orders.

Bar code scanners currently remain the most popular automatic identification system in use. They work to integrate suppliers and customers along the supply chain because all parties read the same labels; in addition, the transfer of goods between parties can be recorded by simple electronic means. Traditionally, laser scanners have been used to read bar codes. The scanners record inventory data and may be directly attached to a computer that uses the data to adjust inventory records and track product movement.

There has been a great deal of recent interest in radio-frequency identification (RFID) technology, due partly to RFID compliance initiatives championed by the U.S. Department of

Defense and Wal-Mart. Although RFID is presently a ＄2 billion industry on a global basis, it is projected to grow dramatically in the coming years, exceeding a ＄25 billion industry by 2015.

Conceptually, RFID involves the use of radio **frequency** to identify objects that have been implanted with an RFID tag. Compared to bar codes, RFID (1) does not require clear line of sight between an object and RFID hardware, (2) can store much larger quantities of data, and (3) offers both read and write capabilities. Potential RFID benefits include inventory reductions, fewer stockouts, labor cost reductions, and the ability to capture tremendous amounts of customer-related data.

One increasingly prominent drawback to RFID involves privacy concerns such as the inappropriate use of the technology. For example, a major retailer embedded RFID chips into a particular line of cosmetic products, and consumers who selected this product from the store shelf were videobeamed, via webcam, to the manufacturer's headquarters.[5] Another drawback to more widespread RFID adoption involves the costs of installing RFID-related hardware and software, particularly the cost of RFID tags, which at the time of publication ranged between 15 and 25 cents apiece (down from approximately 50 cents apiece in 2002) for read-only tags. Some suggest that widespread adoption of RFID will only occur when the price for read-only tags drops below five cents apiece.

New Words

1. perhaps　*adv.*也许;可能
2. comparison　*n.*比较;比喻
3. employee　*n.*受雇者;雇工;雇员
4. invoicing　*n.*开发票
5. pricing　*n.*定价
6. addition　*n.*增加;加法;附加物
7. dramatic　*adj.*戏剧性的;引人注目的;给人深刻印象的;激动人心的
8. description　*n.*描述;刻画;类型;说明书
9. frequency　*n.*频繁;频率

Phrases

1. transaction processing system (TPS)　交易处理系统
2. batch processing　成批处理
3. real-time processing　实时处理
4. purchase order　采购订单
5. advanced shipment notice　预发货通知
6. electronic funds transfer　电子转账
7. bill payment　清算

8. inventory carrying cost　库存持有成本

9. personnel cost　人工成本

10. information float　信息传递时间

11. shipping error　传送错误

12. returned goods　退货

13. lead times　提前期

14. order cycle times　订货周期

15. ordering cost　订货成本

16. automatic identification technology　自动识别系统

17. optical character recognition　光学特征识别

18. machine vision　机器视觉

19. voice-data entry　声音数据录入

20. radio-frequency identification　射频识别

21. point-of-sale（POS）system　销售点系统

22. Universal Product Code（UPC）label　通用产品代码标签

23. food stamp　食品标记

24. radio-frequency identification（RFID）technology　射频识别技术

25. bar code　条形码

Notes

1. Although batch processing might be somewhat out of step with the contemporary emphasis on speed and time reduction, it can be quite effective when real-time processing is not necessary.

虽然成批处理在要求快速短时情况下有些慢,但在不需要实时处理的情况下它还是很有效的。

2. Because EDI provides for the seamless transmission of data across companies (assuming technological compatibility), it can facilitate the integration of and coordination between, supply chain participants.

具备技术能力的公司之间利用 EDI 无缝传输数据,这就促进了供应链参与者的整合和协调。

3. Potential drawbacks to EDI include a lack of awareness of its benefits, high setup costs, lack of standard formats, and incompatibility of computer hardware and software.

EDI 有一些不足,包括缺乏对其好处的认识,高频的准备成本,缺少标准格式,以及缺乏硬件兼容的能力。

4. Ultimately, the idea behind POS systems is to provide data to guide and enhance managerial decision making, as illustrated by the variety of ways that POS data can be used in the restaurant industry.

归根结底,POS 系统真正的含义是提供数据以指导和提高管理决策水平,这可以通过

POS 数据应用于餐馆业经营的多种方式来说明。

5. For example, a major retailer embedded RFID chips into a particular line of cosmetic products, and consumers who selected this product from the store shelf were videobeamed, via webcam, to the manufacturer's headquarters!

例如,一个主要的零售商把 RFID 芯片植入一系列特定的化妆品,在货架上选购商品的顾客会被录像记录,并通过网络存储器将结果发到制造商总部。

Section E   Enterprise Resource Planning（ERP）
企业资源规划

In the last decade, there has emerged a new generation of software systems that link all of the various functional areas within organization. The goal of these systems, which are known as Enterprise Resource Planning (ERP) systems, is to provide a company with a single, uniform software platform and database that will facilitate transactions among the different functional areas within a firm, and in some cases, between firms and their customers and venders. [[1]]

ERP systems didn't just happen overnight. Rather, they are an outgrowth, or the next generation, of Materials Requirements Planning (MRP) systems and Manufacturing Resources Planning (MRP Ⅱ).

ERP systems now link all of functional areas within an organization by providing a common software platform and shared database.

When properly installed and operating, an ERP systems can provide a firm with a significant competitive advantage, which can fully justify the investment of time and money. [2] The benefits of using an ERP system can take many forms, including reduction in the number of errors through the use of a common database, faster customer response time, faster order fulfillment time, and better overall communication within the organization. [3]

For example, Hewlett-Packard's computer system's manufacturing and distribution facility for Europe, which is located in Geuslstein, Germany, achieved significant improvement in operational performance after implementing SAP's ERP system, including on time delivery exceeding 95%, cycle time reduced by 80%, inventories reduced by 30%, operating costs reduced by 30%, and distribution costs reduced by 70%.

New Words

1. decade   *n.* 十年
2. functional   *adj.* 功能的;实用的;起作用的
3. vendor   *n.* 卖主,售卖者
4. manufacturing   *n.* 制造业   *adj.* 制造业的
5. platform   *n.* 台;站台;平台;纲领
6. database   *n.* 数据库;资料库;信息库

7. install   *vt.* 安装;任命;安顿

8. operate   *vt.* 使运作;使运转;使工作

9. competitive   *adj.* 竞争的,比赛的;(价格等)有竞争力的;(指人)好竞争的

10. justify   *vt.* 证明……有理;为……辩护;对……作出解释   *vi.* 整理版面;证明合法

11. fulfillment   *n.* 满足;完成;履行

12. distribution   *n.* 配送

13. facility   *n.* 设备;设施;才能;资质;灵巧;熟练

14. implement   *vt.* 实施,执行;使生效,实现;落实(政策);把……填满

15. delivery   *n.* 传递;交付;递送;分娩;转让;演讲姿态;投球

16. exceed   *vt.* 超过;超出   *vi.* 领先

17. inventory   *n.* 存货(清单)

Phrases

1. Enterprise Resource Planning(ERP)   企业资源规划
2. Materials Requirements Planning(MRP)   物料需求计划
3. Manufacturing Resources Planning(MRP Ⅱ)   制造资源计划

Notes

1. The goal of these systems, which are known as Enterprise Resource Planning(ERP) systems, is to provide a company with a single, uniform software platform and database that will facilitate transactions among the different functional areas within a firm, and in some cases, between firms and their customers and venders.

" which are known as Enterprise Resource Planning(ERP) systems"这是非限定性定语从句,作用是补充说明 systems 的内容,同时,这个句子也是一个插入语,因此,整个句子可以理解为 the goal of these system is to…

ERP 系统的目标就是为企业提供一个统一的、共享的管理框架和数据库共享平台,以便于企业内部各个不同职能部门之间的交流和合作,在其他一些案例里,这也支持企业与其顾客和供应商之间的交流和合作。

2. When properly installed and operating, an EPR system can provide a firm with a significant competitive advantage, which can fully justify the investment of time and money.

When properly installed and operating 此分句的主语是后面的 an EPR system,这是当主句和分句的主语一致时,可以省略分句的主语,避免造成重复。

ERP 系统在正确地安装并投入运行之后,就能为企业带来显著的竞争优势,这充分证明了企业在 ERP 方面所投入的时间和资金是物有所值的。

3. The benefits of using an ERP system can take many forms, including reduction in the number of errors through the use of a common database, faster customer response time, faster order fulfillment times, and better overall communication within the organization.

全句译为:企业实施 ERP 系统之后会带来诸多益处,包括通过使用统一的共享数据

库来减少出错率;提高客户反应速度;加快订单完成时间;有助于支持企业内部各个不同职能部门之间(乃至与顾客和供应商之间)的相互交流和合作。

🎯 Core Concepts 核心概念

1. Virtual logistics is based on logistics network, but more computerized and systematized than logistics operation.

虚拟物流基于物流网络,但比物流更计算机化和系统化。

2. MRP (Material Requirement Planning) is the management system to control the amount of material consumed and to reduce inventory in the manufacturing company.

物料需求计划是制造企业用来控制原料消耗量和减少存货量的管理系统。

3. ERP (Enterprise Resource Planning) is the management system to distribute all resources economically, while satisfying the demand of the market.

企业资源规划是经济地分配所有资源,同时满足市场需求的管理系统。

4. MRP Ⅱ (Manufacturing Resource Planning) is the system to control all elements, including inventory and procurement, cost and working capital, sales order and personnel level.

制造资源计划是控制企业所有元素的系统,包括:库存和采购、成本和运行资本、销售订单和人员水平。

5. The revolution of information started with the introduction of the personal computer, followed by the optical fiber network, the explosion of the Internet and the World Wide Web.

信息革命始于个人计算机的引入,随光纤网络、因特网和万维网而发展。

6. Internet assists market development, operational planning and management decisions in the logistics industry.

因特网辅助物流业的市场发展、运营计划和管理决策。

7. Logistics information system can be made up by three parts: inputs by terminal, data managed by CPU, the outputs managed by optical fiber.

物流信息系统由三个部分组成,包括:输入终端、数据的集中处理和结果的光纤输出管理。

8. Electronic Commerce (EC) is the tool to be used to make deal between the seller and buyer by Internet in a paperless environment.

电子商务是用来在无纸化的网络中处理买方和卖方之间交易的工具。

9. Electronic Data Interchange (EDI) refers to a computer-to-computer information sharing of business documents in a standard format.

电子数据交换是用标准格式记录的企业文档在计算机之间实现的信息共享。

10. EDI is widely applied in the field of commerce with the legal effect.

电子数据交换被广泛应用于有法律影响的商业领域。

11. Intranet is the internal network within an organization that promotes sharing of internal company related information, using similar technology as the Internet.

企业内部网是用来促进公司内部相关信息共享的互联网络,它使用与因特网相同的技术。

12. The World Wide Web is the Internet system to allow users to browse from one Internet site to another and to inspect the information available without using complicated commands and protocols.

万维网是允许用户从一个网络浏览到其他网站的方式来阅览提供的信息,而不使用复杂命令和协议的因特网系统。

Exercises 练习

Ⅰ. Answer the following questions in English.

1. What are the three levels in which information is needed?

2. In what aspects can ICT be instrumental in the tactical level of logistic operation?

3. What is the definition of EDI?

4. The first sentence in the section B probably means _____.

    A. information technology is the most distinctive feature of modern logistics

    B. information technology is of no importance for logistics managers

    C. information technology is the only feature of modern logistics

    D. there are many features of modern logistics among which information technology is of vital importance

5. According to the second paragraph of section B, one-dimensional bar code is _____.

    A. updated

    B. dated

    C. widely used

    D. replaced with two-dimensional bar code

6. According to section B, the writer refers to some types of information that can be transmitted by EDI except _____.

    A. B/L   B. contract   C. involve   D. order

7. According to section B, sometimes managers are misled by the information gathered along the downstream of a supply chain because _____.

    A. information may be distorted or twisted in the process of transmission

    B. too little information is collected

    C. they are too busy to handle MIS

    D. the companies downstream are not willing to cooperate with them

8. The word "block" in the second sentence of Para.5 in section B means _____.

    A. a solid piece of something

    B. a number of quantity of related things dealt with as a unit

C. large buildings

D. metal castings

9. How can communication systems help logistics management in the aftermath of situation such as terrorist attacks and natural disasters?

10. What advances in telecommunications technology do you think as being most beneficial to logistics management? Why?

11. What does wireless communication refer to?

12. What does GPS refer to?

13. What does voice-based order picking refer to?

14. What are the benefits and drawbacks of EDI?

15. Do you believe that EDI is a viable technology for contemporary logistics management? Support your answer.

16. Discuss the relationship between automatic identification technologies and point -of-sale systems.

17. Why are some companies hesitant to adopt RFID technology?

Ⅱ. Choose the best word or phrase that fits the sentence.

1. ICT becomes a tool for integrating and coordinating logistics, supply chains and all the _____ involved in the processes.

  A. factories   B. enterprises   C. businesses   D. plants

2. Information is required for every stage and at every _____ in the supply chain.

  A. standard   B. aspect   C. level   D. respect

3. Information is critical to the efficiency of logistic management because it provides the rapidly conveyed information that logistics managers use to make _____.

  A. decisions   B. choices   C. ideas   D. determinations

4. The term referring to "条形码" is _____.

  A. label   B. bar label   C. bar code   D. bar code label

5. _____ is a method to transmit information electronically with a shared common language.

  A. EDI   B. Bar Code   C. EOS   D. AVNs

6. The term _____ refers to the integrated software and hardware for managing the sales of retail goods.

  A. GPS   B. GIS   C. POS   D. EOS

7. Four basic blocks are needed to build the Internet, namely hosts, _____ and clients and connections.

  A. planners   B. designers   C. routers   D. makers

8. A transaction system is _____ by formalized rules, procedures, and standardized communications; a large volume of transactions; and an operational, day-to-day focus.

A. determined   B. known   C. understood   D. characterized

9. From a logistical _____ , the importance of well-defined and well-executed communication systems was highlighted by the events of September 11, 2002, especially for companies that use or provide airfreight services.

A. prospect   B. perspective   C. purpose   D. prosperous

10. Today, by contrast, many of these technologies are essential for enabling the contemporary logistician _____ perform in the workplace.

A. to   B. in   C. into   D. of

11. Although wireless communication has many logistical applications, we'll take a look _____ two of the more popular types, namely, global positioning systems and voice-based order picking.

A. to   B. at   C. of   D. in

12. Companies that have _____ newer-generation voice-based technology have reported increased productivity and higher pick accuracy.

A. adopted   B. adapted   C. got   D. given

13. Continuing advances in hardware and software have _____ dramatic cost reductions for wireless communication, and one implication is that the technology is no longer limited to those companies with the deepest financial resources.

A. result from   B. come from   C. derive from   D. result in

14. These drawbacks, the dramatic rise of the Internet, and the development of XML (extensible markup language, a fast, flexible text format that facilitates data exchange via the Internet) have resulted in speculation that EDI is an endangered technology and unlikely to be relevant _____ logistics and supply chain management in the future.

A. to   B. with   C. on   D. onto

15. Bar code scanners currently remain the most popular automatic identification system in _____ .

A. time   B. use   C. effect   D. affect

III. Match each word on the left with its corresponding meaning on the right.

A.	B.
1. electronic	(a) not to be dispensed with; essential
2. short-term	(b) of or concerned with electrons
3. replenishment	(c) relating to or extending over a limited period
4. dimensional	(d) (computer science) a device that forwards data packets between computer networks
5. indispensable	(e) the act of transacting within or between groups (as carrying on commercial activities)
6. transmission	(f) of or relating to dimensions

7. router   （g）filling again by supplying what has been used up

8. transaction   （h）the act of changing one thing for another thing

9. interchange   （i）the act of putting something in a certain place

10. positioning   （j）the act of sending a message

Ⅳ. Match the following definitions with the corresponding terms below.

attached	granted	solution	involved	attacks
critical	substitute	basis	by contrast	prominent

1. For example, information at the tactical level is mainly _____ with medium to short-term planning such as forecasting, scheduling and resource planning.

2. The following examples of ICT, once regarded as highly advanced, are now taken for _____ and accepted as normal.

3. Information is _____ to the efficiency of logistic management because it provides the rapidly conveyed information that logistics managers use to make decisions.

4. And EDI is just a good _____ to meeting this demand.

5. Because of the total shutdown of the U.S. aviation system for several days following the terrorist _____, many air shipments were delivered onto trucks, thus delaying many deliveries.

6. Contemporary voice-based systems, _____, are less costly, are more powerful, have better voice quality, and bare less cumbersome for workers to use.

7. A _____ example of a logistics-related TPS is electronic data interchange (EDI), the computer-to-computer transmission of business data in a structured format.

8. The Internet appears to act as a complement to, rather than _____ for, EDI.

9. The scanners record inventory data and may be directly _____ to a computer that uses the data to adjust inventory records and track product movement.

10. Although RFID is presently a $2 billion industry on a global _____, it is projected to grow dramatically in the coming years, exceeding a $25 billion industry by 2015.

Ⅴ. Translate the following sentences into Chinese.

1. One of the major changes in supply chain management over the last decade has been the rises in the importance of information technology in our field.

2. Consumers are becoming increasingly concerned about ecological matters, especially packaging.

3. Although U.K consumers were the most concerned about over-packaging, less than half would change their buying habits.

4. The ways that organizations can use like the Touchwall are limitless, just as the ways used on the Web are limitless.

5. Asia has a reputation for being a haven for counterfeiters, but GSI Hong Kong is working with several companies to test a radio frequency identification system designed to give consumers a convenient and reliable way to distinguish genuine goods from counterfeit products at airport retailers.

Ⅵ. Translate the following sentences into English.

1. 客户服务是所有员工的事情,而不仅仅是直接与客户接触的一线员工,更不仅仅是客户服务部门员工的事情。

2. 现在越来越多的物流公司开始重视客户服务,并将其引入物流公司的经营活动中。

3. 客户资料是物流公司营销活动的起点,其基本思想就是做到对客户了如指掌,并不定期进行意见反馈,征求意见。

4. 为客户来说量身订制物流方案有利于建立战略联盟与伙伴关系。

5. 对客户满意度进行追踪调查和评估,是持续改善服务的关键。

Ⅶ. Fill in the blanks with words from the list below and each word can be used once.

Early on, the system of GPS was designed as a military tool. Now, the system is used in __1__ and many other fields, such as __2__ water vapor in the atmosphere and measuring continental drift. With the development of __3__ map and the 3G technology, GPS applications are now spreading to cell phone, PDA, PC and __4__. The technology is also widely used in logistics and fleet __5__. In logistics, aiming at route-finding and positioning application, GPS products are used in position information service, __6__ automatic piloting, digital map service, Internet map service and other fields. Two hot sourced products in the GPS market are GPS Navigator and Electronic Map. Map __7__ products are divided into piloting map and positioning map, widely used in relative economy construction fields. The data of map comes from __8__ department, surveying and __9__ system, and real test. In recent years, there is a good __10__ in China's logistics industry development and its key technological development. The market of GPS in Asia and the world is entering the fast growth period.

A) mapping	B) vehicles	C) tracking
D) photoing	E) tend	F) digital
G) automobile	H) trend	I) navigation
J) monitor	K) communication	L) navy
M) management	N) database	O) tracing

Chapter 10

Third-Party Logistics
第三方物流

Section A Third-Party Logistics（3PL） 第三方物流

Third-party logistics（3PL）refers to the outsourcing of transportation, warehousing and other logistics-related activities which were originally performed in-house, to a 3PL service provider. [1] More and more **corporations** across the world are outsourcing their logistics activities due to various factors, some of which are outlined below.

A third-party logistics service is something more than **subcontracting** or **outsourcing**. Typically, subcontracting or outsourcing covers one product or one function that is produced or provided by an outside vendor. Examples include automobile companies subcontracting the manufacture of tires, or construction companies subcontracting roofing, or retail companies outsourcing the transportation function. Third-party logistics providers cut across multiple logistics functions and primarily coordinate all the logistics functions and sometimes act as a provider of one or more functions. The primary objectives of third-party logistics providers are to lower the total of cost of logistics for the supplier and improve the service level to the customer. They act as a bridge or facilitator between the first party（supplier or producer）and the second party（buyer or customer）.

As its name implies, 3PL is a kind of logistics service provider expert in logistics industry and capable of professional handling of goods. [2] 3PL differs from those transportation and warehouse providers in that they can provide value adding services with the software they have.[3] In the logistics industry, the hardware is basically the same everywhere. The trucks are the same, the forklifts are the same, and the warehouses are the same. However, what really makes the difference is the software assets such as the management know-how, personnel training program, information technology, global service network, etc.

As more and more manufacturers are outsourcing their logistics operations to the experts, the demand for 3PL increases dramatically. Manufacturers nowadays concentrate more on their core business, outsourcing their logistics operators. Take the example of precision engineering firm Shinei international which started off by leasing some warehousing space from Keppel Logistics. Over the years, this relationship has grown and extended. Today, the company has outsourced its entire logistics operations and management to Keppel Logistics.

The functions of 3PL cover all the aspects of logistics. One of its functions is as a one-stop distribution center, warehousing, trucking and shipping documentation for the client. Together with the flow of goods, the information flows simultaneously. A 3PL company not only provides service to the local manufacturers, but also to the overseas **cargo** buyers. With its worldwide information network, the cargo status is followed step by step and constantly **reflected** in the network, through which the overseas clients can easily see the entire progress. 3PL plays an invaluable role in helping clients review and develop their supply chain management models. It helps both the vendor and the distributor optimize as they can look beyond the individual fragments of the supply chain and see it in its entirety.

Except for the management know-how, variable cost is another major concern for manufacturers in employing 3PL. [4] Take Asian financial crisis as an example. Before it happened, many manufacturers still did most of their own logistics operations. This attitude pretty much changed during the Asian crisis in 1997/98 as companies realized they had to find ways to convert their fixed cost block into variable costs with regard to logistics. Streamlining in difficult times is pretty easy if one can outsource part of the work as one just pay for what he needs. 3PL, as a service provider, concentrates on their expertise while the manufacturers can focus on their own business. [5]

Admittedly, some manufacturers may think of taking back the logistics function due to the previous poor experiences with some 3PLs, [6] which have not bothered to upgrade their operation levels. In the long run, these manufacturers would find it more cost-effective to continue outsourcing these operations but only to a reputable 3PL, which means that those who fail to provide customized service with upgraded operations are destined to get out of the **industries**.

New Words

拓展资源

1. corporation   *n.*企业
2. reflected   *adj.*反射的；reflect 的过去式和过去分词
3. industry   *n.*工业；产业；行业；勤勉；勤劳
4. outsourcing   *n.*外包
5. cargo   *n.*货物
6. subcontracting   *n.*转包契约

Phrases

1. Third party logistics（3PL）　第三方物流
2. global service network　全球服务网络
3. software assets　软件资产
4. personnel training program　人员培训计划

5. one-stop distribution center   一站式分销中心

6. Asian financial crisis   亚洲金融危机

Notes

1. Third-party logistics (3PL) refers to the outsourcing of transportation, warehousing and other logistics-related activities which were originally performed in-house, to a 3PL service provider.

第三方物流是指物流公司把原本由自己承担的运输、仓储及其他相关物流活动承包给物流服务供应商，即第三方物流服务供应商。

2. As its name implies, 3PL is a kind of logistics service provider expert in logistics industry and capable of professional handling of goods.

正如其名字所示，第三方物流是一种物流服务提供者，而且它的服务能力及对物流的熟悉程度更专业。

3. 3PL differs from those transportation and warehouse providers in that they can provide value adding services with the software they have.

第三方物流不同于运输服务及仓储服务提供者的原因在于，它们能够利用已有的软件提供增值服务。

4. Except for the management know-how, variable cost is another major concern for manufacturers in employing 3PL.

对于制造企业来说，除了管理技巧外，采用第三方物流时，可变成本也是一个主要的关注事项。

5. 3PL, as a service provider, concentrates on their expertise while the manufacturers can focus on their own business.

当制造企业聚焦于它们的核心业务时，第三方物流作为一种服务提供者可为它们提供专业的技术服务。

6. Admittedly, some manufacturers may think of taking back the logistics function due to the previous poor experiences with some 3PLs, which have not bothered to upgrade their operation levels.

应该承认，一些制造商认为应该收回物流功能，原因是之前与一些第三方物流有过不愉快的合作，这些第三方物流并未帮助企业提升运营水平。

Section B   Motivation of Third Party Logistics
第三方物流的动机

There are several reasons for the growth of third-party logistics over the past decade. The **transportation** and distribution departments of some of the major **corporations** have been downsizing in order to reduce operating costs. [1] The most logical area to reduce costs is **advisory** functions such as operations research, followed by support functions such as transportation or warehousing. The area where companies want to **strengthen** by investing more is their core competency. Though it may sound like a fad it had been a reality at some of the major corporations. The other reason is from file customer side. Customers demand an **exceptional** service but are not willing to pay **extraordinary** price for it ... This requires file use of faster and frequent transportation services and flexibility in inventory levels. A third-party logistics provider will be in a position to consolidate business from several companies and offer frequent pick-ups and deliveries, whereas **in-house** transportation cannot. Other reasons are as follows:

(1) The company's core business and competency may not be in logistics.

(2) **Sufficient** resources, both **capital** and **manpower**, may not be available for file company to become a world-class logistics operator.

(3) There is an urgency to implement a "world-class" logistics operation or there is insufficient time to develop the required capabilities in-house.

(4) The Company is venturing into a new business with totally different logistics requirements. [2]

(5) Merger or acquisition may make outsourcing logistics operations more attractive than to integrate logistics operations.

In recent years there has been some concern expressed by file users of third-party service providers that they are not being given the expected levels of service and business benefits. Users have also **indicated** that service providers are insufficiently proactive in their approach to the contracted operations—they only aim to provide the minimum and fail to enhance file operations they are responsible for. [3] On the other hand, service providers claim that they are seldom given the opportunity to develop new ideas and offer improvements, because users are not prepared to give them adequate information of their complete, supply chains. One consequence of this has been the idea of using an additional **enterprise** or organization to oversee and take responsibility for all the **outsourced** operations a user might have. This has become known as **fourth-party** logistics.

The need to take a total supply chain approach means that a different type of service provider and a different type of RFQ/ITr **approach** are required. The idea is to aim to provide solutions, not just services. It is important to recognize that there are often several different organizations or participants in a supply chain, that there is a need to develop partnerships and there should be opportunities to integrate and rationalize along the supply chain. [4]

Thus, solutions can be developed by the **co-venture** of fourth-party service provider, to offer:

(1) A total supply chain perspective;

(2) Visibility along the supply chain;

(3) Measurement along the supply chain;

(4) Open systems;

（5）Technical vision；

（6）Flexibility；

（7）Tailored structures and systems.

New Words

1. transportation　*n.*运输；运输工具；运输系统

2. advisory　*adj.*顾问的；咨询的；劝告的　*n.*报告

3. strengthen　*v.*加强；变坚固

4. exceptional　*adj.*异常的；例外的；特别的；杰出的

5. extraordinary　*adj.*非凡的；特别的；特派的

6. sufficient　*adj.*足够的；充分的

7. indicate　*v.*指示；象征；显示；暗示，预示　*v.*表明；指明

8. approach　*v.*靠近；接近；接洽；要求；达到；动手处理　*n.*途径；方法；接近；接洽；要求；路径；进场着陆；相似的事物

9. motivation　*n.*动机

10. corporation　*n.*公司

11. capital　*n.*资金

12. manpower　*n.*人力

13. enterprise　*n.*企业

14. outsource　*v.*外包

15. co-venture　*n.*合资

16. in-house　*adj.*室内的

Phrases

1. operating cost　运营成本

2. core competency　核心竞争力

3. fourth-party service　第四方服务

4. tailored structure　量身订制的结构

Notes

1. The transportation and distribution departments of some of the major corporations have been downsizing in order to reduce operating costs.

一些大型企业的运输和分销部门一直在裁员以降低运营成本。

2. The Company is venturing into a new business with totally different logistics requirements.

公司根据完全不同的物流需求拓展新的业务。

3. Users have also indicated that service providers are insufficiently proactive in their approach to the contracted operations—they only aim to provide the minimum and fail to

enhance file operations they are responsible for.

物流客户认为服务供应商在承包经营方面不够积极—它们只求提供最小量的服务而不能提高运营效率。

4. It is important to recognize that there are often several different organizations or participants in a supply chain, that there is a need to develop partnerships and there should be opportunities to integrate and rationalize along the supply chain.

重要的是要认识到在供应链中往往有几个不同的公司或参与者,因此,有必要发展伙伴关系并利用各种机会整合供应链并将其合理化。

Section C Alliances 联盟

As an **alternative** to acquisitions, many 3PL providers in the United States have developed alliance agreements to broaden their service portfolio and/or area served. In some **instances**, alliances have been formed with other 3PL service providers. In other cases, they have involved a broad range of companies including transportation carriers, freight forwarders, warehousing companies, software vendors, and financial service companies.

The major **challenge** in **pursuing** this strategic option has been to find competent partners. Based upon data we have generated in our annual CEO surveys, the most important considerations in making such relationship work effectively are a shared vision, similar corporate cultures, and a shared commitment to delivering high-quality logistics services. [1]

It should be noted that such alliances by 3 PL providers are not a new development. Sixteen of the 21 companies involved in the 1994 survey indicated that they had at least one alliance partner at that time. Today, nearly all of the major 3PL service providers have multiple alliance partners.

As the industry structure has changed over the ten-year period, the revenue base of the remaining companies has increased dramatically. On average, the companies involved in the 1994 CEO survey reported annual revenues of **approximately** $200 million that year, with only one company generating more than $1 billion. [2] By contrast, the average annual revenue reported by participants in the 2004 survey was $894 million. Five of those companies generated in excess of $1 billion that year, and four more projected exceeding that figure the following year.

It's interesting that in some instances, the growth of 3PL service providers has been restricted by their corporate parents. For example, for a number of years the logistics unit of Federal Express was directed to limit its service offerings to customers that would also generate air cargo for FedEx. Similarly, the CEO of Panalpina, a significant player in the European 3PL industry, once reported that its logistics unit would only consider potential customers that would generate additional forwarding revenues for the parent.

Another corporate restriction was the mandated use of services supplied by other operating units of the 3 PL's corporate family. To illustrate, if a customer requires trucking services in a particular geography, and an operating unit of the 3PL's parent company provides those services in that market, it is "strongly recommended" that the family member be used over a **competitor**. [3] Such artificial restrictions, however, raise concerns in the user community about whose needs are being served in such situations.

New Words

1. alternative   *adj.*两者择一的;供选择的;非主流的   *n.*二者择一;供替代的选择
2. instance   *n.*例子;场合;情况;要求;诉讼程序   *vt.*举例说明
3. challenge   *n.*挑战;邀请比赛;盘问;质疑   *v.*向……挑战;盘问;质疑
4. pursue   *v.*追求;追捕;继续执行;从事
5. approximately   *adv.*大约;近似地
6. competitor   *n.*竞争者;对手

Phrases

1. transportation carrier   运输承运商
2. freight forwarder   货运代理
3. warehousing company   库存公司
4. software vendor   软件供应商
5. financial service company   金融服务公司
6. high-quality logistics service   高品质物流服务
7. multiple alliance partner   多种联盟伙伴
8. annual revenue   年收入
9. Federal Express   联邦快递

Notes

1. Based upon data we have generated in our annual CEO surveys, the most important considerations in making such relationship work effectively are a shared vision, similar corporate cultures, and a shared commitment to delivering high-quality logistics services.

根据我们在每年的 CEO 调查中得到的数据,若建立有效的工作关系,最需要考虑的是共同的理念、相似的企业文化,并共同致力于提供高品质的物流服务。

2. On average, the companies (involved in the 1994 CEO survey) reported annual revenues of approximately $ 200 million that year, with only one company generating more than $ 1 billion.

根据 1994 年 CEO 调查报告,所涉及公司这一年的平均年收入约为两亿美元,只有一家公司的产值超过十亿美元。

3. To illustrate, if a customer requires trucking services in a particular geography, and an operating unit of the 3PL's parent company provides those services in that market, it is

"strongly recommended" that the family member be used over a competitor.

例如,如果客户在某一地区需要卡车运输服务,而第三方物流公司的一个运营部门(一个子公司)正好在那个地区提供这些服务,那么子公司是最好的推荐对象。

Section D   How to Select A 3PL   如何选择第三方物流

Before selecting a third-party logistics provider (3PL), Marc Tanowitz, **principal** with Pace Harmon, an outsourcing advisory services firm, suggests that manufacturers **consider** these five **fundamentals**:

Know Your Demand

Understanding how materials flow through a supply chain is the key to properly **defining** supply chain requirements. Collect detailed historical data to document the costs, units, frequencies and modes utilized as raw materials are converted to sellable units, as it is critical to synchronize planning, material requirements planning (MRP), material delivery, conversion to finished goods and outbound product movement. Modeling the past, with appropriate normalization to accommodate projected future changes, will help manufacturers understand the cost-impacting decisions that drive supply chain requirements and identify which components to outsource or **retain**.

Master (and own) the Forecast

Developing the demand model described above will typically require input and validation from a variety of **stakeholders**, including procurement, manufacturing, distribution and commercial. [1] Participation from these stakeholders is critical to establishing an accurate forecast and articulating key constraints, and ultimately can drive the success of the transaction, as the provider's ability to meet a company's needs and targeted cost structure will be largely dependent on the accuracy of the forecast. An inaccurate forecast likely will result in either excess capacity (or cost) or constrained capacity (and lost sales), with the implications becoming more pronounced as forecast accuracy decreases.

Furthermore, stakeholder understanding of the supply chain performance dependencies is necessary to **ensure** valid root-cause analysis and **issue** resolution in an outsourced environment. [2]

Demand Accountability

Supply chain costs—including transportation, warehousing, handling/labor, working capital and obsolescence—are heavily impacted by business leaders' and stakeholders' decisions. Supply chain leaders may determine where inventory is stored, how much warehouse space to lease/own, or specific transportation carriers and modes, but directives such as customer fulfillment rates and order-to-delivery time drive stocking location decisions, inventory levels and transportation carrier selections. [3] While 3PL providers must be held accountable for optimizing costs within their span of control, internal stakeholders also must take responsibility for the cost implications of their decisions, many of which may limit a 3 PL's ability to truly optimize.

Set Clear and Fair Expectations

A 3PL can improve many aspects of a company's supply chain, but likely will focus on the objectives articulated by its client and reasonably within its control. [4] Set clear objectives drive provider behavior, such as specific cost savings or reporting, escalation and explanation. Engage the 3PL in discussions prior to finalizing objectives, as its experience and input can provide better visibility into the tradeoffs of supply chain decisions.

Measure Business Impact

An outsourced supply chain should provide some combination of increased supply chain effectiveness, reduced cost and overall flexibility. These results can be measured by looking at end-to-end key performance indicators such as inventory turn rates, total cost per unit sold and customer **satisfaction**.

New Words

1. principal   *adj.*主要的;首要的   *n.*本金;资本;校长;主角;委托人;主犯
2. consider   *v.*考虑;思考;认为;体谅;注视
3. fundamentals   *n.*基本原则;名词;fundamental 的复数形式
4. defining   *adj.*定义性的;限定的;动词 define 的现在分词
5. retain   *vt.*保持;保留;记住;聘请
6. stakeholder   利益相关者
7. ensure   *vt.*担保;保证;使安全;确保
8. issue   *n.*议题;问题;期刊号;一次发行额;发行;*v.*发表;公布;正式发给;发行;流出
9. environment   *n.*环境;外界
10. satisfaction   *n.*满意;赔偿;乐事;妥善处理;确信

Phrases

1. raw material   原材料
2. synchronize planning   同步规划
3. material requirements planning (MRP)   物料需求计划
4. outbound product movement   外运商品
5. excess capacity   超额能力
6. inventory turn rate   库存周转价格

Notes

1. Developing the demand model described above will typically require input and validation from a variety of stakeholders, including procurement, manufacturing, distribution and commercial.

上述模式的发展需要各种利益相关者投资和批准,包括采购、制造、分销和商业发展的需求。

2. Furthermore, stakeholder understanding of the supply chain performance dependencies is necessary to ensure valid root-cause analysis and issue resolution in an outsourced environment.

而且,利益相关者必须理解供应链绩效的依赖性以确保对外包环境进行有效的因果分析和解决问题的必要条件。

3. Supply chain leaders may determine where inventory is stored, how much warehouse space to lease/own, or specific transportation carriers and modes, but directives such as customer fulfillment rates and order-to-delivery time drive stocking location decisions, inventory levels and transportation carrier selections.

供应链负责人可能决定存储库存的地点,仓库空间租赁/拥有的数量,或特定的运输载体和模式,但客户履约率和订单交付时间等指令决定了存储方位、库存水平和运输承运人的选择。

4. A 3PL can improve many aspects of a company's supply chain, but likely will focus on the objectives articulated by its client and reasonably within its control.

尽管第三方物流可以改善公司的供应链的许多方面,但也可能会因专注于其客户的某些需求而受其控制。

Section E　China Third Party Logistics Market
中国的第三方物流市场

The total value of China external logistics amounted to RMB 26.8 trillion in the first half of 2006, rising by 15.3% compared to the 1st half of 2005. [1] The figure is amazing!

Structurally, the industrial product logistics developed fastest. The total value of industrial product logistics was RMB 23.4 trillion in 2006. The total value of import logistics was RMB2. 95 trillion in 2006, up 14.2% compared to the 1st half of 2005. The agricultural logistics increased slowest and its growth rate increased by 0.2%. The total value of agricultural product logistics in 2006 reached RMB 461.5 billion.

The total expense of China external logistics was RMB 1687.6 billion in the first half of 2006, rising by 14.7% compared to the 1st half of 2005, as a result of prosperous international and domestic trade. And another reason of high expense of external logistics was the sharp rise of energy cost that caused the common rise of transportation fee. [2] However, the ratio of the total expense of external logistics to GDP had dropped by 0.2% compared to the first half of 2005.

From the view of different functions of logistics, transport cost was RMB 932.9 billion in the first half of 2006, rising by 12.9% compared to the first half of 2005. The storage cost was RMB 531.4 billion, rising by 18.6% compared to the 1st half of 2005.

The market scale of China third-party logistics exceeded RMB 100 billion in 2006, rising by about 30% compared to the previous year. [3] 2006 was the first year to open the logistics market to foreign investment. More and more global logistics corporations began to establish bases or distribution centers in China. Meanwhile, due to the rising price of petroleum and the increasing investment in facility and technology, the operation cost of logistics enterprises will increase dramatically [4]. All these facts meant the intensive competition, but competition would lead to the common decrease of logistics service charges and increased customer service. The logistics enterprises become more and more professional in order to improve their profitability and competitiveness. [5] Therefore, the 3PL market is segmented continuously according to industries, regions and products.

China logistics industry will maintain the rapid growth in the following several years. The promising logistics market in China will provide the investors with great opportunities. [6]

New Words

1. external   *adj.* 外部的
2. Figure   *n.* 数字,数量,数值;图形,图案;人物
3. import   *n.* 进口
4. agricultural   *adj.* 农业的
5. prosperous   *adj.* 繁荣的
6. ratio   *n.* 比率,比例
7. previous   *adj.* 之前的
8. exceed   *v.* 超过,超出,胜过
9. corporation   *n.* 公司
10. petroleum   *n.* 石油
11. enterprise   *n.* 企业;事业;进取心;谋划
12. competition   *n.* 竞争
13. profitability   *n.* 收益性;盈利能力
14. segment   *n.* 部分;弓形;瓣;段;节
15. promising   *adj.* 有前途的;有希望的

Phrases

1. amount to   总计,合计;达到;相当于,等于;取得成就,办成好事

2. industrial product logistics   工业产品物流

3. agricultural logistics   农业物流

4. international trade   国际贸易

5. domestic trade   国内贸易

6. distribution center   分销中心

7. transport cost   运输成本

8. storage cost   存储成本

Notes

1. The total value of China external logistics amounted to RMB 26.8 trillion in the first half of 2006, rising by 15.3% compared to the 1st half of 2005.

2006 年上半年,中国对外物流总值达 26.8 万亿元,比 2005 年上半年增长 15.3%。

2. And another reason of high expense of external logistics was the sharp rise of energy cost that caused the common rise of transportation fee.

外部物流费用高昂的另一个原因是能源成本急剧上升导致运输费普遍上涨。

3. The market scale of China third-party logistics exceeded RMB 100 billion in 2006, rising by about 30% compared to the previous year.

2006 年中国第三方物流市场规模突破 1000 亿元,比上年增长约 30%。

4. Meanwhile, due to the rising price of petroleum and the increasing investment in facility and technology, the operation cost of logistics enterprises will increase dramatically.

与此同时,由于石油价格上涨以及设施和技术投资的增加,物流企业的运营成本将急剧增加。

due to:因为,to 在这里是介词。operation cost:运营成本。

5. The logistics enterprises become more and more professional in order to improve their profitability and competitiveness.

物流企业越来越专业化,以提高其盈利能力和竞争力。

6. The promising logistics market in China will provide the investors with great opportunities.

中国有前途的物流市场将为投资者提供巨大的机遇。

Core Concepts   核心概念

1. Third Party Logistics refers to specialized logistics service providers that provide specific services for suppliers and customers.

第二方物流指专门的物流服务提供者,它为供应商或客户提供专属服务。

2. Third Party Logistics assists the execution of logistic activities.

第三方物流辅助物流活动的执行和运作。

3. Fourth Party Logistics is the planner and manager for logistics network, while Third

Party Logistics is the supplier of logistics service, like transport and storage.

第四方物流是物流网络的计划者和管理者,而第三方物流提供运输存储等物流服务。

4. The bank is a third party in the payment process between the buyers and sellers.

银行是买卖方支付过程中的第三方。

Exercises　练习

Ⅰ. Answer the following questions in English.

1. What does Third-party logistics (3PL) refer to?

2. What are the primary objectives of third-party logistics providers?

3. What are the reasons for the fact that third-party logistics differs from those transportation and warehouse providers?

4. What are the functions of 3PL?

5. What are the reasons for the growth of third-party logistics over the past decade?

6. What solutions do the co-venture of fourth-party service provider offer?

7. How have 3PL providers in the United States done to broaden their service portfolio and/or area served?

8. What is the major challenge in pursuing this strategic option?

9. What do the manufacturers consider when selecting the third-party logistics?

10. Do you think brand name should be taken into consideration in choosing 3PL providers?

Ⅱ. Fill in the bank with the proper words or expressions.

1. More and more corporations across the world are outsourcing their logistics activities _____ various factors, some of which are outlined below.

　　A. due to　　　　B. because　　　C. in that　　　　D. for the reason that

2. Manufacturers nowadays concentrate more _____ their core business, outsourcing their logistics operators.

　　A. in　　　　　B. onto　　　　　C. on　　　　　　D. to

3. _____ the flow of goods, the information flows simultaneously.

　　A. Except　　　B. Instead of　　　C. Together with　　D. Rather than

4. With its worldwide information network, the cargo status is followed step by step and constantly reflected in the network, through _____ the overseas clients can easily see the entire progress.

　　A. that　　　　B. which　　　　C. who　　　　　D. whose

5. This attitude pretty much changed during the Asian crisis in 1997/98 as companies realized they had to find ways to convert their fixed cost block _____ variable costs with regard to logistics.

    A. into   B. to   C. on   D. through

6. _____, these manufacturers would find it more cost-effective to continue outsourcing these operations but only to a reputable 3PL, which means that those who fail to provide customized service with upgraded operations are destined to get out of the industries.

    A. In a short term   B. In the long run

    C. Immediately   D. In the future

7. The most logical area to reduce costs is advisory functions such as operations research, followed by support functions _____ transportation or warehousing.

    A. for example   B. for instance

    C. take an example   D. such as

8. One consequence of this has been the idea of using an additional enterprise or organization to oversee and take responsibility for all the outsourced operations a user might have. This has become known as _____.

    A. first-party logistics   B. second-party logistics

    C. third-party logistics   D. fourth-party logistics

9. Today, nearly all of the major 3PL service providers have _____ alliance partners.

    A. multiple   B. multiply   C. minimum   D. maximum

10. By contrast, the average _____ revenue reported by participants in the 2004 survey was $894 million.

    A. daily   B. weekly   C. monthly   D. annual

11. Such artificial restrictions, however, raise concerns in the user community about _____ needs are being served in such situations.

    A. who   B. which   C. that   D. whose

12. Understanding how materials flow through a supply chain is the key _____ properly defining supply chain requirements.

    A. for   B. to   C. as   D. of

13. Participation from these stakeholders is critical to _____ an accurate forecast and articulating key constraints, and ultimately can drive the success of the transaction.

    A. establish   B. establishing   C. found   D. founding

14. _____ 3PL providers must be held accountable for optimizing costs within their span of control, internal stakeholders also must take responsibility for the cost implications of their decisions, many of which may limit a 3PL's ability to truly optimize.

    A. While   B. Because   C. If   D. Assuming

15. Engage the 3PL in discussions prior to finalizing objectives, _____ its experience and input can provide better visibility into the tradeoffs of supply chain decisions.

    A. which   B. that   C. as   D. who

Ⅲ. Match each word on the left with its corresponding meaning on the right.

A.	B.
1. corporations	(a) the force of workers available
2. subcontracting	(b) happen at the same time
3. personnel	(c) goods carried by a large vehicle
4. manpower	(d) arranged for contracted work to be done by others
5. freight	(e) someone entrusted to hold the stakes for two or more persons betting against one another
6. alliance	(f) group of people willing to obey orders
7. annual	(g) a business firm whose articles of incorporation have been approved in some state
8. synchronize	(h) let for money
9. stakeholders	(i) (botany) a plant that completes its entire life cycle within the space of a year
10. lease	(j) the state of being allied or confederated

Ⅳ. Match the following definitions with the corresponding terms below.

members	role	services	defined	purchased
combination	subcontracting	example	logistics	impacted

1. Examples include automobile companies _____ the manufacture of tires, or construction companies subcontracting roofing, or retail companies outsourcing the transportation function.

2. 3PL plays an invaluable _____ in helping clients review and develop their supply chain management models.

3. Take Asian financial crisis as an _____.

4. Standard TPL _____ contain some easy customized types of operations. The rationale behind routine services is economies of scale and scope.

5. TPL providers can be seen as supportive supply chain _____. This implies that logistics services providers should support alternative supply chain strategies.

6. The name "third-party logistics" refers to a situation where the _____ service provider serves two parts in the supply chain.

7. Contract logistics can be _____ as "a process where by the shipper and the third-party enter into an agreement for specific services at specific costs over some identifiable time horizon".

8. Most logistics services are _____ on a contract basis. The limitation of the dyadic transactional contract is that it might lead to sub optimization.

9. Supply chain costs—including transportation, warehousing, handling/labor, working capital and obsolescence—are heavily _____ by business leaders' and stakeholders' decisions.

10. An outsourced supply chain should provide some _____ of increased supply chain effectiveness, reduced cost and overall flexibility.

Ⅴ. Translate the following sentences into Chinese.

1. Currently, users are focusing on outsourcing activities such as transportation, warehouse, and customs clearance.

2. In the 1999 and 2000 surveys of the CEOs of 20 of the leading 3PL providers, the CEOs identified e-commerce as the most significant opportunity available to the industry.

3. 3PL providers are embracing the Web to provide technical support and linkages to clients even if they are not heavily involved in supporting e-commerce activities for clients.

4. The logistics industry is actually in the clearly stages of a massive wave of even greater consolidation that will reward a small number of third-party logistics companies with tremendous values.

5. Many observers have predicted that the logistics provider industry will continue to expand at a rate of 15-20 percent annually.

Ⅵ. Translate the following sentences into English.

1. 第三方物流是供应方和需求方之间的纽带,它以满足顾客的需求为目标。

2. 信息技术是第三方物流发展的基础,在物流服务过程中,信息技术发展实现了信息实时共享,促进了物流管理的科学化,提高了物流服务效率。

3. 第三方物流是通过合同形式来规范物流经营者和物流消费者之间的关系的。

4. 物流设计、物流操作过程、物流管理都应该是专业化的,物流设备和物流设施都应该是标准化的。

5. 第三方物流企业根据消费者的要求,提供有针对性的个性服务和增值服务。

Ⅶ. Fill in the blanks with words from the list below and each word can be used once.

Many foreign firms team up with Chinese partners in offering 3PL services. For instance, Mitsui OKK Lines (MOL) of Japan and Fuji __1__ operate a logistics and warehousing company in Suzhou to take care of all the logistics involved in making the Fuji film __2__ across the China market. UPS's JV logistics company plans to open 19 offices in China. DHL and Sinotrans have __3__ the agreement by 50 years.

Other foreign companies such as Excel Logistics, TNT and Nippon Express are setting up offices or __4__ JV deals in Shenzhen and Guangzhou. The US $ 30 million logistics JV between TNT and Shanghai Automotive Industry Corp (Group) is the first of its kind in China specializing in the automobile ___5___ . APL Logistics has formed JVs with two local transport giants in Shanghai and Shenyang to develop the mainland logistics market. APL Logistics currently has ___6___ companies in 10 cities around China's north, central and south parts.

While many foreign companies team up with local partners, some ___7___ to go it alone. Typically these companies provide 3PL service to foreign and ___8___ companies. The Maersk Group, since receiving the green light to enter the China market in 2001, has set up 11 branches across the country. It has also opened its first ___9___ center in Shanghai, with plans to set up 10 more. Meanwhile, Nippon Express has formed logistics companies in Dalian, Shenzhen and Shanghai to facilitate business ___10___ in China. NYK Lines (China) has also established a branch in Shanghai, and is now moving to set up Logistics companies in Tianjin, Qingdao, Fuzhou, Xiamen, Guangzhou and Dalian. OOCL has located its China headquarters in Shanghai with 21 offices all over the country.

A) domestic	B) branch	C) distribution
D) negotiating	E) jointly	F) sector
G) employers	H) subsidiaries	I) top
J) prefer	K) extended	L) available
M) excellent	N) expansion	O) process

Chapter 11

International Logistics
国 际 物 流

Section A Definition of International Logistics
国际物流的概念

It is increasingly difficult to separate the practices of **domestic** and international logistics. International logistics—logistics activities associated with goods that are sold across national boundaries— occurs in the following situations:

1. A firm exports a portion of a product made or grown—for example, paper-making machinery to Sweden, wheat to Russia, or coal to Japan.

2. A firm imports raw materials—such as pulpwood from Canada—or manufactured products—such as motorcycles from Italy or Japan.

3. Goods are partially assembled in one country and then shipped to another, where they are further assembled or processed. For example, a firm stamps electronic components in the United States. It ships them to a free trade zone in the Far East, where low-cost labor assembles them, and then the assembled components are returned to the United States to become part of the finished product.

4. The firm is global in outlook and sees almost all nations as being markets, sources of supply, or sites for markets or for assembly operations.

5. Because of geography, a nation's **domestic** commerce crosses foreign borders, often in bond. For example, goods moving by truck between Detroit and Buffalo or between the Lower 48 states and Alaska, through Canada, travel in bond, which means that the carrier handling them has a special legal **obligation** to keep them sealed and to make certain that they are not released for sale or use within the country through which they are traveling. [1] Products shipped in bond are not subject to normal duties of the country through which they are passing.

Until World War Ⅱ, the concepts of international trade were simple. Industrialized powers maintained political and **economic** colonies that were sources of raw materials, cheap labor, and markets for manufactured products. When dealing with those colonies, manufacturers in the parent country bought low and sold high. World War Ⅱ brought an end to the colonial system; since then, emerging nations have attempted to develop their own political and economic systems with varying degrees of success. As emerging nations attempt to flex their political and economic muscles, they cause changes in the traditional ways of conducting international business.

Developing nations often insist that an increasing **proportion** of assembling and manufacturing be conducted within their own borders. Because the national governments of these countries play a substantial role in expanding their economies, these governments are able to exert considerable influence over outside firms desiring to do business within their borders. [2] National governments want their share of the supply chain's activity, and these governments are becoming more insistent that much of their foreign trade be carried on vessels or planes owned by companies headquartered within their boundaries. Governments want local firms to have at least a fair share of revenues from the sale of freight forwarding services, marine insurance, and other distribution functions.

Traditionally, the United States has been a major exporter of manufactured goods and agricultural products. Because of its wealth, the United States has also imported many consumer goods. Over the past 25 years, the United States has seen increasing annual trade deficits, which signifies that the dollar value of imports exceeds the dollar value of exports. Some of the key contributors to the U.S. trade deficit involve heavy importation of clothing, crude oil, office equipment, televisions and related electronic equipment, as well as automotive vehicles. [3] Moreover, the United States currently runs trade deficits with the majority of its key trading partners; for example, during 2006, the U.S. trade deficit with China was approximately $230 billion.

It's important to recognize that international logistics is both more costly and more challenging than domestic logistics. One reason for the increased cost is that the relevant documentation requirements for international shipments are more substantial (i.e., a greater number of documents) and more complex than those associated with domestic shipments. [4] In addition, international logistics is characterized by greater distances between origin and destination points, which means that managers must consider trade-offs between transportation and inventory holding costs. Although faster transportation between origin and destination will lead to lower inventory holding costs, faster transportation is generally associated with higher transportation costs, and the converse is true for slower transportation options.

The challenges associated with international logistics come from a number of sources. Economic conditions, such as changes in the relative value of **currencies**, have a **profound** effect on international trade patterns. When one country's currency is weak relative to other currencies, it becomes more costly to import products, but exports often surge; when one country's currency is strong relative to other currencies, the reverse occurs. [5] Differences between countries in regulations, laws, and legal systems also add to the challenges of international logistics, and the degree of enforcement of existing regulations and laws is not uniform from country to country.

拓展资源

New Words

1. domestic   *adj.*家庭的;国内的;驯养的   *n.*佣人;家仆
2. obligation   *n.*义务;责任
3. economic   *adj.*经济学的;经济的;有利可图的
4. proportion   *n.*部分;比例;均衡;(复)规模   *vt.*使成比例;使均衡;分摊
5. profound   *adj.*深奥的;渊博的;极度的;意义深远的
6. currency   *n.*货币

Phrases

1. international logistics   国际物流
2. finished product   最终产品
3. assembly operations   装备作业
4. in bond   保税
5. trade deficit   贸易赤字
6. crude oil   原油
7. holding cost   持有成本

Notes

1. For example, goods moving by truck between Detroit and Buffalo or between the Lower 48 states and Alaska, through Canada, travel in bond, which means that the carrier handling them has a special legal obligation to keep them sealed and to make certain that they are not released for sale or use within the country through which they are traveling.

例如,在底特律和布法罗之间往来的货物,或在美国低纬度的 48 个州和阿拉斯加州之间途经加拿大往来的货物是以保税的方式以卡车运送的,也就是说负责这些货物的承运人要承担特殊的法律责任,将货物密封并确保在途经其他国家时不把货物拆开进行销售或使用。

2. Developing nations often insist that an increasing proportion of assembling and manufacturing be conducted within their own borders. Because the national governments of these countries play a substantial role in expanding their economies, these governments are able to exert considerable influence over outside firms desiring to do business within their borders.

发展中国家坚持在本国进行的装配和制造越来越多。因为这些国家的中央政府在其经济发展过程中起着重要的作用,所以这些政府能够对希望在其境内从事贸易的外国企业施加重大的影响。

3. Some of the key contributors to the U.S. trade deficit involve heavy importation of clothing, crude oil, office equipment, televisions and related electronic equipment, as well as automotive vehicles.

造成美国贸易赤字的一些重要成因包括服装、原油、办公设备、电视和相关电子设备以及机动车辆的大量进口。

4. One reason for the increased cost is that the relevant documentation requirements for international shipments are more substantial (i.e., a greater number of documents) and more complex than those associated with domestic shipments.

成本增加的一个原因是国际货运相关单证的要求比国内货运要更多(也就是单证数量更多)而且更复杂。

5. When one country's currency is weak relative to other currencies, it becomes more costly to import products, but exports often surge; when one country's currency is strong relative to other currencies, the reverse occurs.

当一个国家的货币相对其他货币处于弱势时,进口产品变得成本更高,但出口通常会猛增;而当一个国家的货币相对其他货币处于强势时,会出现相反的情形。

Section B　Risk in International Logistics　国际物流风险

In addition to time to market and inventory risks, events of recent years have forced companies to adapt to the new supply chain reality of expecting the unexpected. Companies are not only responding to current **volatility** and **geopolitical** risks, but also developing new risk management approaches based upon the realization that decades of globalizing supply chains has come at a price: a heightened and different risk profile.

Geopolitical threats

The 2003 **SARS** crisis and the second Gulf War were major events in and of themselves; they were also **consecutive** and made huge impacts on supply chain continuity and execution feasibility. [1] Trade routes had to be altered and global travel was limited. In addition to that, structurally heightened government security measures and screening are indicators of risks involved in international logistics. Logistics making the global economy a reality can never be a given and a non-issue that deserves no second thought.

Transportation breakdowns

Transportation may be a commodity, which does not mean that it is a given and that nothing can go wrong. A several-week strike in the US west coast ports in 2002 lasted long enough to almost cripple the US economy. With hundreds of cargo ships floating outside the ports shipments were not arriving at US destinations. This meant that factories were shut down and stores were emptying. It also had a ripple effect on global trade overall. For example: return shipments were not happening because no ships were leaving the ports either. With so many ships and containers tied up other routes could not be served either. And in fact a resulting global shortage of containers caused a slowdown of shipments in many other port regions. So shipments on other routes, in different harbours and even shipments using different modalities were affected.

Risk and security concerns are not a one-time issue but require a continuous risk management process [2]. Helferich and Cook (2003) found that this is much needed because for example：

- only about 61 percent of US firms have disaster recovery plans；
- among those that do typically cover data centers, only about 12 percent cover total organizational recovery；
- few plans include steps to keep a supply chain operational；
- only about 28 percent of companies have formed crisis management teams, and even fewer have supply chain security teams；
- an estimated 43 percent of businesses that suffer a fire or other serious damage never reopen for business after the event. [3]
- According to Helferich and Cook (2003) this can partially be explained by the fact that there are competing business issues, and managers might not recognize their vulnerability and might assume that the government will bail them out. Peck (2003) has published a **self-assessment** for supply chain risk and an operational level tool kit.

New Words

1. industrialized   *adj.*工业化的；动词 industrialize 的过去式和过去分词形式
2. volatility   *n.*挥发性；挥发度；轻快；(性格)反复无常
3. consecutive   *adj.*连续的；连贯的
4. geopolitical   *adj.*地理政治学的
5. SARS   *n.*Severe Acate Respiratory Syndromes 的缩写，传染性非典型肺炎
6. self-assessment   *n.*自我评估

Phrases

1. the second Gulf War   第二次海湾战争
2. execution feasibility   执行可行性
3. global economy   全球经济
4. the US west coast ports   美国西海岸港口
5. disaster recovery plans   灾难恢复计划
6. crisis management teams   危机管理小组

Notes

1. The 2003 SARS crisis and the second Gulf War were major events in and of themselves；they were also consecutive and made huge impacts on supply chain continuity and execution feasibility.

2003 年 SARS 危机和第二次海湾战争本身就是重大事件。同时对供应链的连续性和执行可行性带来了可持续和重大的影响。

2. Risk and security concerns are not a one-time issue but require a continuous risk management process.

风险和安全问题不是一个一次性问题,而是需要一个持续的风险管理过程。

3. An estimated 43 percent of businesses that suffer a fire or other serious damage never reopen for business after the event.

估计有43%的企业遭受火灾或其他严重损伤之后就倒闭了。

Section C Political Restriction on Trade 贸易的政治限制

Political restrictions on trade can take a variety of forms. Many nations ban certain types of shipments that might jeopardize their national security; for example, the United States does not ship military equipment or strategic materials to certain nations. [1] Likewise, individual nations may band together to pressure another country to not be an active supplier of materials that could be used to build nuclear weapons. Some nations **restrict** the **outflow** of **currency** because a nation's economy will suffer if it imports more than it exports over a long term. These regulations are not concerned with specific commodities; rather, they are concerned with restricting the outflow of money. All imports require advance approval, and goods that arrive without prior approval are not allowed to enter.

A relatively common political restriction on trade involves **tariffs**, or taxes that governments place on the importation of certain items. Tariffs are often established to protect local manufacturers, producers, or growers, and once tariff **barriers** are built, they are not easily torn down. [2] Sometimes, the tariff the importing nation charges differs according to the nation from which the good is coming. From an international sourcing standpoint, this influences the choice of production site.

Another group of political restrictions on trade can be **classified** as nontariff **barriers**, which refer to restrictions other than tariffs that are placed on imported products. [3] One type of nontariff barrier is an import quota, which limits the amount or product (either in units or by value) that may be imported from any country during a period of time. The health and safety of a country's population often provides "convenient" reasons for applying nontariff barriers. Many nations are concerned with stopping the spread of plant and animal diseases and therefore **inspect** various commodities or products to make certain that they do not contain these problems. If material is found to be infested, it cannot enter the country until it is cleaned. Entry of other products may be prohibited because they do not meet safety standards. For example, because of the danger of earthquakes in Japan, upright refrigerators must be built so that they will remain upright, even when tilted as much as 10 degrees.

Another political restriction on trade, due to political tensions, involves **embargoes**, or the prohibition of trade between particular countries. [4] For example, U.S. trade with Cuba has been banned since the late 1950s (corresponding to Fidel Castro's rise to Cuban prime **minister** and installation of a **socialistic** government). In a similar fashion, because of long-standing political tensions, Israel and several Arab nations do not trade with each other, and this embargo has been extended to include nations that are sympathetic, or provide support, to Israel.

New Words

1. restrict　*vt.*限制;约束
2. currency　*n.*货币;流通
3. tariff　*n.*关税
4. barrier　*n.*栅栏;障碍物;屏障
5. classified　*adj.*分类的;类别的;机密的
6. inspect　*v.*检查;视察
7. minister　*n.*外交使节;部长;大臣;牧师　*v.*照顾;给予帮助
8. socialistic　*adj.*社会主义的
9. outflow　*n.*外流
10. embargo　*n.*禁运

Phrases

1. nuclear weapon　核武器
2. specific commodity　特定商品
3. nontariff barrier　非关税壁垒
4. imported quota　进口配额
5. safety standard　安全标准
6. upright refrigerator　立柜式冰箱
7. long-standing political tension　长期政治紧张

Notes

1. Many nations ban certain types of shipments that might jeopardize their national security; for example, the United States does not ship military equipment or strategic materials to certain nations.

很多国家会禁止运送某些可能危害国家安全的货物。例如,美国不许将军用设备或战略物资运往一些特定的国家。

2. Tariffs are often established to protect local manufacturers, producers, or growers, and once tariff barriers are built, they are not easily torn down.

关税的设立通常是为了保护本地的制造商、生产商或种植者,而且一旦建立了关税堡垒,就不容易被消除。

3. Another group of political restrictions on trade can be classified as nontariff barriers, which refer to restrictions other than tariffs that are placed on imported products.

另外一种对贸易的政治限制可以归类为非关税壁垒,指的是施加在进口产品之上除关税之外的限制。

4. Another political restriction on trade, due to political tensions, involves embargoes, or the prohibition of trade between particular countries.

另外一种对贸易的政治限制是因为政治关系紧张而导致的禁运,或特定国家之间的贸易禁止。

Section D Government's Role in International Transport
政府在国际贸易中的作用

As in other aspects of international business, governments are more **involved** in international transportation than they are in domestic transportation. One reason for this is that ocean carriers and international airlines can operate as extensions of a nation's economy, and most of the revenue they receive flows into that nation's economy. [1] To that nation, international **carriage** functions as an export with **favorable** effects on the nation's balance of payments. However, to the nation on the other end of the shipment, the effect is opposite because it must import the transport service, and this has an adverse impact on its balance-of-payments position. Some nations with very weak balance-of-payments positions issue an import license, or permit, on the condition that the goods move on a vessel or plane flying that nation's flag, which means it is importing only the goods, not the transportation service required to carry them. [2] Situations such as this dictate carrier choice.

With respect to water transportation, many nations provide subsidies, train their own merchant marine officers, absorb portions of the costs of building commercial vessels, and engage in other activities to promote their own merchant fleets. [3] Governments also support their own carriers through cargo preference rules, which require a certain **percentage** of traffic to move on a nation's flag vessels.

Historically, many international airlines were owned and operated by their national government; examples include Air India, Air China, and Alitalia (owned by the Italian government). However, over the past 20 years some government-owned international carriers have moved to the private sector, a process called **privatization**. A successful example of this process is British Airways (formerly British Overseas Airways Corporation, or BOAC), which was privatized by the British government in the late 1980s.

New Words

1. involved   *adj.*涉及的;牵连的;复杂的;感情投入的;有密切关系的;动词 involve 的过去式和过去分词

2. carriage   *n.*四轮马车;客车车厢;运输;运费;举止;托架

3. favorable   *adj.*有利的;顺利的;良好的;赞同的

4. percentage   *n.*百分率;比例;部分;好处

5. privatization   *n.*私有化

Phrases

1. international transportation   国际运输
2. domestic transportation   国内运输
3. balance of payment   收支差额
4. commercial vessel   商船队
5. cargo preference   货物优先运送
6. British Overseas Airways Corporation（BOAC）   英国海外航空公司

Notes

1. One reason for this is that ocean carriers and international airlines can operate as extensions of a nation's economy, and most of the revenue they receive flows into that nation's economy.

其中一个原因是远洋承运人和国际航空公司可以被视为一个国家的经济延伸,而且他们的大多数收入会流入那个国家的经济系统。

2. Some nations with very weak balance-of-payments positions issue an import license, or permit, on the condition that the goods move on a vessel or plane flying that nation's flag, which means it is importing only the goods, not the transportation service required to carry them.

一些国际收支差额地位非常低的国家会签发一种进口许可证,或通行证,但条件是货物是通过悬挂该国国旗的船或飞机来运输的,这意味着其进口的只是货物,而不是运送它们所需的运输服务。

3. With respect to water transportation, many nations provide subsidies, train their own merchant marine officers, absorb portions of the costs of building commercial vessels, and engage in other activities to promote their own merchant fleets.

至于水路运输,许多国家会提供补贴,培训它们自己的商船指挥官,负担建造商船的一部分成本,以及参与其他活动来促进本国商船队的发展。

Section E   International Logistics Strategies   国际物流战略

Just as international logistics services are a **component** of the entire value and are dependent on other value activities, the international logistics strateg y is an element of the internationalization strategy of manufacturing companies.[1] The decision about which international logistics strategy to choose can be made only within the context of the overarching internationalization strategy.

International logistics activities increase as indirect **exports** become direct exports. They reach their peak when a company **assembles** products abroad or conducts some form of international production.[2] They decrease as other types of international production are conducted and global management is performed.

The international market entry of a production company is used here as an example. The following table (Table 11-1) shows how an international logistics, strategy can be **formulated** in the selection of an international strategy of a manufacturing company.

Extending logistics activities beyond a country's borders **represents** something more to a company than lengthening its transport distances.[3] For instance, it must determine how the goods are to be shipped abroad. Another question that must be **addressed** is whether the company itself will become active internationally or whether an external expert will be brought in. In the end, all of these questions can be answered only within the context of the company's **overarching** strategy for its international activities. A strategy can be developed only by considering all factors.[4]

Table 11-1 International Logistics Strategy

International strategy of a manufacturing company	International logistics strategy
Indirect exports by a domestic export company and/or an International Import company.	The company does not create a special international system. Rather, it manages the flow of goods and information with its national logistics system or with external logistics system.
Direct exports through licensed production abroad	The company can avoid creating an international system. Unlike indirect exports, though, more influence can be exerted on the supplier service being offered. This is because the supplier requirements that must be fulfilled can be part of the license contract.
Direct exports with direct investment in an international logistics system	As part of direct exports, the company making the investment can operate a traditional logistics system with one or more warehouses serving inventory or distribution functions. International customers are supplied directly from the country of origin with the help of fast means of transport.
International assembly or production through joint ventures or a company's own plant	Atypical example of international assembly is "CKD production" in the automotive industry. Vehicle components of defined production steps are turned into subsets and exported on certain countries for assembly. The supply operation for CKD assembly plants places special demands on packaging, fright costs and delivery scheduling. If the international operation consists of production being undertaken in a customer's country for this one particular nation, then the company making the investment will face no new logistics problems.
Global companies with centralized and/or decentralized management	Global markets with homogeneous products can lead to lower logistics unit costs if costs associated with order processing, packaging, inventories and warehousing fall as a result of standardization. They can also generate higher logistics unit cost if the communication and transport costs of supplying world markets rise.

New Words

1. component　*n.* 组成部分;成分;部件
2. export　*n.* 出口;输出;出口产品;输出品
3. assemble　*v.* 装配;组装
4. formulate　*v.* 制订;规划;构想;准备
5. represent　*v.* 代表
6. address　*v.* 设法解决;处理;对付
7. overarching　*adj.* 非常重要的;首要的

Phrases

1. international logistics service　国际物流服务
2. manufacturing company　制造公司
3. domestic export company　国内出口公司
4. International Import company　国际进口公司
5. centralized management　集中管理
6. decentralized management　分散管理

Notes

1. Just as international logistics services are a component of the entire value and are dependent on other value activities, the international logistics strategy is an element of the internationalization strategy of manufacturing companies.

正如国际物流服务是整个价值活动的组成部分并依赖于其他价值活动一样,国际物流战略也是制造企业国际化战略的一个组成部分。

2. International logistics activities increase as indirect exports become direct exports. They reach their peak when a company assembles products abroad or conducts some form of international production.

随着间接出口变为直接出口,国际物流活动也随之增加。当一家公司在国外组装产品或进行某种形式的国际生产时,国际物流活动达到了顶峰。

3. Extending logistics activities beyond a country's borders represents something more to a company than lengthening its transport distances.

将物流活动扩展到一个国家的边界之外,对一个公司来说,比延长运输距离更重要。

4. In the end, all of these questions can be answered only within the context of the company's overarching strategy for its international activities. A strategy can be developed only by considering all factors.

最后,所有这些问题只能在公司国际活动的总体战略框架内得到回答。只有综合考虑所有因素,才能制定出战略。

🎯 Core Concepts　核心概念

1. International logistics is a result of international commercial activities, cross border investment, and importing and exporting activities.

国际物流是国际商业活动,跨国投资及进出口活动的结果。

2. International transport is the major part in international logistics.

国际运输是国际物流活动的主要部分。

3. International transport is dominated by water carriers. It is used to transport more than 70% of the total trading volume in value and 95% by weight.

国际运输中水运占支配地位,它占70%贸易总值和95%贸易总量。

4. International transportation by trucks is limited between the joint border countries (regions) like US and Mexico or closely located WTO members like mainland China, Hong Kong and Macao.

采用卡车进行国际运输限于边界相邻的国家(地区)间,如美国和墨西哥;或者位置相近的WTO成员间,如中国内地、香港和澳门地区。

📝 Exercises　练习

Ⅰ. Answer the following questions in English.

1. What is the definition of International logistics?

2. Explain how developing nations ensure that an increasing proportion of supply chain activities are conducted within their borders.

3. Discuss some of the challenges associated with international logistics.

4. What are the risks that the international logistics are facing?

5. What are some key political restrictions on cross-border trade?

6. Discuss the roles that a particular country's government might play in international transport.

Ⅱ. Fill in the bank with the proper words or expressions.

1. Goods are partially assembled in one country and then shipped to another, _____ they are further assembled or processed.

　　A. which　　　　B. that　　　　　C. as　　　　　　D. where

2. The firm is global in outlook and sees almost all nations as being markets, _____ of supply, or sites for markets or for assembly operations.

　　A. sources　　　B. resources　　　C. sauce　　　　D. causes

3. Until World War Ⅱ, the concepts of international trade were simple. Industrialized

powers maintained political and economic colonies that were sources of _____ materials, cheap labor, and markets for manufactured products.

  A. crude   B. original   C. raw   D. previous

  4. National governments want their share of the supply chain's activity, and these governments are becoming more insistent that much of their foreign trade _____ carried on vessels or planes owned by companies headquartered within their boundaries.

  A. was   B. were   C. is   D. be

  5. Because of its wealth, the United States has also _____ many consumer goods.

  A. exported   B. grown   C. imported   D. manufactured

  6. The challenges _____ with international logistics come from a number of sources.

  A. associated B. related   C. along   D. together

  7. Logistics making the _____ economy a reality can never be a given and a non- issue that deserves no second thought.

  A. local   B. global   C. national   D. domestic

  8. So shipments on other _____ in different harbours and even shipments using different modalities were affected.

  A. ways   B. methods   C. routes   D. clues

  9. These regulations are not _____ with specific commodities; rather, they are concerned with restricting the outflow of money.

  A. associated B. consistent C. concerning D. concerned

  10. From an international sourcing _____, this influences the choice of production site.

  A. opinion   B. standpoint C. idea   D. point

  11. Many nations are concerned with stopping the spread of _____ and animal diseases and therefore inspect various commodities or products to make certain that they do not contain these problems.

  A. biology   B. living   C. creature   D. plant

  12. With _____ to water transportation, many nations provide subsidies, train their own merchant marine officers, absorb portions of the costs of building commercial vessels, and engage in other activities to promote their own merchant fleets.

  A. respect   B. aspect   C. concern   D. reference

  13. Historically, many international airlines were _____ and operated by their national government.

  A. owed   B. owned   C. controlled D. dominated

  14. Governments also support their own carriers through cargo _____ rules, which require a certain percentage of traffic to move on a nation's flag vessels.

  A. reference   B. persistence C. preference D. liking

  15. However, over the past 20 years some government-owned international carriers have moved to the private sector, a process called _____.

A. private　　　　B. public　　　　C. common　　　　D. privatization

Ⅲ. Match each word on the left with its corresponding meaning on the right.

A.	**B.**
1. exert	(a) the act of performing
2. deficit	(b) put to use
3. documentation	(c) a sheltered port where ships can take on or discharge cargo
4. currency	(d) self-evaluation
5. execution	(e) an unstable situation of extreme danger or difficulty
6. harbor	(f) the property of being an amount by which something is less than expected or required
7. crisis	(g) a government tax on imports or exports
8. self-assessment	(h) a principle that limits the extent of something
9. restriction	(i) the metal or paper medium of exchange that is presently used
10. tariff	(j) confirmation that some fact or statement is true through the use of documentary evidence

Ⅳ. Match the following definitions with the corresponding terms below.

safety	balance	assembled	challenges	boundaries
unexpected	band	earthquakes	political	domestic

1. It is increasingly difficult to separate the practices of _____ and international logistics. International logistics—logistics activities associated with goods that are sold across national boundaries.

2. Goods are partially in one country _____ and then shipped to another, where they are further assembled or processed.

3. World War Ⅱ brought an end to the colonial system; since then, emerging nations have attempted to develop their own _____ and economic systems with varying degrees of success.

4. National governments want their share of the supply chain's activity, and these governments are becoming more insistent that much of their foreign trade be carried on vessels or planes owned by companies headquartered within their _____.

5. The _____ associated with international logistics come from a number of sources. Economic conditions, such as changes in the relative value of currencies, have a profound effect on international trade patterns.

6. In addition to market and inventory risks, events of recent years have forced companies to adapt to the new supply chain reality of expecting the _____.

7. Likewise, individual nations may _____ together to pressure another country to not

be an active supplier of materials that could be used to build nuclear weapons.

8. The health and _____ of a country's population often provides "convenient" reasons for applying nontariff barriers.

9. For example, because of the danger of _____ in Japan, upright refrigerators must be built so that they will remain upright, even when tilted as much as 10 degrees.

10. To that nation, international carriage functions as an export with favorable effects on the nation's _____ of payments.

Ⅴ. Translate the following sentences into Chinese.

1. The United States is the world's largest economy and the largest exporter and importer.

2. The theme of this year's Report is "Trade in a Globalizing World".

3. The 2008 Report provide as a reminder of what we know about the gains from international trade and highlights the challenges arising from higher levels of integration.

4. The 2008 Report asks why some countries have managed to take advantages of falling trade costs and greater policy-driven trading opportunities while others have remained largely outside international commercial relations.

5. The 2008 report addresses a range of interlinking questions, including a consideration of what constitutes globalization, what drives it, what benefits it brings, what challenge it poses.

Ⅵ. Translate the following sentences into English.

1. 经济全球化是指世界经济活动超越国界,通过对外贸易、资本流动、技术转移、提供服务、相互依存、相互联系而形成的全球范围内的有机经济整体。

2. 经济全球化趋势已成为世界经济和国际形势发展的一个突出特点。

3. 跨国公司在全球范围内的企业生产过程布局达到了新的水平。

4. 跨国公司内部生产、贸易和投资应分别占世界生产的2/3、世界贸易总量的70%和世界投资总额的80%以上。

5. 在中国对外贸易的构成中,加工贸易比重已占中国进出口总额的50%以上。

Ⅶ. Fill in the blanks with words from the list below and each word can be used once.

DHL is a leading global ___1___ delivery and logistics service provider. Founded in 1969 and ___2___ in Brussels, Belgium, DHL is part of the Deutsche Post World Net (DPWN) group, one of the largest shipping consortia in the world. Since 2003, DPWN has ___3___ its ___4___ including DHL, Danzas Air and Ocean, and Euro Express, to form the new DHL, which now ___5___ 220 countries and ___6___ with over 120,000 delivery points, its own fleet of 250 planes, 60,000 miscellaneous ground ___7___, 118 hubs, and over 170,000 ___8___ around the world. In 1998 it was voted the "most globalized company" by Global Finance magazine.

The operational performance of DHL Taiwan is often ranked among the ___9___ 15 of all of

DHL's overseas operations, and has been recognized by DHL's global headquarters. It is clear from the ___10___ performance achieved by DHL Taiwan in these global performance assessments that Chinese Taiwan occupies an important position in the global shipping business.

A) headquartered	B) vehicles	C) express
D) employees	E) consolidated	F) regions
G) employers	H) subsidiaries	I) top
J) outstanding	K) solid	L) high
M) excellent	N) serves	O) process

Chapter 12

Logistics Documentation
物 流 文 件

Section A   The Letter of Credit   信用证

A letter of credit is a document issued mostly by a financial institution, such as a bank, which usually provides an **irrevocable** payment **undertaking** (it can also be **revocable**, **confirmed**, **unconfirmed**, **transferable** or others) to a beneficiary against complying documents as stated in the Letter of Credit. [1] On the other hand, it also assures the buyer that he is not required to pay until the seller ships the goods. [2] It is thus a **catalyst** that provides the buyer and the seller with mutual protection in dealing with each other.

Letter of Credit is abbreviated as LC or L/C, and often is referred to as a documentary credit, abbreviated as DC or D/C.

The Benefits of Using a Letter of Credit in International Trade

Firstly, it improves negotiating status: Issuing of L/C means that importer provides the exporter with conditional payment commitment of the bank in addition to **commercial** credit. [3] It improves credit and negotiating status of the importer, so may be able to negotiate for a lower purchase price and better terms. [4]

Secondly, it ensures that the goods supplied are the goods ordered.

Thirdly, it reduces occupied capital.

Parties of a Letter of Credit

拓展资源

Applicant: on behalf of a buyer.

Beneficiary: the seller who is to receive the money.

Issuing bank: a bank that gives payment undertaking.

Advising bank: usually a foreign **correspondent** bank of the issuing bank that will advise the beneficiary.

Confirming bank: the correspondent bank that may **confirm** the letter of credit for the beneficiary.

The Operation of Handling a Letter of Credit

The process of handling a letter of credit is illustrated by Figure 12-1.

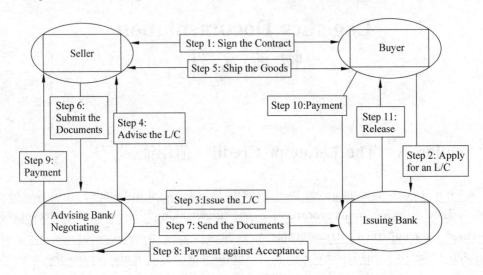

Figure 12-1　The Process of Handling a Letter of Credit

New Words

1. catalyst　*n.*催化剂;刺激因素

2. commercial　*adj.*商业的　*n.*商业广告

3. correspondent　*n.*通讯记者;通信者　*adj.*与……一致的;相应的

4. confirm　*v.*证实;批准;确定

5. undertaking　*n.*事业

6. irrevocable　*adj.*不能撤销的

7. revocable　*adj.*可撤销的

8. confirmed　*adj.*认证的

9. unconfirmed　*adj.*未认证的

10. transferable　*adj.*可转让的

11. applicant　*n.*申请人

12. beneficiary　*n.*受益人

Phrases

1. letter of credit　信用证

2. mutual protection　相互保护

3. documentary credit　(DC 或 D/C)跟单信用证

4. issuing bank　开证行

5. advising bank   通知行

6. confirming bank   确认行

Notes

1. A letter of credit is a document issued mostly by a financial institution, such as a bank, which usually provides an irrevocable payment undertaking (it can also be revocable, confirmed, unconfirmed, transferable or others) to a beneficiary against complying documents as stated in the Letter of Credit.

信用证多数是由金融机构开具的,比如银行,通常能为受益人在提交信用证规定文件时提供不可撤销的支付担保(它也可以是可撤销的、可保兑的、不可保兑的、可转换的或其他类型)。

2. On the other hand, it also assures the buyer that he is not required to pay until the seller ships the goods.

另一方面,它也可以保证买方直到卖方发出货物之后才支付货款。

3. Issuing of L/C means that importer provides the exporter with conditional payment commitment of the bank in addition to commercial credit.

开具信用证意味着进口商向出口商提供一种商业信用之外的有条件的银行支付承诺。

4. It improves credit and negotiating status of the importer, so may be able to negotiate for a lower purchase price and better terms.

它改进了进口商的信用和谈判地位,所以可以(与出口商)谈判争取更低的购买价格与更好的条款。

📚 Section B   Contract   合同

Contract has different names called, and it is called Sales Confirmation or Agreement. Contract is some terms **restricted** formed between buyer and seller about criterion to buying and selling, and both of sides will have responsibility for each other as long as contract is signed. In the international trade, contract is used along with letter of credit generally. Its main contents of contract including:

1) Name of contract both in (Chinese and English) such as Sales Confirmation or Contract.

2) Name and address of buyer and seller.

3) No. and date of contract.

4) Name of commodity, specification, shipping mark and packaging.

5) Delivery quantity.

6) Terms of price, unit price and amount .

7) Terms of shipping, such as time of shipping, port of loading and port of **destination**.

8) Terms of payment.

9) Insurance and claim.

10) Signature of buyer and seller.

New Words

1. restricted   *adj.*有受限制的;(土地)对公众不完全开放的;保密的;*v.*限制(restrict 的过去式)

2. destination   *n.*目的,目标;目的地,终点;[罕用语]预定,指定

Phrases

1. name of contract   合同名称

2. name and address of buyer and seller   买卖双方的名称、地址

3. No. and date of contract   合同编号、日期

4. name of commodity, specification, shipping mark and packaging   货物名称、规格型号、唛头及包装

5. delivery quantity   交易数量

6. terms of price, unit price and amount   价格条款、单价和总金额

7. terms of shipping, such as time of shipping, port of loading and port of destination   装运条款,如装运日期、起运港、目的地

8. terms of payment   付款条件

9. insurance and claim   保险和索赔

10. signature of buyer and seller   买卖双方签署

Section C   Issue of Document Credit   开具跟单信用证

Issue of a Documentary Credit		
		BKCHCNBJA08E SESSION: 000 ISN: 000000 BANK OF CHINA (GUANGDONG) NO. 5, ZHONGSHAN ROAD, YUEXIU DISTRICT, GUANGZHOU, CHINA
Destination Bank		BANK OF OSAKA (NEW YORK) NO. 216, AUMAHU, AKI GUN, OSAKA, JAPAN
Type of Documentary Credit	40 A	IRREVOCABLE
Letter of Credit Number	20	LC06E0087/06
Date of Issue	31G	060916
Date and Place of Expiry	31D	061015 JAPAN
Applicant Bank	51D	BANK OF CHINA GUANGDONG BRANCH
Applicant	50	VICTORY CORPORATION, C.P.O.BOX 110 OSAKA JAPAN
Currency Code, Amount	32B	USD 500 000.00

Available with …by …	41D	ANY BANK BY NEGOTIATION
Drafts at	42C	45 DAYS AFTER SIGHT
Drawee	42D	BANK OF CHINA GUANGDONG BRANCH
Partial Shipments	43P	NOT ALLOWED
Transshipment	43T	NOT ALLOWED
Shipping on Board/ Dispatch/Packing in Charge at/from		44A OSAKA, JAPAN
Transportation to	44B	GUANGDONG PORT, P.R.CHINA
Latest Date of Shipment	44C	060927

Description of Goods or Services: 45A-MEDICAL EQUIPMENT PACKED WITH WOODEN CASES
USD50,000/SET CFR GUANGZHOU
QUANTITY: 10 SETS
Documents Required: 46A
1. SIGNED COMMERCIAL INVOICE IN 5 COPIES.
2. FULL SET OF CLEAN ON BOARD OCEAN BILLS OF LADING MADE OUT TO ORDER AND BLANK ENDORSED, MARKED "FREIGHT PREPAID" NOTIFYING GUANGDONG OCEAN CY CO., LTD. TEL: (86)20-3880 ××××
3. PACKING LIST/WEIGHT MEMO IN 4 COPIES INDICATING QUANTITY/GROSS AND NET WEIGHTS OF EACH PACKAGE AND PACKING CONDITIONS AS CALLED FOR BY THE L/C.
4. CERTIFICATE OF QUALITY IN 3 COPIES ISSUED BY PUBLIC RECOGNIZED SURVEYOR.
5. BENEFICIARY'S CERTIFIED COPY OF FAX DISPATCHED TO THE ACCOUNTEE WITH 3 DAYS AFTER SHIPMENT ADVISING NAME OF VESSEL, DATE, QUANTITY, WEIGHT, VALUE OF SHIPMENT, L/C NUMBER AND CONTRACT NUMBER.
6. CERTIFICATE OF ORIGIN IN 3 COPIES ISSUED BY AUTHORIZED INSTITUTION.
7. CERTIFICATE OF HEALTH IN 3 COPIES ISSUED BY AUTHORIZED INSTITUTION.

Additional Instructions: 47 A
1. CHARTER PARTY B/L AND THIRD PARTY DOCUMENTS ARE ACCEPTABLE.
2. SHIPMENT PRIOR TO L/C ISSUING DATE IS ACCEPTABLE.
3. BOTH QUANTITY AND AMOUNT 10 PERCENT MORE OR LESS ARE ALLOWED.

Charges	71B	ALL BANKING CHARGES OUTSIDE THE OPENING BANK ARE FOR BENEFICIARY'S ACCOUNT.
Period of Presentation	48	DOCUMENT MUST BE PRESENTED WITHIN 15 DAYS AFTER THE DATE OF ISSUANCE OF THE TRANSPORT DOCUMENTS BUT WITHIN THE VALDITY OF THE CREDIT
Confirmation Instructions	49	WITHOUT

Instructions to the Paying/Accepting/Negotiating Bank:
1. ALL DOCUMENTS TO BE FORWARDED IN ONE COVER, UNLESS OTHERWISE STATED ABOVE.
2. DISCREPANT DOCUMENT FEE OF USD 50.00 OR EQUAL CURRENCY WILL BE DEDUCTED FROM DRAWING IF DOCUMENTS WITH DISCREPANCIES ARE ACCEPTED.

"Advertising Through" Bank	57A	BANK OF OSAKA (NEW YORK) NO. 216, AUMAHU, AKI _ GUN, OSAKA, JAPAN

Notes

1. Issue of a Documentary Credit　开具跟单信用证

2. Destination Bank　通知行

3. Letter of Credit Number　信用证号

4. Date of Issue　开证日期

5. Date and Place of Expiry　信用证失效日期和地点

6. Applicant Bank　申请开证行

7. Currency Code，Amount　信用证结算的币种和金额

8. Drafts at：45 DAYS AFTER SIGHT　汇票支付期限：45 天期限

9. Drawee　汇票支付人

10. Partial Shipments　分批装运

11. Latest Date of Shipment　最迟装船日期

12. Transshipment　转运

13. MEDICAL EQUIPMENT PACKED WITH WOODEN CASES USD50，000/SET CFR GUANGZHOU QUANTITY：10 SETS. 以木板箱包装的医疗设备，每套 CFR 广州价格 50，000 美元，共 10 套。

14. SIGNED COMMERCIAL INVOICE IN 5 COPIES. 签章的商业发票一式五份。

15. FULL SET OF CLEAN ON BOARD OCEAN BILLS OF LADING MADE OUT TO ORDER AND BLANK ENDORSED，MARKED "FREIGHT PREPAID" NOTIFYING GUANGDONG OCEAN CY CO.，LTD. TEL：(86)20-3880×××. 一整套已装船清洁提单，抬头为空白背书，且注明"运费已付"，通知人为广东海洋 CY 有限公司，电话(86)20-3880×××。

16. PACKING LIST/WEIGHT MEMO IN 4 COPIES INDICATING QUANTITY/GROSS AND NET WEIGHTS OF EACH PACKAGE AND PACKING CONDITIONS AS CALLED FOR BY THE L/C.装箱单/ 重量清单一式四份，指明数量或每箱毛重、净重以及信用证要求的包装情况。

17. CERTIFICATE OF QUALITY IN 3 COPIES ISSUED BY PUBLIC RECOGNIZED SURVEYOR.由 UBLIC RECOGNIZED SURVEYOR（检验机构）签发的质量证明书一式三份。

18. BENEFICIARY'S CERTIFIED COPY OF FAX DISPATCHED TO THE ACCOUNTEE WITH 3 DAYS AFTER SHIPMENT ADVISING NAME OF VESSEL，DATE，QUANTITY，WEIGHT，VALUE OF SHIPMENT，L/C NUMBER AND CONTRACT NUMBER.受益人证明的传真件，在船开后的三天内已将船名、日期、货物的数量、重量、价值、信用证号和合同号通知付款人。

19. CERTIFICATE OF ORIGIN IN 3 COPIES ISSUED BY AUTHORIZED INSTITUTION. 当局签发的原产地证明一式三份。

20. CERTIFICATEOF HEALTH IN 3 COPIES ISSUED BY AUTHORIZED INSTITUTION.

当局签发的健康/检疫证明一式三份。

21. Additional Instructions 附加指示

22. CHARTER PARTY B/L AND THIRD PARTY DOCUMENTS ARE ACCEPTABLE.租船提单和第三方单据可以接受。

23. SHIPMENT PRIOR TO L/C ISSUING DATE IS ACCEPTABLE.装船期在信用证内有效期内可接受。

24. BOTH QUANTITY AND AMOUNT 10 PERCENT MORE OR LESS ARE ALLOWED.允许数量和金额公差在10%左右。

25. ALL BANKING CHARGES OUTSIDE THE OPENING BANK ARE FOR BENEFICIARY'S ACCOUNT.开证之外的所有银行费用都由受益人承担。

26. DOCUMENTS MUST BE PRESERVED WITHIN 15 DAYS AFTER THE DATE OF ISSUANCE OF THE TRANSPORT DOCUMENTS BUT WITHIN THE VALDITY OF THE CREDIT.文件资料需在运单开出15天内提交,但必须在信用证有效期之内。

27. Instructions to the Paying/Accepting/Negotiating Bank：对付款行、议付行、承兑行的指示

28. ALL DOCUMENTS TO BE FORWARDED IN ONE COVER, UNLESS OTHERWISE STATED ABOVE.所有文件一次寄出,除非以上另有陈述。

29. DISCREPANT DOCUMENT FEE OF USD 50.00 OR EQUAL CURRENCY WILL BE DEDUCTED FROM DRAWING IF DOCUMENTS WITH DISCREPANCIES ARE ACCEPTED.接受不符合点,但需要扣除50美元或其他等值货币。

Section D　E-logistics Document　电子物流文件

E-Documents enable the business to store and manage all information and existing transactions in one **database**, as well as set up individual **portals** for employees, customers, suppliers and **distributors** in a way you want. [1]

On 15 May, 2002, European e-Logistics **hub** Transwide has launched a twDoc e-solution for electronic transport documents.

TwDoc creates an electronic version of the **CMR**, the standard European document in the road transport industry, sharing instantly all data and events recorded on the CMR between supply chain partners.

Transport documents are still often completed manually and, as they travel with the shipments, very little information is available during transit. The CMRs come back to **headquarters** days or weeks later and often need to be **manually** entered into different IT systems. Manual signatures on the CMRs are often the trigger to send invoices as they form the legal **proof** of delivery. Errors arise due to incorrect completion of the document, illegible entries, and linguistic misunderstandings. Post event reporting is also difficult and time consuming, as each individual shipment document must be consulted and noted manually.

The solution is currently being used by Solvin, a joint venture between Solvay and BASF, logistics partners such as De Dijcker and Solvin cusomers such as Deceuninck. Users from these companies **access** twDoc on **PCs** or **PDAs** to create and sign electronic CMRs, from loading and delivery points located in four different European countries.

"TwDoc is dramatically increasing the transparency and efficiency of our logistics processes," said Stephane Metzler, **Statistical** and Logistics Manager of Solvin. "One standard real time platform for in-transit shipments enables us to save costs while providing an unprecedented level of proactive service to both internal and external customers. [2] TwDoc is becoming an essential pillar of our customer satisfaction strategy."

With electronic CMRs, twDoc increases visibility throughout the transport execution process by providing a unique and common source of information. When a shipment is picked up or is in-transit, the ETA (Estimated Time of Arrival) can be immediately provide to the end customer (whether point-of-delivery, warehouses, headquarters, etc). Non-conformities are available online giving clear information about the exact contents of the shipment.

Using electronic signature technology, twDoc enables validation of all information such as real time electronic proofs of pick-up and delivery. [3] It allows complete tracking of the data source and indicates the time of all updates. Dispute resolution becomes easier and more straightforward as irrefutable data is provided. All events trigger optional notifications, giving management by exception its full meaning. [4]

New Words

1. distributor   *n.*分发器,承销商
2. manually   *adv.*用手;手动地
3. proof   *n.*证明;证据;校样   *adj.*防……的;耐……的. *vt.*检验;给……做防护措施
4. access   *n.*入口;通道   *n.*接近(的机会);使用权   *vt.*进入;(计算机)存取
5. statistical   *adj.*统计的;统计学的
6. portal   *n.*入口
7. hub   *n.*网络集线器;网络中心

Phrases

1. E-Documents   电子单据,电子文书
2. database   数据库,资料库
3. electronic version   电子版
4. CMR Code Martrix Reader   代码矩阵阅读器
5. a joint venture   合资企业
6. PCs personal computer   个人电脑
7. PDAs personal digital assistant   个人数字助理
8. management by exception   管理例外

Notes

1. E-Documents enable the business to store and manage all information and existing transactions in one database, as well as set up individual portals for employees, customers, suppliers and distributors in a way you want.

电子文书使企业利用一个数据库就能储存和管理所有的信息和现有交易,也可以按照需要为职员、顾客、供应商和分销商建立单独的入口。

2. One standard real time platform for in-transit shipments enables us to save costs while providing an unprecedented level of proactive service to both internal and external customers.

为运输中的货物建立标准的实时平台,使我们在为内外部客户提供空前的高水平服务的同时节约了成本。

3. Using electronic signature technology, twDoc enables validation of all information such as real time electronic proofs of pick-up and delivery.

运用电子信号技术,广域文档能让我们确认所有的信息,例如收货和运送的实时电子证明。

4. All events trigger optional notifications, giving management by exception its full meaning.

所有事件都有可选告示,从而给例外管理以完整而丰富的内涵。

📚 Section E　How to Write A Good Business Letter
如何写好商业信件

How to write a good letter? It seems difficult to answer this question as business letters deal with so many subjects and are written in so many different circumstances. [1] Some basic principles should be followed.

Firstly, a business letter should be short and to the point.

Before writing a letter, the writer should take a few minutes to list all of the specific points he needs to cover. The letter indicates that the writer has a good grasp of his subject-matter, containing everything that needs to be said and nothing that needs to be omitted. [2] The presentation of the message of the letter should be clear.

Secondly, the writer is as positive, helpful and constructive as circumstances allow him to be. [3]

The writer should consider the needs and the business situation of the reader, putting himself in the reader's position. There is thus a greater chance that the reader will read the letter to the end with interest. Generally speaking, the tone and content of the letter should be appropriate, friendly, formal and factual. [4] Discriminatory or emotional language should be avoided. Make sure that you avoid language that is specific to gender, race or religion in all business letters. For example, "workforce" is better than "manpower", or use "salesperson" rather than "salesman".

Thirdly, use standard or formal layout.

The commonest layout for the business letter today is known as the blocked. [5] The blocked letter style is now popular in the United States and is being increasingly adopted in Britain. In this style all the lines, including those for the date, inside name and address, salutation, subject heading, each paragraph and complimentary close, begin at the left-hand margin with no indentation at all. Business letters with the full block form are always along with open punctuation or mixed punctuations. That means punctuation is often dispensed with in the inside name and address and the salutation. But a comma is necessary between the day and year in the date line and the full stop is retained after the abbreviation such as company, Inc. and Ltd. [6]

Semi-blocked form with each paragraph adopting indented style is the traditional British practice.[7] The heading and the date are usually placed on the right-hand side. In this style the inside name and address is typed in block form, but the paragraphs forming the body of the letter are all indented six or ten spaces. The closing, signature, and printed name are all indented to the right half of the page. The traditional indentation of paragraphs makes clear separation of paragraphs and is thus easy for reading. [8]

Sample (Full Block Style)

CHINA O&R COMPANY
××× Ti Yu Xi Road
Guangzhou (Post Code 510620)
Tel: (020) 38 ××××××
Fax: (020) 38 ××××××

Date: 12 Sep., 2007
Ref: Enquiry for price
The Sales Manager
SL Company
LONDON CC9N 8HA
Dear Sir/Lady
We have learned from Jordan that you manufacture a range of high-fashion dresses in a variety of styles. We operate a quality retail business in China and our sales volume is large. We have chain stores all over the nation.
Would you please provide me a copy of your dress catalogue with details of your prices and payment terms?
Yours faithfully,
Sandra Jones
Manager

New Words

1. circumstance　*n.* 环境,状况,事件
2. grasp　*n.* 把握,抓紧;抓住,紧握,领会
3. omit　*v.* 省略,疏忽,遗漏
4. positive　*adj.* 肯定的,积极的,绝对的;正面的,正数的,阳性的
5. constructive　*adj.* 建设性的,构造上的
6. tone　*n.* 音调,语气,品质;　*vt.* 调和,以特殊腔调说
7. formal　*adj.* 正式的,正规的
8. discriminatory　*adj.* 歧视的,差别对待的
9. emotional　*adj.* 感情的, 情绪的
10. gender　*n.* 性别
11. race　*n.* 种族;赛跑;　*vt.* 赛跑;竞赛
12. religion　*n.* 宗教;宗教信仰
13. workforce　*n.* 劳动力;工人总数
14. manpower　*n.* 人力
15. salesperson　*n.* 售货员
16. indent　*n.* 契约,订货单;　*vt.* 缩排,缩进
17. indentation　*n.* 刻痕(印压,缩进);缩进
18. punctuation　*n.* 标点符号
19. dispense　*v.* 分发;省略
20. comma　*n.* 逗号
21. abbreviation　*adj.* 缩写

Phrases

1. business letter　商业信函
2. be short and to the point　言简意赅
3. have good grasp of　很好地掌握
4. discriminatory or emotional language　歧视性/情感性语言
5. standard or formal layout　正规的格式
6. full block form　齐头式
7. semi-blocked form　半齐头式
8. a range of high-fashion dresses in a variety of styles　系列时尚、多款式的女装
9. chain stores　连锁店

Notes

1. It seems difficult to answer this question as business letters deal with so many subjects and are written in so many different circumstances.

由于商业信函有多种主题而且写作环境多样,这个问题显得难以回答。

2. The letter indicates that the writer has a good grasp of his subject-matter, containing everything that needs to be said and nothing that needs to be omitted.

商业信函反映了作者对主题的良好把握,包含了所有要说的内容而没有冗长啰嗦。

3. Secondly, the writer is as positive, helpful and constructive as circumstances allow him to be.

其次,在条件允许的情况下,作者应尽可能积极、有帮助及有建设性。

4. Generally speaking, the tone and content of the letter should be appropriate, friendly, formal and factual.

一般来说,信中的内容和语气要合适、友好、正规和真实。

5. The commonest layout for the business letter today is known as the blocked.

如今使用最普遍的商业信函格式是齐头式。

6. But a comma is necessary between the day and year in the date line and the full stop is retained after the abbreviation such as company, Inc. and Ltd.

但是日期中的年月日之间的逗号和缩写形式之后的点号——比如"company, Inc.和Ltd."——是必需的。

7. Semi-blocked form with each paragraph adopting indented style is the traditional British practice.

半齐头式是一种传统英式的格式,每个段落都采用缩进格式。

8. The traditional indentation of paragraph makes clear separation of paragraphs and is thus easy for reading.

传统的段落缩进格式使段落分隔清晰,因而方便阅读。

🎯 Core Concepts　核心概念

1. Letter of credit (L/C) is used exclusively by the buyer. It is a letter issued by the bank employed by the buyer which authorizes the bearer (the supplier or seller) to draw a stated amount of money from the issuing bank.

信用证是由银行根据买方要求开立的,受益人可以凭信用证从开证银行取得一定金额的货款。

2. Letter of Credit is issued by the buyer's bank for the importer's benefits.

信用证是为了保证进口方的利益由买方银行开立的。

3. Bill of Lading is a document title.

提单是物权凭证。

4. Ocean Bill of Lading is a receipt for goods loaded in the ship.

海运提单是货物装船的收据。

5. Bill of Lading is evidence of the contract of carriage between carrier and shipper.

提单是承运人和托运人之间运输合同的证明。

6. Seaway Bill is different from Ocean B/L. The latter is negotiable but the former is not.
海运单不同于海运提单，后者可以转让而前者不能。

7. NVOCC is also a carrier because it can issue B/L.
无船承运人也是承运人因为他可以签发提单。

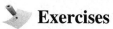 **Exercises** 练习

Ⅰ. Answer the following questions in English.

1. What is the definition of a letter of credit?

2. What are the benefits of using a letter of Credit in international trade?

3. What are the parties of a letter of credit?

4. What does contract refer to?

5. What does the main contents of contract include?

6. What are the advantages of e-documents?

7. How do we usually deal with transport documents?

8. What are the disadvantages of handling documents manually?

9. What is the use of manual signatures on the CMRs?

10. What do you think of twDoc?

Ⅱ. Fill in the bank with the proper words or expressions.

1. Secondly, it _____ that the goods supplied are the goods ordered.

　　A. assures　　　B. sure　　　　C. ensures　　　D. make certain

2. On the other hand, it also _____ the buyer that he is not required to pay until the seller ships the goods.

　　A. assures　　　B. makes sure　　C. ensures　　　D. make certain

3. Contract has different names _____, and it is called Sales Confirmation or Agreement.

　　A. call　　　　B. calling　　　C. called　　　D. a call

4. In the international trade, contract is used _____ letter of credit generally.

　　A. as well　　　B. and　　　　C. aside with　　D. along with

5. E-Documents _____ the business to store and manage all information and existing transactions in one database, as well as set up individual portals for employees, customers, suppliers and distributors in a way you want.

　　A. able　　　　B. unable　　　C. enable　　　D. make

6. TwDoc creates an electronic version of the CMR, the _____ European document in the road transport industry, sharing instantly all data and events recorded on the CMR between supply chain partners.

A. ordinary   B. common   C. standard   D. normal

7. Errors _____ due to incorrect completion of the document, illegible entries, and linguistic misunderstandings.

A. rise   B. raise   C. raise   D. arise

8. One standard _____ time platform for in-transit shipments enables us to save costs while providing an unprecedented level of proactive service to both internal and external customers.

A. true   B. false   C. genuine   D. real

9. Using electronic signature _____, twDoc enables validation of all information such as real time electronic proofs of pick-up and delivery.

A. skill   B. technique   C. technology   D. way

10. The solution is currently being usedby Solvin, a joint _____ between Solvay and BASF, logistics partners such as De Dijcker and Solvin cusomers such as Deceuninck.

A. enterprises   B. company   C. corporation   D. venture

Ⅲ. Match each word on the left with its corresponding meaning on the right.

A.	B.
1. credit	(a) capable of being moved or conveyed from one place to another
2. mutual	(b) an organized body of related information
3. applicant	(c) common to or shared by two or more parties
4. undertaking	(d) the recipient of funds or other benefits
5. revocable	(e) money available for a client to borrow
6. transferable	(f) capable of being revoked or annulled
7. beneficiary	(g) (usually plural) the office that serves as the administrative center of an enterprise
8. database	(h) a principle that limits the extent of something
9. headquarters	(i) any piece of work that is undertaken or attempted
10. exception	(j) a deliberate act of omission

Ⅳ. Match the following definitions with the corresponding terms below.

visibility	responsibility	due to
protection	status	available

1. It is thus a catalyst that provides the buyer and the seller with mutual _____ in dealing with each other.

2. It improves credit and negotiating _____ of the importer, so may be able to negotiate for a lower purchase price and better terms.

3. Contract is some terms restricted formed between buyer and seller about criterion to

buying and selling, and both of sides will have _____ for each other as long as contract is signed.

4. Transport documents are still often completed manually and, as they travel with the shipments, very little information is _____ during transit.

5. Errors arise _____ incorrect completion of the document, illegible entries, and linguistic misunderstandings.

6. With electronic CMRs, twDoc increases _____ throughout the transport execution process by providing a unique and common source of information.

Ⅴ. Translate the following phrases or sentences into Chinese.

1. revocable L/C/irrevocable L/C

2. confirmed L/C unconfirmed L/C

3. sight L/C/usanceL/C

4. transferable L/C or assignable L/C or transmissible L/C/ untransferable L/C

5. divisible L/C/ undivisibe L/C

6. A quality agreement and material specification must be the main contents of any contract with new suppliers.

7. Companies should utilize a comprehensive risk model to systematically focus on key supply needs.

8. Organizations should require their high risk suppliers to disclose supply chain details at the start of the partnership.

9. Particulars furnished by Shipper, Carrier have no means or times to check.

10. We regret to say that we cannot anti-date your B/L because that will constitute a fraud to bona fide third party.

Ⅵ. Translate the following phrases or sentences into English.

1. 进口商接到到货通知后,一般可以派车到港口提货。

2. 在当前市场竞争十分激烈的情况下,出口商必须加快货运,以快取胜。

3. 和国内物流相比,单证在国际物流中发挥着更为特殊的作用。

4. 当你填写好订舱单后,应注意如何分发这 10 联单。第一联是你自己的,第 2、3、4 联交给船务公司,第 5、6、7、8 联用于报关。

Ⅶ. Fill in the blanks with words from the list below and each word can be used once.

Bills of lading are not new things. They are universally used in sea ___1___ and combined transport. What is a bill of lading? A bill of lading is a type of ___2___ that is used to acknowledge the receipt of a ___3___ of goods. It also ___4___ the title of the goods.

Who is the party that issues the bill of lading? Generally, a transportation company or

_____5_____ issues this document to a shipper. It indicates the particular _____6_____ on which the goods have been placed, the destination of the goods, and the terms for delivering the shipment to its final _____7_____ .

An ocean bill of lading is a document that provides terms between an _____8_____ and the carrier for the shipment of goods to a foreign location _____9_____ . Ocean bills of lading may be _____10_____ or non-negotiable. If the consignee is named in the document, it is non-negotiable. In that case, the carrier is required to deliver the goods only to the person who is mentioned as the consignee in the document.

A) carry	B) represents	C) express
D) exporter	E) carrier	F) document
G) import	H) overseas	I) vessel
J) destination	K) process	L) negotiable
M) shipment	N) transport	O) consignee

附录 A

汉英物流术语解释

汉 语 术 语	英 语 术 语	解　　释
物品	Article	经济活动中涉及实体流动的物质资料。
物流	Logistics	物品从供应地向接收地的实体流动过程。根据实际需求,将运输、储存、装卸、搬运、包装、物流加工、配送、信息处理等基本功能实施的有机结合。
物流活动	Logistics Activity	物流诸功能的实施与管理过程。
物流作业	Logistics Operation	实现物流功能时所进行的具体操作活动。
物流模数	Logistics Modulus	物流设施与设备的尺寸基准。
物流技术	Logistics Technology	物流活动中所采用的自然科学与社会科学方面的理论、方法,以及设施、设备、装置与工艺的总称。
物流成本	Logistics Cost	物流活动中所消耗的物化劳动和活劳动的货币表现。
物流管理	Logistics Management	为了以最低的物流成本达到用户所满意的服务水平,对物流活动进行的计划、组织、协调与控制。
物流中心	Logistics Center	从事物流活动的场所或组织。应基本符合下列要求:(1)主要面向社会服务;(2)物流功能健全;(3)完善的信息网络;(4)辐射范围大;(5)少品种、大批量;(6)存储、吞吐能力强;(7)物流业务统一经营、管理。
物流网络	Logistics Network	物流过程中相互联系的组织与设施的集合。
物流信息	Logistics Information	反映物流各种活动内容的知识、资料、图像、数据、文件的总称。
物流企业	Logistics Enterprise	从事物流活动的经济组织。
物流单证	Logistics Documents	物流过程中使用的所有单据、票据、凭证的总称。
物流联盟	Logistics Alliance	两个或两个以上的经济组织为实现特定的物流目标而采取的长期联合与合作。
供用物流	Supply Logistics	为生产企业提供原材料、零部件或其他物品时,物品在提供者与需求者之间的实体流动。

续表

汉 语 术 语	英 语 术 语	解　　释
生产物流	Production Logistics	生产过程中,原材料、在制品、半成品、产成品等在企业内部的实体流动。
销售物流	Distribution Logistics	生产企业、物流企业出售商品时,物品在供方与需方之间的实体流动。
回收物流	Returned Logistics	不合格物品的返修、退货以及周转使用的包装容器从需方返回到供方所形成的物品实体流动。
废弃物物流	Waste Material Logistics	将经济活动中失去原有使用价值的物品,根据实际需要进行收集、分类、加工、包装、搬运、储存等,并分送到专门处理场所时所形成的物品实体流动。
绿色物流	Environmental Logistics	在物流过程中抑制物流对环境造成危害的同时,实现对物流环境的净化,使物流资源得到最充分的利用。
企业物流	Internal Logistics	企业内部的物品实体流动。
社会物流	External Logistics	企业外部的物流活动的总称。
军事物流	Military Logistics	用于满足军队平时与战时需要的物流活动。
国际物流	International Logistics	不同国家(地区)之间的物流。
第三方物流	Third-Part Logistics(TPL)	由供方与需方以外的物流企业提供物流服务的业务模式。
定制物流	Customized Logistics	根据用户的特定要求而为其专门设计的物流服务模式。
虚拟物流	Virtual Logistics	以计算机网络技术进行物流运作与管理,实现企业间物流资源共享和优化配置的物流方式。
增值物流服务	Value-added Logistics Service	在完成物流基本功能基础上,根据客户需求提供的各种延伸业务活动。
供应链	Supply Chain	生产及流通过程中,涉及将产品或服务提供给最终用户活动的上游与下游企业,所形成的网链结构。
装箱单	Packing List (sometimes As packing note)	列出运输所需的材料,例如发票、买方、收货人、原产地、航班日期、装货港口/机场、卸货港口/机场、交货地点、装运标志/货柜编号、货品重量/体积,以及全部有关货品的详情,包括装箱资料。
空运提单	(AWB) Air Waybill	航运公司。这是用于空运货物的一种运货单。空运提单说明运输的条件,作为交付货品的收据,但不是所有权证明文件或可转让的文件。

续表

汉 语 术 语	英 语 术 语	解　　释
运输商空运提单	（HAWB）House Air Waybill	航空公司。这是空运代理行发出的空运托运单,提供货物说明及记录,但并非所有权证明文件。
条码	Bar Code	由一组规则排列的条、空及字符组成的、用以表示一定信息的代码。同义词：条码符号 Bar Code Symbol［GB/T4122.1—1996 中 4.17］
汇票	Bill of Exchange, or Draft（B/E）	这是无条件的书面指示。出口商在该指示中要求进口商即时或在未来日期支付某一金额给抬头人或持票人。
本票	Promissory Note	这是可转让的财务文件,证明海外买方须付款给持票人。
信托收据	（T/R）Trust Receipt	银行凭此文件向买方发放货品(货品仍属银行所有)。买方取得货品后,必须将货品与本身其他资产分别开来,随时准备银行收回。
提单	（B/L）Bill of Lading	航运公司。这是货品拥有人与运输公司之间的合约。顾客通常需要提单的正本,以证明货品属他所有,有权提取货品。提单分两种：不可转让的直接提单,以及可转让或付货人指示提单(亦是所有权证明文件),后者可在货物过境时买卖或交易,以及用于多种融资交易。
跟单信用证	D/C Documentary Credit	这个是按买方要求开立的银行文件,证明开证银行向卖方保证,只要符合跟单信用证所列的具体要求,便会支付某一金额。
备用信用证	Standby Credit	客户与其银行作出的安排,使客户享有在该银行兑现某一金额内的支票的便利。或出口商与进口商的安排,承诺若完成不了合约内容,出口商需要赔偿进口商部分损失,这又叫履约保证书。通常用于大宗的交易如原油、肥料、鱼苗、糖及尿素等。
托收指令	Collection Instruction	只是出口商向其银行发出的指示,授权银行根据合约条款代出口商收款。
电子数据交换	Electronic Data Interchange	通过电子方式,采用标准化的格式,利用计算机网络进行结构化数据的传输和交换。
有形损耗	Tangible Loss	可见或可测量出来的物理性损失、损耗。
无形损耗	Intangible Loss	由于科学技术进步而引起的物品贬值。
国际铁路联运	International Through Railway Transport	使用一份统一的国际铁路联运票据,由跨国铁路承运人办理两国或两国以上铁路的全程运输,并承担运输责任的一种连贯运输方式。

续表

汉 语 术 语	英 语 术 语	解　释
国际多式联运	International Multimodal Transport	按照多式联运合同,以至少两种不同的运输方式,由多式联运经营人将货物从一个国境内的接管地点运至另一国境内指定交付地点的货物运输。
大陆桥运输	Land Bridge Transport	用横贯大陆的铁路或公路作为中间桥梁,将大陆两端的海洋运输连接起来的连贯运输方式。
班轮运输	Liner Transport	在固定的航线上,以既定的港口顺序,按照事先公布的船期表航行的水上运输方式。
海运提单	Sea Waybill	货运代理行。这是货物收据,内含付货人与航运公司之间的运输合约。海运提是不可转让的文件,并非所有权证明文件。
租船运输	Shipping By Chartering	根据协议,租船人向船舶公司所有人租赁船舶用于货物运输,并按商定运价,向船舶所有人支付运费或租金的运输方式。
船务代理	Shipping Agency	根据承运人的委托,代办与船舶进出港有关的运输方式。
货运担保	Shipping Guarantee	货运代理行。这是通常由航运公司预先印备的表格,由进口商银行向航运公司担保交还运输文件正本,顾客便于凭这文件提货,而不必出示提单正本。这文件通常与信托收据一并使用,以保障银行对货物的控制权。
国际货运代理	International Freight Forwarding Agent	接受进出口货物收货人、发货人的委托,以委托人或自己的名义,为委托人办理国际货物运输及相关业务,并收取劳务报酬的经济组织。理货、货物装卸中,对照货物运输票据进行的理(点)数、计量、检查残缺、指导装舱记载、核对标记、检查包装、分票、分标志和现场签证等工作。
装运通知	Shipping Advice	由出口商(卖主)发给进口商(买主)的。
装运须知	Shipping Instructions	由进口商(买主)发给出口商(卖主)的。
国际货物运输保险	International Transportation Cargo Insurance	在国际贸易中,以国际运输中的货物为保险标的的保险,以对自然灾害和意外事故所造成的财产损失获得补偿。
报关	Customs Declaration	由进出口货物的收发货人或其代理人向海关办理进出境手续的全过程。
进出口检验	Commodity Inspection	简称"商检"。确定进出口商品的品质、规格、重量、数量、包装、安全性能、卫生方面的指标及装运技术和装运条件等项目实施检验和鉴定,以确定其是否与贸易合同、有关标准规定一致,是否符合进出口国有关法律和行政法规的规定。

续表

汉 语 术 语	英 语 术 语	解 释
普及特惠税制度产地来源证表格甲(即特惠税政)	Certificate of Origin Generalised Systems of Preferences (GSP) From A or as From A	该文件证明出口国产品根据普及特惠税供给国的普及特惠税制度享有进口税优惠(减免或免税)。一般来说,货品必须同时符合受惠国的产地规则与供给国普及特惠税制度的产地标准,才可获发表格甲。中国香港目前是加拿大及挪威普及特惠税制度下的受惠者。而中国则是澳大利亚、欧盟、加拿大、捷克、日本、波兰、俄罗斯、斯洛伐克等国的普及特惠税受惠者。
经济订货批量	Economic Order Quantity	通过平衡采购进货成本和保管仓储成本核算,以实现总库存成本最低的最佳订货量。
定量订货方式	Fixed-Quantity System(FQS)	库存量下降到预定的最低的库存数量(订货点)时,按规定数量(一般以经济订货批量为标准)进行订货补充的一种库存管理方式。
定期订货方式	Fixed-interval System(FIS)	按预先确定的订货间隔期间进行订货补充的一种库存管理方式。
电子订货系统	Electronic Order System(EOS)	不同组织间利用通信网络和终端设备以在线联结方式进行订货作业与订货信息交换的体系。
配送需求计划	Distribution Requirements Planning (DRP)	一种既保证有效地满足市场需要又使得物流资源配置费用最省的计划方法,是 MRP 原理与方法在物品配送中的运用。
配送资源计划	Distribution Resource Planning (DRP Ⅱ)	一种企业内物品配送计划系统管理模式。是在 DRP 的基础上提高各环节的物流能力,达到系统优化运行的目的。

英汉物流术语翻译

英语术语	汉语术语	解　释
ATA Carnet	暂时过境证	这是国际海关文件,用来申请将货品(如国际交易会的展品、货办及专业设备)暂时运进《暂时过境证海关公约》的缔约国时面交关税。
Bar Code	条码	由一组规则排列的条、空及字符组成的,用以表示一定信息的代码。同义词：条码符号 Bar Code Symbol[GB/T 4122.1—1996 中 4.17]
Certificate of Origin	产地来源证	这是证明货品制造地点、性质、数量、价值的证明书。工业贸易署及五个贸易机构。
Import/Export Declaration	进出口报关单	这是在货物进出港口时向海关关长递交的报关说明书,用于申报货品的详情,包括付运货品的性质、目的国、出口国等,其主要作用是汇编贸易统计资料。
Import/Export Licensee	进出口证	这是由有关政府部门签发的文件,授权某些受管制货品进出口及出口。
International Import Certificate	国际进口证	这是目的地政府签发的证明,证明进出口的战略物品会在指定的国家出售。中国香港地区只为符合出口国规定的货物签发国际进口证。
Delivery Verification Certificate	货物抵境证明书	这是目的地政府签发的说明,证明指定的战略物品已抵达指明的国家。中国香港地区只为符合出口国规定的货物签发货物抵境证明书。
Landing Certificate	卸货证明书	这是目的地政府签发的说明,证明指定的商品已抵达指明的国家。中国香港地区的卸货证明书由政府统计处签发。申请时需提交下列文件：进口报关单及收据、提单、海运提单及舱单、供应商发票以及装箱单(若有)。
Customs Invoice	海关发票	这是进口国海关指定的文件,说明货品的售价、运费、保险、包装资料、付款方式等,以便海关估价。
Commercial Invoice	商业发票	这是出口商要求进口商根据销售合约支付货款的正式文件。商业发票应说明所售货品的详情、付款方式及贸易条款。商业发票也在货品清关时使用,有时供进口商安排外汇时使用。

续表

英语术语	汉语术语	解　释
Consular Invoice	领事发票	这是有些国家要求的文件,载明付运货品的详情,例如托运人、收货人、价值说明等。此文件由驻外国领事馆人员签署证明,供该国海关人员核实付运货品的价值、数量及性质。
Customized Logistics	定制物流	根据用户的定制要求而为其专门设计的物流服务模式。
(D/R) Dock Receipt or Mate's Receipt	码头收货单或大副收据	付货人/运输公司。这是确定码头/货仓已收妥待运货物的收据。码头收据单是拟备提单所需的文件,但不是处理付款事宜时按法律规定必须具备的文件。
External Logistics	社会物流	企业外部的物流活动总称。
Electronic Date Interchange	电子数据交换	通过电子方式,采用标准化的格式,利用计算机网络进行结构化数据的传输和交换。
Fumigation Certificate	熏蒸证书	这是虫害防治证书,证明有关产品已经获认可的熏蒸服务商所提供的检疫及付运前熏蒸程序。美国、加拿大和英国的海关都要求来自中国香港地区及中国内地的实木包装材料附有熏蒸证书。
Health Certificate	卫生证明书	这是出口农产品或食品时,由主管国家发出的文件,证明农产品或食品符合出口国的有关范例,以及在付运前检验时完整无损、适合人使用。
House Bill of Lading(Groupage)	运输商提单(拼箱提单)	这是由货运代理商发出的提单,很多时候都不是所有权证明文件。付运人如选用运输商提单,应在采用信贷服务前向银行说明是否可接纳做信用证用途。与个别托运相比,拼箱提单的优点包括包装较少、保费较低、过境较快、损失风险及费用较低。
Inspection Certificate	检验证明书	由独立公证人(检验公司)或出口商就买方或有关国家要求的付运货品规格(包括品质、数量及/或价钱等)发出的报告。
Insurance Policy/Certificate	保险单/保险证明书,分保单	保险单是证明付运货品已投保的保险文件,详述有关保险额的资料。保险证明书证明付运货品已受保于某一开口保单,保障货品在付运途中免受损失或损害。
Intangible Loss	无形损耗	由于科学技术进步而引起的物品贬值。
Logistics Network	物流网络	物流过程中相互联系的组织与设施的集合。
Logistics Information	物流信息	反映物流各种活动内容的知识、资料、图像、数据、文件的总称。
Logistics Enterprise	物流企业	从事物流活动的经济组织。
Logistics Documents	物流单证	物流过程中使用的所有单据、票据、凭证的总称。

续表

英 语 术 语	汉 语 术 语	解　释
Logistics Alliance	物流联盟	两个或两个以上的经济组织为实现特定的物流目标而采取的长期联合与合作。
Phytosanitary Certificate	植物检疫证	国际间通常规定的植物或种植物料须附有出口国发出的植物检疫证,证明付运货品大致上没有疾病或害虫,并符合进口国现行的植物检疫规例。在中国香港地区应向渔民处申请植物检疫证。
Packing List	装箱单	详列付运货品装箱资料的文件。
Pro Forma Invoice	估价发票	这是货物付运时由供应商提供的发票,作用是通知买家即将付运商品的种类、数量、价值及进口规格(重量、大小及类似的特点)。估价发票不是用来要求买方付款的,但可用于申请进口证、安排外汇或其他财务安排。
Production Logistics	生产物流	生产过程中,原材料、在制品、半成品、产成品等,在企业内部的实物流动。
Production Testing Certificate	产品检测证明书	这是证明产品在品质、安全、规格等各方面均符合国际或个别国家技术标准的证明书。
Quotation	报价单	指售货的报价,应清楚说明价钱、品质详情、货品数量、贸易条款、交货条件、付款方式。
Returned Logistics	回收物流	不合格物品的返修、退货以及周转使用的包装容器从需方返回到供方所形成的物品实体流动。
Sales Contract	销售合约	是买房与卖方之间的合约,订明交易细规,具法律约束力,因此在签署前最好先征询法律意见。
(S/O) Shipper Order	发货通知单或出仓纸	说明货物详情及付款人各项要求的文件,是拟备其他运输单据(如提单、空运提单等)所需的基本文件。
Supply Logistics	供应物流	为生产企业提供原材料、零部件或其他物品时,物品在提供者与所需求者之间的实体流动。
Supply Chain	供应链	生产及流通过程中,涉及将产品或服务提供给最终用户活动的上游与下游企业,所形成的网链结构。
Tangible Loss	有形损耗	可见或可测量出来的物理性损失、消耗。
Value-added Logistics Service	增值物流服务	在完成物流基本功能基础上,根据客户需求提供的各种延伸业务活动。
Waste Material Logistics	废弃物物流	将经济活动中失去原有使用价值的物品,根据实际需要进行收集、分类、加工、包装、搬运、储存等并分送到专门处理场所时所形成的物品实体流动。

附录 C

英汉物流常用词汇

英　文	中　文
abc classificiation	abc 分类法
accomplish a bill of lading（to）	付单提货
actual displacement	实际排水量
ad valorem freight	从价运费
addendum（to a charter party）	（租船合同）附件
additional for alteration of destination	变更卸货港附加费
additional for optional destination	选卸港附加费
address commission（Addcomm）	回扣佣金
adjustment	海损理算
advanced B/L	预借提单
advanced shipping notice（ASN）	预先发货通知
air express	航空快递
airway bill	航空运单
all in rate	总运费率
all purposes（A.P）	全部装卸时间
always afloat	始终保持浮泊
American Bureau of Shipping（A.B.S.）	美国船级社
anchorage dues	锚泊费
annual survey	年度检验
anti-dated B/L	倒签提单
arbitration award	仲裁裁决
arbitrator	仲裁员
area differential	地区差价
assembly	组配

续表

英　文	中　文
automatic replenishment (ar)	自动补货系统
automatic warehouse	自动化仓库
average adjuster	海损理算师
average bond	海损分摊担保书
average guarantee	海损担保书
back (return) load	回程货
back to back charter	转租合同
backfreight	回程运费
bale or bale capacity	货舱包装容积
ballast (to)	空载行驶
bar code	条形码
bareboat (demise) charter party	光船租船合同
barge	驳船
barratry	船员的不轨行为
barrel handler	桶抓手
base cargo (1)	垫底货
base cargo (2)	起运货量
beam	船宽
bearer (of a B/L)	提单持有人
bearer B/L	不记名提单
bill of lading	提单
blank endorsement	空白备书
boatman	缆工
bonded warehouse	保税仓库
book space	洽订舱位
booking note	托运单(定舱委托书)
boom of a fork-lift truck	铲车臂
both ends (Bends)	装卸两港
both to blame collision clause	互有过失碰撞条款
bottom	船体

续表

英　文	中　文
bottom stow cargo	舱底货
bottomry loan	船舶抵押贷款
breakbulk	零担
breakbulk cargo	零担货物
broken stowage	亏舱
brokerage	经纪人佣金
bulk cargo	散装货
bulk carrier	散货船
bulk container	散货集装箱
bundle（Bd）	捆(包装单位)
bunker adjustment factor（Surcharge）（BAS or BS）	燃油附加费
bunker escalation clause	燃料涨价条款
buoy	浮标
Bureau Veritas（B.V.）	法国船级社
business logistics	企业物流
cabotage	沿海运输
canal transit dues	运河通行税
capsize vessel	超宽型船
captain	船长
car carrier	汽车运输船
car container	汽车集装箱
cargo hook	货钩
cargo manifest	载货清单(货物舱单)
cargo sharing	货载份额
cargo superintendent	货物配载主管
cargo tank	货箱
cargo tracer	短少货物查询单
cargo worthiness	适货
carryings	运输量
certificate of seaworthiness	适航证书

续表

英　文	中　文
cesser clause	责任终止条款
chargeable weight	计费重量
charter party（C/P）	租船合同(租约)
charter party B/L	租约项下提单
chartered carrier	包机运输
chassis	集装箱拖车
claims adjuster	理赔人
classification certificate	船级证书
classification register	船级公告
classification society	船级社
classification survey	船级检验
clean（petroleum）products	精炼油
clean B/L	清洁提单
clean the holds（to）	清洁货舱
closing date	截止日
closure of navigation	封航
collapsible flattrack	折叠式板架集装箱
combination of rate	分段相加运价
Commodity classification rates（CCR）	等价货物运价
common carrier	公共承运人
completely knocked down（CKD）	全拆装
compulsory pilotage	强制引航
computer assisted ording(CAO)	计算机辅助订货系统
conference	公会
congestion	拥挤
congestion surcharge	拥挤费
con-ro ship	集装箱/滚装两用船
consecutive single trip C/P	连续单航次租船合同
consecutive voyages	连续航程
consign	托运

续表

英 文	中 文
consignee	收货人
consignment	托运;托运的货物
consignor	发货人
consolidation	集中托运
consolidation（groupage）	拼箱
consortium	联营
constants	常数
construction rate	比例运价
container barge	集装箱驳船
container freight station（CFS）	集装箱货运站
container leasing	集装箱租赁
container load plan	集装箱装箱单
container yard（CY）	集装箱堆场
containerised	已装箱的,已集装箱化的
containerization	集装箱化
containership	集装箱船
contamination（of cargo）	货物污染
continuous replenishment program（CRP）	连续补充库存计划
contract logistics	合同物流
contract of affreightment（COA）	包运合同
Contributory value	分摊价值
Conventional container ship	集装箱两用船
conveyor belt	传送带
corner casting（fitting）	集装箱(角件)
corner post	集装箱(角柱)
crane	起重机
crawler mounted crane	履带式(轨道式)起重机
crew list	船员名册
cross docking	交叉配送(换装)
Currency adjustment factor（CAF）	货币贬值附加费

续表

英　文	中　文
custom of the port（COP）	港口惯例
customary assistance	惯常协助
customary quick despatch（CQD）	习惯快速装运
customization logistics	定制物流
cycle stock	订货处理周期
daily running cost	日常营运成本
damage for detention	延期损失
dangerous cargo list	危险品清单
dead weight cargo tonnage（DWCT）	净载重吨
deadfreight	亏舱费
deadweight（weight）cargo	重量货
deadweight cargo（carrying）capacity	载货量
deadweight tonnage（all told）（DWT or D.W.A.T）	总载重吨位(量)
deaiweight scale	载重图表
deck cargo	甲板货
declaration of ship's deadweight tonnage of Cargo	宣载通知书
declared value for carriage	运输声明价值
declared value for customs	海关声明价值
delivery of cargo（a ship）	交货(交船)
delivery order（D/O）	提货单(小提单)
demurrage	滞期费
demurrage half despatch（D1/2D）	速遣费为滞期费的一半
derrick	吊杆
despatch or despatch money	速遣费
destuff	卸集装箱
Det Norske Veritas（D.N.V.）	挪威船级社
deviation	绕航
deviation surcharge	绕航附加费
direct additional	直航附加费
direct B/L	直航提单

续表

英　文	中　文
direct discharge	(车船)直卸
direct store delivery(DSD)	店铺直送
direct transshipment	直接转船
dirty(Black)(petroleum)products (D.P.P.)	原油
disbursements	港口开支
discharging port	卸货港
disponent owner	二船东
distribution centre(DC)	配送(分拨)中心
distribution processing	流通加工
distribution requirement planning(DRP Ⅰ)	配送需求计划
distribution resource planning (DRP Ⅱ)	配送资源计划
dock	船坞
dock receipt	场站收据
docker	码头工人
door to door	门到门运输
downtime	(设备)故障时间
draft (draught)	吃水;水深
draft limitation	吃水限制
dropping outward pilot (D.O.P.)	引航员下船时
dry cargo	干货
dry cargo(freight) container	干货集装箱
dry dock	干船坞
dunnage and separations	垫舱和隔舱物料
economic order quantity(EOQ)	经济订货批量
efficient customer response (ECR)	有效客户反应
efficient deck hand (E.D.H.)	二级水手
electronic data interchange (EDI)	电子数据交换
electronic order system (EOS)	电子订货系统
elevator	卸货机
enter a ship inwards (outwards)	申请船舶进港(出港)

英　文	中　文
enterprise resource planning（ERP）	企业资源计划
entrepot	保税货
equipment	设备(常指集装箱)
equipment handover charge	设备使用费
equipment interchange receipt（EIR）	集装箱设备交接单
estimated time of completion（ETC）	预计完成时间
estimated time of departure（ETD）	预计离港时间
estimated time of readiness（ETR）	预计准备就绪时间
estimated time of sailing（ETS）	预计航行时间
europallet	欧式托盘
even if used（E.I.U.）	即使使用
excepted period	除外期间
exception	异议
exceptions clause	免责条款
excess landing	溢卸
expiry of laytime	装卸欺瞒
extend a charter	延长租期
extend suit time	延长诉讼时间
extension of a charter	租期延长
extension to suit time	诉讼时间延长
extreme breadth	最大宽度
fairway	航道
feeder service	支线运输服务
feeder ship	支线船
ferry	渡轮
first class ship	一级船
fixed-interval System（FIS）	定期订货方式
fixed-quantity System（FQS）	定量订货方式
fixture note	租船确认书
flag of convenience（FOC）	方便旗船

续表

英　　文	中　　文
floating crane	浮吊
floating dock	浮坞
force majeure	不可抗力
fork-lift truck	铲车
forty foot equivalent unit（FEU）	四十英尺集装箱换算单位
four-way pallet	四边开槽托盘
free in（FI）	船方不负责装费
free in and out（FIO）	船方不负责装卸费
free in and out, stowed and trimmed（FIOST）	船方不负责装卸、理舱和平舱费
free out（FO）	船方不负责卸费
freeboard	干舷
freight all kinds（FAK）	包干运费
freight canvasser	揽货员
freight collect（freight payable at destination）	运费到付
freight manifest	运费舱单
freight prepaid	运费预付
freight quotation	运费报价
freight rate（rate of freight）	运费率
freight tariff	运费费率表
freight ton（FT）	运费吨
freighter	货船
fresh water load line	淡水载重线
fridays and holidays excepted（F.H.E.X.）	星期五和节假日除外
full and complete cargo	满舱满载货
full and down	满舱满载
full container load（FCL）	整箱货
full container ship	全集装箱船
full-service distribution Company（FSDC）	全方位物流服务公司
fumigation charge	熏蒸费
gantry crane	门式起重机(门吊)

续表

英　文	中　文
Gencon	金康航次租船合同
general average	共同海损
general average act	共同海损行为
general average contribution	共同海损分摊
general average sacrifice	共同海损牺牲
general cargo (generals)	杂货
general cargo rates (GCR)	普通货物运价
general purpose container	多用途集装箱
geographical rotation	地理顺序
georgraphical Information System (GIS)	地理信息系统
Germanischer Lloyd (G.L.)	德国船级社
global positioning system (GPS)	全球定位系统
goods collection	集货
goods shed	料棚
goods shelf	货架
goods stack	货垛
goods yard	货场
grabbing crane	抓斗起重机
grain or grain capacity	散装舱容
greenwich mean time (G.M.T.)	格林尼治时间
gross dead weight tonnage	总载重吨位
gross registered tonnage (GRT)	注册(容积)总吨
gross weight(GW)	毛重
grounding	触底
gunny bag	麻袋
gunny matting	麻垫
Hague rules	海牙规则
Hague-Visby Rules	海牙-维斯比规则
Hamburg Rules	汉堡规则
hand hook	手钩

续表

英　　文	中　　文
handymax	杂散货船
handy-sized bulker	小型散货船
harbour	海港
harbour dues	港务费
hatch (hatch cover)	舱盖
hatchway	舱口
head charter (charter party)	主租船合同
head charterer	主租船人
heavy fuel oil (H.F.O)	重油
heavy lift	超重货物
heavy lift additional (surcharge)	超重附加费
heavy lift derrick	重型吊杆
heavy weather	恶劣天气
high density cargo	重货
hire statement	租金单
hold	船舱
home port	船籍港
homogeneous cargo	同种货物
hook	吊钩
hopper	漏斗
house airway bill (HAWB)	航空分运单
house B/L	运输代理行提单
house bill of lading	运输代理行提单
hovercraft	气垫船
husbandry	维修
ice-breaker	破冰船
identity of carrier clause	承运人责任条款
idle	(船舶、设备)闲置
idle formality	例行手续
immediate rebate	直接回扣

续表

英　文	中　文
import entry	进口报关
in apparent good order and condition	外表状况良好
indemnity	赔偿
inducement	起运量
inducement cargo	起运量货物
inflation adjustment factor (IAF)	通货膨胀膨胀调整系数
infrastructure (of a port)	(港口)基础设施
inherent vice	固有缺陷
inland container depot	内陆集装箱
institute warranty limits (IWL)	(伦敦保险人)协会保证航行范围
insufficient packing	包装不足
intaken weight	装运重量
itegrated logistics	综合物流
International Air Transport Association (IATA)	国际航空运输协会
International Association of Classification Societies (IACS)	国际船级社协会
International Civil Aviation Organization (ICAO)	国际民用航空组织
International Maritime Dangerous Goods Code (IMDG)	国际海上危险品货物规则(国际危规)
International Maritime Organization (IMO)	国际海事组织
International Transport Workers' Federation (ITF)	国际运输工人联合会
inventory control	存货控制
inventory cycle time	库存周期
inward	进港的
inward cargo	进港货物
itinerary	航海日程表
jettison	抛货
joint service	联合服务
joint survey	联合检验
jumbo derrick	重型吊杆
jurisdiction (litigation) clause	管辖权条款
Just in time (JIT)	准时制

续表

英　文	中　文
knot	航速(节)
laden	满载的
laden draught	满载吃水
landbridge	陆桥
landing charges	卸桥费
landing,storage and delivery	卸货、仓储和送货费
lash	用绳绑扎
lashings	绑扎物
latitude	纬度
lay up	搁置不用
lay-by berth	候载停泊区
laydays (laytime)	装卸货时间
laydays canceling (Laycan 或 L/C)	销约期
laytime saved	节省的装卸时间
laytime statement	装卸时间计算表
laytime statement	装卸时间记录
lead time	备货时间
lean logistics	精益物流
leg (of a voyage)	航段
length overall (overall length,LOA)	(船舶)总长
less container load (LCL)	拼箱货
letter of indemnity	担保书(函)
lien	留置权
lift-on lift-off (LO-LO)	吊上吊下
light displacement	轻排水量
lighter	驳船
limitation of liability	责任限制
line (shipping line)	航运公司
liner (liner ship)	班轮
liner in free out (LIFO)	运费不包括卸货费

续表

英　文	中　文
liner terms	班轮条件
liner transport	班轮运输
lloyd's Register of Shipping	劳埃德船级社
load (loaded) displacement	满载排水量
loading hatch	装货口
loading list	装货清单
loadline (load line)	载重线
log abstract	航海日志摘录
log book	航行日志
logistics	物流
logistics activity	物流活动
logistics alliance	物流联盟
logistics centre	物流中心
logistics cost	物流成本
logistics industry	物流产业
logistics modulus	物流模数
logistics network	物流网络
logistics operation	物流作业
long form B/L	全式提单
long length additional	超长附加费
long ton	长吨
longitude	经度
losgistics resource planning (lrp)	物流资源计划
low density cargo	轻货
lump sum charter	整笔运费租赁
lump-sum freight	整船包价运费
maiden voyage	处女航
main deck	主甲板
main port	主要港口
manifest	舱单

续表

英　　文	中　　文
manufacturing resource planning（MRP Ⅱ）	制造资源计划
maritime declaration of health	航海健康申明书
maritime lien	海事优先权
marks and numbers	唛头
master airway bill（MAWB）	航空主运单
Material requirement planning（MRP Ⅰ）	物料需求计划
mate's receipt	大副收据;收货单
maximum freight	最高运费
mean draught	平均吃水
measurement cargo	体积货物
measurement rated cargo	按体积计费的货物
measurement rules	计量规则
merchant	（班轮提单）货方
merchant haulage	货方托运
merchant marine	商船
metric ton	公吨
minimum freight	最低运费
misdelivery	错误交货
misdescription	错误陈述
mixed cargo	混杂货
mobile crane	移动式起重机
more or less（MOL）	增减
more or less in charterer's option（MOLCHOP）	承租人有增减选择权
more or less in owner's option（MOLOO）	船东有增减选择权
mother ship	母船
multideck ship	多层甲板船
multi-modal（Inter-modal, combined）transport B/L	多式联运提单
multi-purpose cargo ship	多用途船
multi purpose terminal	多用途场站
named B/L	记名提单

续表

英　文	中　文
narrow the laycan	缩短销约期
net registered tonnage（NRT）	注册(容积)净吨
net weight	净重
New Jason clause	新杰森条款
New York Produce Exchange charter-party（NYPE）	纽约土产交易所制定的定期程租船合同格式
newbuilding	新船
Nippon Kaiji Kyokai（NKK）	日本船级社
No cure no pay	无效果无报酬
no customs valuation（NCV）	无声明价值
no value declared（NVD）	不要求声明价值
nominate a ship	指定船舶进行航行
non-conference line（Independent line, Outsider）	非公会成员的航运公司
non-delivery	未交货
non-negotiable bill of lading	不可流通的提单
non-reversible laytime	不可调配使用的装卸时间
non-vessel owning(operating) common carrier（NVOCC）	无船承运人
not always afloat but safe aground	不保持浮泊但安全搁浅
not otherwise enumerated（N.O.E.）	不另列举
note protest	作海事声明
notice of Readiness（NOR）	船舶准备就绪通知书
notice of redelivery	还船通知书
notify party	通知方
ocean（Liner, Sea）waybill	海运单
off hire	停租
oil tanker	油轮
on board（Shipped）B/L	已装船提单
on deck B/L	甲板货提单
on-carriage	货运中转
on-carrier	接运承运人
one-way pallet	单边槽货盘

续表

英　文	中　文
open hatch bulk carrier	敞舱口散货船
open rate	优惠费率
open rated cargo	优惠费率货物
open side container	侧开式集装箱
open top container	开顶集装箱
operate a ship	经营船舶
optical character recognition	光学文字识别
optional cargo	选港货物
order B/L	指示提单
order picking	拣选
ore/bulk/oil carrier	矿石/散货/油轮
out of gauge	超标(货物)
outport	小港
outsourcing	业务外包(外协,外购)
outturn	卸货
outturn report	卸货报告
outward	出港的
outward cargo	出港货
over weight surcharge	超重附加费
overheight cargo	超重货物
overlanded cargo or overlanding	溢卸货
overload	超载
overstow	堆码
overtime（O/T）	加班时间
overtonnaging	吨位过剩
owner's agents	船东代理人
package limitation	单位(赔偿)责任限制
packing list	装箱单
pallet	托(货)盘
pallet truck	托盘车

英　　文	中　　文
palletized	托盘化的
panamax	巴拿马型船
paramount clause	首要条款
parcel	一包,一票货
per freight ton (P. F. T.)	每运费吨
performance claim	性能索赔
perishable goods	易腐货物
permanent dunnage	固定垫舱物
phosphoric acid carrier	磷酸船
physical production	产品配送
piece weight	单重
pier	突码头
pier to pier	码头至码头运输
piggy-back	驮背运输
pilferage	偷窃
pilot	引航员
pilotage	引航
pilotage dues	引航费
platform	平台
platform flat	平台式集装箱
point of sale(pos)	销售实点(信息)系统
pooling	(班轮公司间分摊货物或运费)分摊制
port	港口,船的左舷
port congestion surcharge	港口拥挤附加费
port of refuge	避难港
port surcharge	港口附加费
portable unloader	便携式卸货机
post fixture	订约后期工作
post-entry	追补报关单
preamble	(租船合同)前言

续表

英　文	中　文
pre-entry	预报单
pre-shipment charges	运输前费用
pre-stow	预装载
private carrier	私人承运人
private form	自用式租船合同
pro forma charter-party	租约格式
produce carrier	侧开式集装箱
product（products）carrier	液体货运输船
promotional rate	促销费率
prospects	预期
protecting（protective, supervisory）agent	船东利益保护人
Protection and Indemnity Club（association）（P.& I. Club, Pandi club）	船东保赔协会
protective clauses	保护性条款
protest	海事声明
pumpman	泵工
purchase	（吊杆）滑车组
quarter ramp	船尾跳板
quarter-deck	后甲板
quay	码头
quick response（QR）	快速反应
quote	报价
radio frequency（RF）	无线射频
ramp	跳板
ramp/hatch cover	（跳板）舱口盖
rate	费率
rate of demurrage	滞期费率
rate of discharge（discharging）	卸货率
rate of freight	运费率
rate of loading	装货
received for shipment B/L	备运（收妥待运）提单

续表

英　　文	中　　文
receiving dates	收货期间
recharter	转租
recovery agent	追偿代理
redelivery（redly）	还船
redelivery certificate	还船证书
refrigerated（reefer）ship	冷藏船
refrigerated（reefer）container	冷藏集装箱
register	登记,报到
register（registered）tonnage	登记吨位
registration	登记,报到
Registro Italiano Navale（R.I.）	意大利船级社
release a bill of lading	交提单
release cargo	放货
remaining on board（R.O.B.）	船上所有
removable deck	活动甲板
reporting point（calling-in-point）	报告点
reposition containers	调配集装箱
respondentia loan	船货抵押贷款
return cargo	回程货
return load	回程装载
return trip C/P	往返航次租船合同
reversible laytime	可调配的装卸时间
roads（roadstead）	港外锚地
rolling cargo	滚装货物
rolling hatch cover	滚动舱单
roll-on roll-off（Ro-ro）	滚上滚下
roll-on roll-off ship	滚装船
rotation	港序
round the world（service）（R.T.W.）	全球性服务
round voyage	往返航次

续表

英　　文	中　　文
run aground	搁浅
running days	连续日
safe aground	安全搁浅
safe berth（s.b）	安全泊位
safe port（S.P）	安全港口
safe working load	安全工作负荷
safety radio-telegraphy certificate	无线电报设备安全证书
safety stock	安全库存
said to contain（s.t.c.）	(提单术语)内货据称
sail	航行,离港
sailing schedule（card）	船期表
salvage agreement	救助协议
salvage charges	救助费
salve	救助
salvor	救助人
Saturdays,Sundays and holidays excepted（S.S.H.E.X.）	星期六、日与节假日除外
Saturdays,Sundays and holidays included（S.S.H.I.N.C）	星期六、日与节假日包括在内
Scancon	斯堪人航次租船合同
Scanconbill	斯堪人航次租船合同提单
scantlings	构件尺寸
scheduled airline	班机运输
scrap terminal	废料场
seaworthiness	船舶适航
secure（to）	固定
segregated ballast tank	分隔压载水舱
self-sustaining ship	自备起重机的集装箱船
self-trimming ship（self-trimmer）	自动平舱船
self-unloader	自卸船
semi-container ship	半集装箱船
semi-trailer	半拖车

续表

英　　文	中　　文
separation	隔票
service contract	服务合同
shears（shear-legs）	人字(起重)架
sheave	滑轮
shelter-deck	遮蔽甲板船
shift	工班
shift（to）	移泊,移位
shifting charges	移泊费
shipbroker	船舶经纪人
shipping	航运,船舶,装运
shipping instructions	装运须知
shipping line	航运公司
shipping order（S/O）	装货单（下货纸）
ship's gear	船上起重设备
ship's rail	船舷
ship's tackle	船用索具
shipyard	造船厂
shore	货撑
shore gear	岸上设备(岸吊)
short form B/L	简式提单
short sea	近海
short shipment	短装
shortage	短少
shortlanded cargo	短卸货物
shut out（to）	短装
side door container	侧门集装箱
side-loading trailer	侧向装卸拖车
similar Substitute（sim.sub.）	相似替换船
single deck ship（s.d.）	单层甲板船
single hatch ship	单舱船

续表

英　　文	中　　文
single trip C/P	单航次租船合同
sister ship	姐妹船
skid	垫木
skip	吊货盘
sliding hatch cover	滑动舱盖
sling	吊货索(链)环,吊起
slop tank	污水箱
slops	污水
slot	箱位
societal logistics	社会物流
sorting	分拣
special commodity quotation（SCQ）	特种商品报价
special equipment	特殊设备
specific commodity rates（SCR）	特种货物运价
specific gravity(s.g.)	比重
spiral elevator	螺旋式卸货机
spreader	横撑(集装箱吊具)
squat	船身下沉
stacking	堆码
stale B/L	过期提单
starboard（side）	右舷
statement of facts	事实记录
stem	船艏,装期供货
stem a berth	预订泊位
stereoscopic warehouse	立体仓库
stern	船尾
stevedore	装卸工人
stevedoring charges	装卸费用
stevedor's（docker's,hand）hook	手钩
stiff	稳性过大

续表

英　文	中　文
stowage factor	积载因素(系数)
stowage plan	货物积载计划
stranding	搁浅
strengthened hold	加固舱
strike clause	罢工条款
strike-bound	罢工阻碍
strip (destuff) a container	卸集装箱
strip seal	封条
stuff (to)	装集装箱
sub-charterer	转租人
sub-freight	转租运费
subject (sub.) details	有待协商的细节
subject (sub.) stem	装期供货待定
subject free (open)	待定条款
subrogation	代位追偿权
substitute	替代船,替换
substitution	换船
suit time	起诉期
summer draught	夏季吃水
summer freeboard	夏季干舷
supply chain	供应链
supply chain management(scm)	供应链管理
supply chian integration	供应链整合
support ship	辅助船
tackle	索具(滑车)
tally	理货
tally clerk	理货员
tally sheet (book)	理货单
tank car	槽车
tank cleaning	油舱清洗

英　　文	中　　文
tank container	液体集装箱
tank terminal（farm）	油罐场
tanker	油轮
tariff	费率表
tarpaulin	油布
tender	稳性过小
terminal chassis	场站拖车
terminal handling charge	场站操作费
third-party logistics（tpl）	第三方物流
through B/L	联运提单
through rate	联运费率
tier limit（limitation）	层数限制
time bar	时效丧失
time charter	期租
time charter party	定期租船合同
time sheet	装卸时间表
to be nominated（TBN）	指定船舶
tolerated outsider	特许非会员公司
tomming（down）	撑货
tones per centimeter（TPI）	每厘米吃水吨数
tones per day（TPD）	每天装卸吨数
tones per inch（TPI）	每英寸吃水吨数
top stow cargo	堆顶货
total deadweight（TDW）	总载重量
tracer	（货物）查询单
tractor	牵引车
trading limits	航行范围
trailer	拖车
tramp transport	不定期（租船）运输
transfer（equipment handover）charge	设备租用费

续表

英　　文	中　　文
transhipment (transshipment , trans-shipment)	转船
transit cargo	过境货物
transporter crane	轨道式起重机
transship (trans-ship)	转船
transshipment B/L	转船提单
tray	货盘
trim	平舱
trim a ship	调整船舶吃水
tug	拖轮
turn round (around , or turnaround) time	船舶周转时间
turn time	等泊时间
tween deck	二层甲板
twenty equivalent unit (TEU)	二十尺集装箱换算单位
twin hatch vessel	双舱口船
two-way pallet	两边开槽托盘
ultra large crude carrier (ULCC)	超大型油轮
unclean (Foul , Dirty) B/L	不清洁提单
uncontainerable (uncontainerisable) cargo	不适箱货
under deck shipment	货舱运输
unit load	成组运输
unit load devices (ULD)	集装设备
unitisation	成组化
universal bulk carrier (UBC)	通用散装货船
unload	卸货
unmoor	解缆
unseaworthiness	不适航
utilization	整箱货
valuation charges	声明价值费
valuation form	货价单
valuation scale	货价表

续表

英　　文	中　　文
value-added logistics service	增值物流服务
value-added network	增值网
vehicle /train ferry	汽车/火车渡轮
vendor managed inventory（VMI）	供应商管理库存
ventilated container	通风集装箱
ventilation	通风
ventilator	通风器
vessel	船舶,船方
vessel sharing agreement（V.S.A.）	船舶共用协议
virtual logistics	虚拟物流
virtual warehouse	虚拟仓库
void filler	填充物
voyage（trip）charter	航次租船
voyage account	航次报表
voyage charter party	航次租船合同
voyage charter party on time basis	航次期租合同
warehouse	仓库
warehouse layout	仓库布局
warehouse management system（WMS）	仓库管理系统
waybill	货运单
weather permitting（W.P）	天气允许
weather working day	晴天工作日
weather working days（W.W.D）	良好天气工作日
weather-bound	天气阻挠
weight cargo	重量货
weight or measure（measurement）（W/M）	重量/体积
weight rated cargo	计重货物
well	货井,井区
wharf	码头
wharfage（charges）	码头费

续表

英　文	中　文
when where ready on completion of discharge（w.w. r c.d.）	何时何处还船
whether in berth or not（w.i.b.o.n.）	无论靠泊与否
whether in free pratique or not（w.i.f.p.o.n.）	无论是否通过检验
whether in port or not（ w.i.p.o.n.）	不论是否在港内
white（clean，clean petroleum）products	精炼油
wide laycan	长销约期
with effect from（w.e.f）	自生效
workable（working）hatch	可工作舱口
working day	工作日
working day of 24 consecutive hours	连续 24 小时工作日
working day of 24 hours	24 小时工作日
working time saved（w.t.s.）	节省的装卸时间
yard（shipyard）	造船厂
zero inventory	零库存

附录 D

物流英语基本概念

一、物流基本概念

1. Logistics is referred to the article flow, but not including the flow of the people.

物流是指物品流动,但不包括人员流动。

2. The concept of article in logistics includes tangible goods and intangible service, such as customer service, freight agents and logistics network design.

物流中,物品的概念包括有形的货物和无形的服务,如客户服务、货运代理及物流网络设计。

3. Logistics documents generally refer to documentations required to complete all processes of logistics, such as contracts, bills, and notes.

物流单证一般是指完成整个物流过程所需的文件,如合同、票据、签单。

4. The external logistics is about the macro economic activities, like international trade and global investment.

社会物流主要关于宏观经济活动,如国际贸易和全球投资。

5. The four key procedures in the internal logistics are supply, production, distribution and reverse.

企业物流的四个关键步骤是:供应、生产、销售和回收。

6. Supply chain management (SCM) is a system applied to maximize profits for all parties in the whole logistic system and other economic systems.

供应链管理(SCM)是一个系统,应用于将整个物流系统与其他经济体系的所有各方的利益最大化。

7. A standardized logistic system ensures better time management, location choices and distribution capacities.

一个标准化的物流管理系统应确保更好的时间管理、地点选择和分配能力。

8. Distribution capacity is value added in the logistic system.

配送能力是物流系统的增值(服务)。

9. Logistics system includes customer service, packaging, transportation, storage, distribution processing and information control.

物流系统包括客户服务、包装、运输、仓储、流通加工和信息控制。

10. Market share is the proportion of sales of a good or service provided by one company to

the industry sales of such good or service.

市场份额是指一家公司提供的商品或服务等占行业销售的该商品或服务的比例。

11. The need for outsourcing creates Third Party Logistics.

外包需求催生第三方物流。

12. Customer relationship management (CRM) is software to manage the relationship and communication between customers and suppliers.

客户关系管理(CRM)是管理软件,用于管理客户及供应商之间的沟通与关系。

13. Exclusive distribution refers to the fact that there is only one wholesaler or retailer who selling a product or providing a certain service.

独家分销是指,只有一个批发商或零售商销售某种产品或提供某种服务。

14. A logistic model is a standardized module that is used to regulate the cargo transportation, manage logistics facilities and equipments.

物流模型是一个标准化的模块,用于调节货物运输、管理物流设施和设备。

15. Letter of credit (L/C) is used exclusively by the buyer. It is a letter issued by the bank employed by the buyer which authorizes the bearer (the supplier or seller) to draw a stated amount of money from the issuing bank.

信用证(L/C)使用时完全由买方承担。它是由受雇于买方的银行发行的一封信,授权信用证的持有者从发信银行提取指定额度的资金。

16. A logistics center consists of a series of integrated logistic activities, processes, equipments, and information network.

物流中心由一系列的综合物流活动、过程、设备、信息网络组成。

17. Third party logistics refers to specialized logistics service providers that provide specific services for suppliers and customers.

第三方物流是指专业化的物流服务提供商,为供应商和客户提供具体服务。

18. Customized logistics refer to a logistic system or process specifically designed to cater to an individual customer's requirements and needs.

定制物流是指一个专门设计的物流系统或过程,可迎合个别客户的要求和需要。

19. Logistics alliance refers to the long term cooperation and business relationship between logistics supplier and customers.

物流联盟是指物流供应商和客户之间的长期合作和业务关系。

20. Bridge transport refers to containers transported by railway using the bridges that link both ends separated by river or oceans.

桥运输是指借助于链接被河流或海洋隔开的两端的桥梁,通过铁路运输的集装箱。

21. International logistics is a result of international commercial activities, cross border investment, and importing and exporting activities.

国际物流是国际商业活动、跨境投资、进口和出口活动的结果。

22. Time value in logistics refers to the differences in value of the same goods at different time.

物流的时间价值是指同一商品在不同时间的价值差异。

23. Location value in logistics refers to the differences in value of the same goods in different locations.

物流的空间价值是指同一商品在不同地点的价值差异。

24. Logistics vehicles include ships, trucks, trains and aircrafts used in the logistics process.

物流运输工具包括在物流过程中使用的船只、卡车、火车和飞机。

25. The main differences between the traditional and modern logistic systems are the usage of containers and information technologies.

传统与现代物流系统的主要区别是对集装箱和信息技术的使用。

26. Integrated logistics management was the early stage of Supply Chain Management (SCM).

综合物流管理是供应链管理(SCM)的早期阶段。

27. International transport is the major part in international logistics.

国际运输是国际物流的重要组成部分。

28. Third party logistics assist the execution of logistic activities.

第三方物流协助物流活动的执行。

29. Fourth party logistics is the planner and manager for logistics network, while Third Party Logistics is the supplier of logistics service, like transport and storage.

第四方物流是物流网络策划者和管理者,而第三方物流是物流服务供应商,如运输和储存。

30. Supply chain is the relationship between suppliers and customers. In the supply chain, suppliers rank before buyer, seller and customers.

供应链是供应商与客户的关系。在供应链中,供应商排名在买方、卖方和客户之前。

31. Logistics activities, especially transportation have a major impact on the environment.

物流活动,特别是运输对环境有重大影响。

32. Logistics is a combination of applied technology and business management.

物流是应用技术和业务管理的结合。

33. Insurance is very important to logistics because of the potential hazards and dangers in the process, such as fire, theft, handling damage and even the natural disasters.

对物流而言,保险非常重要,因为物流过程中有潜在危害和危险,如火灾、盗窃、损坏,甚至自然灾害。

34. Costs for logistics are similar to all other businesses and include fixed cost, variable cost and management cost.

物流成本与所有其他商业活动类似,包括固定成本、可变成本和管理成本。

35. The process to handle export and import with the international customs is the customs declaration.

与国际海关处理出口和进口的过程即报关。

36. Customer services link all logistics activities effectively.

客户服务有效地连接所有的物流活动。

37. The bank is a third party in the payment process between the buyers and sellers.

银行是在买家和卖家之间付款过程中的第三方。

38. Letter of credit is issued by the buyer's bank for the importer's benefits.

信用证由买方银行以进口商的名义签发。

39. Industry competition leads to more efforts to improve customer service.

行业竞争导致了更多努力,以改善客户服务。

40. For small and medium-sized companies, logistics management is still largely decentralized.

对于小型和中型公司,物流管理在很大程度上仍是分散的。

41. Customer service is specially set up to provide services to handle and inquiry and respond to demands from customers.

客户服务是专门设立提供服务,以处理、询问和响应来自客户的需求。

42. Safety is always the top concern for warehouses to handle goods.

安全始终是仓库货物处理最关心的问题。

43. Logistics information refers general logistics knowledge, materials, images, data and documentation.

物流信息是指一般的物流知识、资料、图像、数据和文件。

44. Most large companies locate in the Central Business District of a city.

大多数大型公司位于一个城市的中央商务区。

45. In a bull market, market prices for most goods will continuously go up.

在牛市中,大多数商品市场价格将不断上升。

46. The payment of most global transactions is carried out in the form of letter of credit.

大多数全球交易的付款采用信用证的形式。

47. Distribution processing value is the value added by changing the length, thickness and package of goods.

配送加工价值是通过改变货物的长度、厚度和包装产生的增值。

48. Communication links the entire logistics process with customers.

通信将整个物流过程与客户连接。

49. Demand forecasting helps managers to use their resources effectively.

需求预测可以帮助管理者有效地利用其资源。

50. The process to operate and manage logistics is logistics control activities.

操作和管理物流的过程就是物流控制活动。

51. Supply logistics is the procedure in which orders are taken from customers and purchases are delivered to the warehouse belonged of the customers.

供应物流是一种程序,在其中,订单从客户获取,购买的物品则被配送到客户所属的仓库。

52. Distribution processing is different from a manufacturing process.

流通加工不同于制造过程。

53. Distribution logistics is the delivery of process in which final products are delivered from sellers to buyers.

配送物流是最终产品从卖方交付给买家的运送过程。

二、储存功能

1. Storage is a process in which goods are stored, protected and managed.

存储是货物的储存、保护和管理过程。

2. Every manufacturer and wholesaler need inventory.

每个制造商和批发商都需要存货。

3. Fixed quantity system (FQS) is more accurate and convenient than fixed interval system (FIS).

定量订货方式比定期订货方式更准确、更方便。

4. "Twenty-eighty" analysis method is the same as ABC classification.

"20—80"分析法与 ABC 分类法相同。

5. Zero inventory is guaranteed by the full market supply and just-in-time (JIT).

充分的市场供应和 JIT 管理可以保证零库存。

6. Procurement is the process in which materials for production are ordered from customers.

采购是客户订购生产资料的过程。

7. Supply chain links all suppliers and customers along a system in which products and services are delivered.

供应链通过一个产品和服务交付系统,连接所有供应商和客户。

8. Cycle stock is the maximum inventory based on the maximum needs.

周转库存是基于最大需求的最大库存。

9. Safe stock refers to minimum inventory level given the forecasted market demand.

安全库存是指基于预测市场需求的最低库存水平。

10. The average time when the goods is moved in and out of warehouse is inventory cycle time.

物品移入和移出仓库的平均时间是库存周转时间。

11. Inventory control is the method to keep the best inventory level and position with the minimum cost to satisfy the demand.

库存控制是保持最佳库存水平和位置的方法,以最低成本满足需求。

12. When the inventory is reduced to a specific level, purchase for new parts and material will start. It is called the Order Point System.

当库存减少到一个特定水平,新零部件和原材料采购将启动。这就是所谓的订货点制度。

13. Zero stock is means zero inventory.

零库存是指零存货。

14. Inspection is the operation to check the quantity, quality and package of the goods according to the contract and specific standards.

检验是按合同和具体标准,检查货物的数量、质量和包装。

15. Goods that are stored in warehouses for distribution and sales are called inventory.

存放在仓库待配送和销售的货物被称为库存。

16. Warehouse rental represent a very significant proportion of total warehouse cost.

仓库租金占总仓储成本的一个非常重要的比例。

17. The size of warehouses is determined by the needs of the customer groups, such as their inventory level planning.

仓库大小取决于客户群体的需要,如他们的库存水平规划。

18. Commodity inspection is the process in which exported and imported goods are examined for their quantity, quality, package, place of production, safety and hygiene conditions.

商检是检查进出口商品的数量、质量、包装、生产、安全和卫生条件的过程。

19. Electronic order system (EOS) is responsible for taking customer orders and the information sharing between companies connected to the transactions.

电子订货系统(EOS)负责获取客户订单、负责交易有关的公司之间的信息交流。

20. The purpose of just-in-time (JIT) is to meet demand instantly, with perfect quality and punctuality.

JIT 的目的是及时满足需求,并保证质量和守时。

21. Goods handling may account for only 50% of the direct labor cost in warehouse and 70% in distribution center.

在仓库,搬运货物只占 50% 的直接劳动力成本,在配送中心,则占 70%。

22. Zero stock is the best way for inventory control.

零库存是库存控制的最佳途径。

三、运输功能

1. Liner transport has three specific components: fixed ports, fixed routes and announcing shipping time in advance.

班轮运输有三个具体内容:固定港口、固定航线、提前宣布发船时间。

2. Shipping by chartering is used for transporting low value goods.

租船航运用于输送低价值货物。

3. The broker company in ocean transportation is called shipping agency.

在海洋运输中,经纪公司被称为船务代理。

4. Air freight costs 5 times more than transportation by trucks and 20 times more than by rail. But it is more reliable, punctual and predictable under normal operating condition.

空运费用是卡车运输的 5 倍以上,是铁路的 20 倍,但在正常作业条件下,更可靠、准时和可预测。

5. Bulk container is used to load bulk cargo.

散货集装箱用于装载散装货物。

6. Cargo is freight carried by a ship, an aircraft, or another vehicle, upon the agreement for the delivery of goods.

货物是根据配送协议采用船只、飞机或其他工具运送的货品。

7. Tanker container is mainly used to transport oil and gas.

油轮集装箱主要用于运输石油和天然气。

8. Deadhead means a vehicle, such as an aircraft and truck that transports no passengers or freight during a single trip.

空回头车指如飞机、卡车等交通工具在单程中没有运输乘客或货物。

9. Back haul is the distance traveled from the delivery destination point back to the departure point.

回程是从交货目的地回到出发点的距离。

10. Bill of Lading is a document title.

提单是一个物权凭证。

11. Ocean Bill of Lading is a receipt for goods ioaded in the ship.

海运提单是船上装载货物的收据。

12. Shipper and carrier are two parties in a shipping contract.

托运人和承运人是运输合同中的两方。

13. Usually, the buyer in the trading contract is consignee.

通常，交易合约中的买方是收货人。

14. Liner sails in the fixed route between fixed ports and sends sailing information in advance.

班轮在固定港口之间按固定航线航行，并提前发送信息。

15. Brokers are agents who coordinate shippers and carriers by providing timely information about rates, routes and service capabilities.

经纪是代理，通过提供有关费率、路线和服务能力的及时信息，撮合托运人和承运人。

16. TEU and FEU both are containers which are used in ocean transportation frequently.

TEU 和 FEU 都是在海洋运输中经常使用的容器。

17. Bill of Lading is the evidence of the contract of carriage between carrier and shipper.

提单是承运人和托运人之间运输合同的证据。

18. Seaway Bill is different from Ocean B/L. The latter is negotiable but the former is not.

Seaway Bill 与 Ocean B/L 不同，后者是可以转让的，前者不可。

19. Transport agencies include air and surface freight forwarders, shippers' associations and transport brokers.

运输代理，包括空中和地面货运代理、船运协会和运输经纪人。

20. Freight forwarders purchase long distance service from water, rail, air even and truck

carriers.

货运代理购买水路、铁路、航空甚至和卡车的长途服务。

21. International Railway Bill can be used in land bridge transport.

国际铁路法案可以用在陆桥运输。

22. Transportation using multiple transportation means is also called combined transport.

使用多种运输方式的运输也被称为联运。

23. NVOCC is also a carrier because it can open B/L.

无船承运人,也是一个承运人,因为它可以开立 B/L。

24. Transportation creates location value in logistics.

运输创造物流的位置(空间)价值。

25. Transport does not need to change packages of goods or stop in any place between the departure point and destination location.

运输并不需要改变货物包装或停止在出发点和目的地之间的任何地方。

26. Door-to-door delivery refers to carrier picking up the goods from the shipper's warehouse and delivers it to consignee's warehouse.

送货上门,是指承运人从托运人的仓库获取货物并把它送到收货人的仓库。

27. Containerization can speed up the logistics process, such as handling, loading and unloading, storing and transport.

集装箱化可以加快物流过程,如搬运、装卸、贮存和运输。

28. Domestic intercity truck is the motor carrier service between the different cities domestically.

国内城际卡车提供在国内不同城市的汽车运输服务。

29. A fleet is group of vehicles or ships owned or operated as a unit.

船队是作为一个单位被拥有或操作的一组车辆或船。

30. Transportation is usually the biggest logistic costs for most companies.

运输通常是大多数企业最大的物流成本。

31. Truck enjoys the great advantages in the transit time and frequency compared to other transportation means.

与其他运输方式相比,卡车在中转时间和频率方面有很大优势。

32. The railroad represents the biggest usage in the land transport in China.

在中国,铁路是陆路运输的最大使用形式。

33. There are three kinds of freight in transport: full-car load, Less-than-truck load and Container.

有三种货物运输形式:整车运输、零担运输和集装箱。

34. Water transport can carry the greatest amount of goods for the longest distance with the lowest cost.

水路运输可以最低的成本运送最大量的商品至最远距离。

35. Air transport has the distinct advantage in the terms of fast delivery and enjoys the

lowest ratio of loss and damage.

在快速配送、最低的损失和破坏比例方面,航空运输具有明显优势。

36. The most economic feasible products transported by pipeline are crude oil, natural gas and refined petroleum one.

通过管道运输的最经济可行的产品是原油、天然气和成品油。

37. International transport is dominated by water carriers. It is used to transport more than 70% of the total trading volume in value and 95% by weight.

国际运输以水运为主体,它运送总交易价值的 70%和总重量的 95%。

38. International transportation by trucks is limited between the joint border countries(regions) like US and Mexico or closely located WTO members like mainland China, Hong Kong and Macao.

采用卡车进行国际运输限于边界相邻的国家(地区)间,如美国和墨西哥;或者位置相近的 WTO 成员间,如中国内地、香港和澳门地区。

39. Grouping small shipment into large ones is the primary method to lower cost per unit of weight in transportation.

将小型运输组合成大型运输,是降低单位运输重量成本的主要方法。

40. Transportation decision is referred to the transportation models and carriers selected for delivery, vehicle routing, scheduling, and freight grouping.

运输决策是指为配送、路线、调度和货运分组选择的运输模式和承运人。

41. Container logistics management is becoming a core strategy for large shipping company for its fast loading and unloading process, safe transportation and goods storage.

集装箱物流管理正在成为大型航运企业的快速装卸过程、货物安全运输和储存的核心战略。

42. The primary factor to influence transport cost is distance and competition.

影响运输成本的主要因素是距离和竞争。

43. Containerization ensures quick transit between ships and other transport vehicles such as trucks and freight rail cars.

集装箱化保证了货物在船舶和其他运输车辆如卡车和火车之间的快速中转。

四、物流信息管理

1. Automated warehouse must be managed by information system.

自动化立体仓库必须由信息系统管理。

2. The application of bar code is of primary importance in the Bar Code System.

条码的应用在条码系统是至关重要的。

3. Bar code scanner is called bar code reader.

条形码扫描仪被称为条码阅读器。

4. Firewall in the computer system is not a physical wall, but is a computer language to protect the network from invasion and damage.

电脑系统的防火墙不是一个实体的墙,而是一个计算机语言,可防止网络入侵和破坏。

5. Virtual logistics is the management by computer technology and Internet.

虚拟物流是利用计算机技术和网络管理。

6. Data warehousing is virtual data system in computer technology.

数据仓库是计算机技术中的虚拟数据系统。

7. Using 13 digits, the bar code store the information of goods.

条码使用13位数字存储商品信息。

8. Global positioning system directs the mobile equipments, like trucks, ships and aircrafts by satellite tracking.

全球定位系统通过卫星跟踪,指示移动设备如卡车、船舶和飞机。

9. The main application of E-selling is in B2B and B2C.

电子商务的主要应用是 B2B 和 B2C。

10. B2E refers to business to employee and business to executives.

B2E 是指企业对员工和企业对管理人员。

11. In the logistics information system, EDI plays the most important role.

在物流信息系统,电子数据交换起着至关重要的作用。

12. The logistics network is virtual network.

物流网络是虚拟的网络。

五、配送功能

1. Delivery refers to sending goods to the destination specified by buyers and collection of the transportation costs.

发送货物交付,是指将货物运送至买方指定目的地并征收运输成本。

2. Joint distribution refers to delivering goods for different shippers using the same vehicle by the most economic route.

联合配送是指使用最经济的路线,同车交付不同托运人的货物。

3. Distribution is one of functions in logistics, which deliver goods to customers directly according to the order in the most economic way.

配送是物流的职能之一,根据订单以最经济的方式将货物交付客户。

4. Distribution includes logistics activities related to the sales and delivery of goods.

配送包括与销售和交付货物有关的物流活动。

5. Distribution center is a short-term storage center located close to a major market to facilitate the rapid processing of orders and shipment of goods to customers.

配送中心是一个短期的仓储中心,位于靠近主要市场的位置,以便于向客户提供订单快速处理和货物装运。

6. The national distribution center is linked to the metropolitan's outer expressway, providing easy access to and from key ports, roads and other distribution channels for importers.

全国配送中心与大都市的外围高速公路连接在一起,为进口商提供主要港口、道路及其他分销渠道的方便进出通道。

7. The regional distribution center provides customized solution for supply chain management, warehousing and sea, air freight transport in the international logistics market.

区域配送中心,提供个性化的供应链管理、仓储和国际物流市场的船运空运的解决方案。

8. The distribution centers focus on maximizing the profit impact of fulfilling customer delivery requirement and distribution processing.

配送中心的重点在通过满足客户的交付需求和配送加工,使利益最大化。

六、包装功能

1. Packaging performs two basic functions, marketing and delivery in logistics.

包装执行两个基本功能,市场营销和物流配送。

2. The purpose of sales package is for sales and convenient use.

销售包装的目的是为销售和使用带来方便。

3. In logistic and transportation process, it is very important to package the goods appropriately for protection and safety purposes.

在物流和运输过程中,对货物进行适当包装以达到保护和安全目的非常重要。

4. Vacuum packaging is used to protect goods from deterioration or contamination, like food and medicine.

真空包装是用来保护如食品和药品之类的货物免于变质或污染。

5. Palletizing refers to the process of loading goods in pallet.

码垛是指用托盘装载货物的过程。

6. Palletizing is to load goods onto a pallet and wrap to form a handling and loading unit.

码垛是将货物加载到一个托盘上并包装,以形成一个处理和运载单位。

7. The No.1 function of packaging is to protect goods.

包装的第一位的功能是保护货物。

8. In marketing, the package also aims for promoting and advertising the attractiveness of goods to be sold.

在市场营销中,包装的目的还在于提高和广告待售商品的吸引力。

七、物流设施、物流工具和物流操作

1. The area for unloading goods in warehouse is receiving space.

仓库中卸载货物的区域是收货区。

2. Forklift truck is very convenient equipment for loading and unloading goods.

叉车是非常方便的装卸货物的设备。

3. Container is a large packaging box.

集装箱是一个大包装箱。

4. A twenty-foot unit is called a standard container.

一个 20 英尺单位称为一个标准集装箱。

5. Yard is a warehouse without roof and wall for containers storage.

堆场是一个没有屋顶和墙壁的集装箱存储仓库。

6. Stereoscopic warehouse has three parts: warehouse, high store shelf and stacker.

立体仓库有三个部分：仓库,高货架和堆垛机。

7. Automatic guided vehicle (AGV) can move goods to a specific location without the help of rail.

自动导引车(AGV)可以无须铁轨帮助移动货物到特定位置。

8. Conveyor can move the solid goods fluidly.

输送带可以流畅地移动固体货物。

9. Full container ship is only used for goods to be transported in container.

全集装箱船仅用于用集装箱运输的货物。

10. Customs broker is a company representing the customers to declare and store the goods.

海关经纪公司是一家代表客户申报和储存货物的公司。

11. Cargo inspection is not only to examine the goods quantity, but also quality.

货物检验不仅检验货物的数量,也检验质量。

12. Deconsolidation center is a logistics center where most inbound goods are in truck loads and most outbound goods are in small pieces.

分货中心是一个物流中心,其中,大部分入境货物以整卡车装载,大部分出境货物是一小块一小块的。

13. Deliver cycle is the time between acceptance of the order and delivery of the goods.

交付周期是接受订单和交货之间的时间。

14. Factory price does not contain the cost of freight or distribution.

工厂价格不包含运费或配送成本。

15. Less-than Container is the mode which can be used to ship goods for more than one shippers and consignees.

零担集装箱是可用于为不止一个托运人和收货人运送货物的模式。

16. The station to transfer goods from one carrier to another is gateway.

将货物从一个承运者转移至另一个承运者的站点称为门户。

17. Boned warehouse is the place to store the goods imported or in transit, without paying duty under custom's supervision.

保税仓库是在海关监管下,无须付费存储进口或过境货物的地方。

18. Conveyors are used widely in the operations of warehouse and distribution center and form the basic handling device for a number of selection systems.

输送机广泛用于仓库和配送中心的运作,并是形成大量选择系统的基本处理设备。

19. Dispatch area is the place where goods are stored and ready to be delivered.

调度区是货物存放并随时可以交付的地方。

20. Rack is the same as goods shelves which are used to place stored goods in high density area.

Rack 货架与 goods shelves 货架一样,用于在高密度区域放置存货。

2l. Standardized containers are storage and transportation equipments that may load the cargo of 16 to 26 tons or in 30 to 60 cubic meters.

标准化集装箱是储存和运输设备,可装载 16~26 吨或者 30~60 立方米的货物。

八、逆向物流

1. Recycle logistics is the part of reverse logistics.

回收物流是逆向物流的一部分。

2. Reverse logistics is the process to handle returned goods, recycle useful materials and dispose waste goods.

逆向物流是处理退货、回收有用材料和处置废物的流程。

3. When the non-qualified goods are returned or from buyer to seller, we call it reverse logistics.

当不合格品被退回或由买方给卖方,我们称之为逆向物流。

4. Green logistics is very important to the environmental protection.

绿色物流对环境保护非常重要。

5. Scrap disposal is the part of reverse logistics.

废料处理是逆向物流的一部分。

6. Recycle logistics is the process to sort, treat and collect the valuable parts from used products.

回收物流是从使用过的产品中搜寻、处理和收集有用零件的过程。

7. Reverse logistics makes goods flow from customers to suppliers.

逆向物流使货物从客户向供应商流动。

8. Averagely, retailers and manufacturers predict approximately 5%~10% of their merchandise will be returned.

平均而言,零售商和制造商预测约 5%~10%的商品将被退回。

九、其他

1. Saving or reducing expenditure in business operations is called cost control.

储蓄或减少经营开支是所谓的成本控制。

2. If the goods is damaged or lost in the process of logistics, the shipper may claim to carrier.

如果货物损坏或在物流过程中丢失,托运人可以向承运人索赔。

3. Tally is to count and inspect goods in logistics.

理货即在物流中计数和检验货物。

4. Handling or carrying is the operation to move the goods horizontally.

搬运是指水平移动货物的操作。

5. Loading and unloading may be the most frequent activities in logistics, but its related costs are hard to estimate.

装卸是物流中最频繁的活动,但其相关成本很难估计。

6. Loading and unloading is the operation moving the goods by labor or equipment to the transported vehicles, storage places or other locations in the logistic process.

装卸作业是由工人或设备将货物移动到运输车辆、贮存场所或物流过程中的其他地点。

7. CIF and FOB are two major terms in the international trade.

CIF 和 FOB 是国际贸易中的两个重要条款。

8. Virtual logistics is based on logistics network, but more computerized and systematized than logistics operation.

虚拟物流基于物流网络,但比物流运作更计算机化、系统化。

9. MRP (material requirement planning) is the management system to control the amount of material consumed and to reduce inventory in the manufacturing company.

MRP(材料需求计划)是管理系统,用以控制消耗材料的数量和减少制造公司的库存。

10. ERP (enterprise resource planning) is the management system to distribute all resources economically, while satisfying the demand of the market.

ERP(企业资源计划)是管理系统,用以经济地分配所有资源,同时满足市场需求。

11. MRP Ⅱ (manufacturing resourse planning) is the system to control all elements, including inventory and procurement, cost and working capital, sales order and personnel level.

MRP Ⅱ 是一个系统,用来控制所有元素,包括库存和采购,成本和周转资金,销售秩序和人员的水平。

12. Performance monitoring system is essential to the warehouse management.

绩效监测系统对仓库管理是必不可少的。

13. The advantage of crane on a forklift truck is to lift and move heavy materials, but is can be rather inflexible.

与叉车相比,起重机的优点是可以抬起和移动沉重的材料,但相对不太灵活。

14. The revolution of information started with the introduction of the personal computer, followed by the optical fiber network, the explosion of the Internet and the World Wide Web.

信息革命来源于个人计算机的普及,及其后的光纤网络、因特网和万维网的爆炸性发展。

15. Internet assists market development, operational planning and management decisions in the logistics industry.

互联网有助于物流业的市场发展、业务规划和管理决策。

16. Handling/carrying and loading/unloading are the most frequent activities in the logistics.

搬运和装卸是物流中最频繁的活动。

17. Parts and service support are components of after sales service.

零部件和服务支持是售后服务的组成部分。

18. Logistics information system can be made up by three parts: inputs by terminal, data managed by CPU, the outputs managed by optical fiber.

物流信息系统可以由三个部分组成：终端输入，CPU 管理的数据，光纤管理的输出。

19. Electronic commerce (EC) is the tool to be used to make deal between the seller and buyer by Internet in a paperless environment.

电子商务(EC)是一种工具，用于使卖方和买方在无纸化环境下通过互联网络形成交易。

20. Electronic data interchange (EDI) refer to a computer-to-computer information sharing of business documents in a standard format.

电子数据交换(EDI)是指商业文件的计算机到计算机信息交流的标准格式。

21. Virtual warehousing is not real logistics network but an information network based on warehouse management.

虚拟仓储不是真正的物流网络，而是基于仓库管理的信息网络。

22. EDI is widely applied in the field of commerce with the legal effect.

EDI 广泛应用于商业领域，具有法律效力。

23. Data warehouse is a consolidated database maintained separately from different organizations' production system databases.

数据仓库是一个综合数据库，由不同组织的生产系统数据库分别维护。

24. Intranet is the internal network within an organization that promotes sharing of internal company related information, using similar technology as the Internet.

内联网是指一个组织的内部网络，利用类似互联网的技术，旨在促进公司内部相关信息的共享。

25. The World Wide Web is the Internet system to allow users to browse from one Internet site to another and to inspect the information available without using complicated commands and protocols.

万维网是互联网系统使用户能够从一个互联网网站浏览到另一个，无须使用复杂的命令和协议检阅可得到的信息。

26. Container terminal connects sea and land, transfers container to and from ships.

集装箱码头连接大海和陆地，转移集装箱上下船舶。

27. Distribution center is a large and highly automated multi-store building destined to receive goods from various suppliers, take orders, fill them in container efficiently, deliver goods to the customer as quickly and satisfyingly as possible.

配送中心是一个庞大而高度自动化的多库建筑，定位于接受来自不同供应商的商品，接受订单，将商品高效地放入集装箱，将货物尽快和尽可能令人满意地送到客户。

28. B2C is the Internet commerce designed for direct communications and commercial relationship between a firm and its end customer. B2B is managed to the communication and relationship between business entities.

B2C 是互联网电子商务,为企业和它的最终客户之间的直接沟通和商业关系而设计。B2B 则是为业务实体之间的沟通和关系而设计。

参 考 文 献

1. Donald J Bowersox, David J Closs, M Bixby Cooper. Supply Chain Logistics Management[M]. NY: McGraw-Hill, 2009.

2. John L Burbidge. Production Flow Analysis for Planning Group Technology[M]. Oxford: Oxford University Press, 1997.

3. Shad Dowlatshahi. Developing a theory of reverse logistics interfaces[J]. Sustainable Business, 2000, 30 (3).

4. Elizabeth A Williamson, David K Harrison, Mike Jordan. Information systems development within supply chain management[J]. International Journal of Information Management, 2004, 24.

5. 程世平.物流专业英语[M].北京:机械工业出版社,2008.

6. 闫静雅.物流专业英语[M].北京:机械工业出版社,2010.

7. 张国宾.物流专业英语[M].北京:北京理工大学出版社,2010.

8. 王淑云.现代物流(双语)[M].北京:人民交通出版社,2010.

9. 刘如意.物流英语[M].北京:中国人民大学出版社,2009.

10. 吴健,黄金万,傅莉萍.现代物流专业英语[M].北京:机械工业出版社,2008.

11. 光昕,欧阳斌.国际物流英语[M].北京:北京理工大学出版社,2010.

12. 毛立群,王宪.物流专业英语[M].北京:高等教育出版社,2010.

13. 张庆英,李郁.物流专业英语教程[M].北京.电子工业出版社,2010.

教师服务

感谢您选用清华大学出版社的教材！为了更好地服务教学，我们为授课教师提供本书的教学辅助资源，以及本学科重点教材信息。请您扫码获取。

▶▶ 教辅获取

本书教辅资源，授课教师扫码获取

扫描二维码
获取练习答案

教师扫描二维码
获取授课课件

▶▶ 样书赠送

物流与供应链管理类重点教材，教师扫码获取样书

 清华大学出版社

E-mail: tupfuwu@163.com
电话：010-83470332 / 83470142
地址：北京市海淀区双清路学研大厦 B 座 509

网址：http://www.tup.com.cn/
传真：8610-83470107
邮编：100084